CURRENT ISSUES

Critical Policy Choices
Facing the U.S. and the World

Close Up Press

Chief Operating Officer
Rick Rockelli

Publisher
George W. Dieter

Managing Editor
Amy E. Talbot

Art Director
Tisha L. Finniff

Graphic Designer
Trisha J. Stehouwer

Writers
Tiffany Farrell
Marcia A. Friedman
Pherabe Kolb
Tim Walker

Copy Editor
Gretchen E. Matthews

Cover Photos
© DLILLC/Corbis
AP Photo/Chris O'Meara
AP Photo/Matt York

© 2007 Close Up Foundation
Printed in the United States of America.

Educate. Inspire. Empower.

Close Up is the nation's leading civic education provider. Since 1971, we've made it our mission to educate, inspire, and empower individuals to become active citizens in our democracy. Each year, through our Washington, D.C.-based experiential learning programs and our multi-media publications, we help more than 1 million students and teachers in 15,000 schools nationwide develop the skills needed to begin a lifetime of active citizenship.

Our 31st edition of *Current Issues* gives you a host of new information on the hottest issues and debates in the U.S. today. Look for cutting-edge discussions on the war in Iraq, stem cell research, immigration, global warming, and much more.

Plus, we are pleased to announce the launch of additional *Current Issues* materials at **closeup.org.** Here, you'll find a chapter on the Middle East, which we've chosen to make available electronically to provide updated content on this volatile region. You can also read *Face the Music,* an in-depth look at music downloading.

Welcome to *Current Issues 2007-08,* a key part of Close Up's critical work to help create citizens for life.

Timothy S. Davis
President and CEO

Close Up Foundation
44 Canal Center Plaza
Alexandria, VA 22314
closeup.org

PREFACE

Welcome to the 2007-08 edition of *Current Issues,* the nation's most popular social studies classroom supplement and the textbook of Close Up's Washington, D.C., programs.

For more than three decades, *Current Issues* has covered a multitude of hot topics and continues to be an unparalleled resource for unbiased debate on the most critical issues facing the nation today. From the Cold War politics of the 1980s and the technology-driven economics of the 1990s, to debates over immigration and the war on terrorism today, *Current Issues* provides readers with the knowledge and skills to make sense of the headlines. At the same time, this book serves an even higher purpose: to encourage the important work of creating citizens for life.

This edition of *Current Issues* presents key facts and differing viewpoints in an insightful and balanced manner that will help you form your own opinions. It covers domestic and foreign policy issues in 20 concise chapters, providing basic background information on and analysis of key issues.

This year, for the first time, we are pleased to offer additional *Current Issues* materials at **closeup.org**. Here, you can read a special electronic chapter on the Middle East. You will also find more issue briefings on other hot topics that you will want—and need—to know about.

Teachers can register at **closeup.org** for access to peer-driven lesson plans and teaching materials.

To a large degree, lively dialogue between the federal government and the American people will determine the nation's future. Reading and discussing *Current Issues* will help ensure that when it comes time to vote in an election or take a stand on an issue, you will be able to do so from a thoughtful and informed perspective.

CONTENTS

Foreign Policy Issues

THE FEDERAL GOVERNMENT

"We the People." The U.S. Constitution begins with these famous words. They emphasize a guiding principle in the founding and functioning of the United States—that of a nation run by the will of its citizens. The United States is a republic, governed by democratically elected representatives who deal with complex national issues on behalf of the American people. The Constitution outlines the rights and responsibilities of citizens and the structure of government. Within that framework, government officials formulate public policy—the plans that address the nation's wants and needs and that govern relations with other countries.

In the United States, the federal government consists of three branches: the executive, the legislative, and the judicial. Each plays a different role in creating and implementing public policy. In short, the legislative branch makes the laws, the executive branch implements the laws, and the judicial branch interprets the laws. Although these three mandates are distinct, by constitutional design the branches must work together. The Constitution prevents any one branch from gaining too much power through a system known as "checks and balances," in which each branch is given the authority to overrule the others in certain circumstances. This complex and delicate dance between the branches is designed to ensure that the nation's policies reflect the will of the majority of citizens, while not overlooking the rights and wants of those in the minority.

The executive branch, often referred to as "the administration" or "the White House," includes the president, the cabinet departments, and federal agencies. This branch carries out the laws of the United States and advances the president's policy agenda. Examples of cabinet departments include the Department of Defense and the Department of Education; examples of federal agencies include the Environmental Protection Agency and the Social Security Administration. Each year, the executive branch sends Congress a budget proposal, designed to shape government spending for the coming year, and proposes other laws and policy changes. Once those proposals are enacted into law, it is the job of the executive branch to execute them and oversee their implementation.

The legislative branch, Congress, is primarily charged with establishing public policy and making decisions about how federal money should be spent. The Constitution gives senators and representatives the power to establish defense, trade, and other policies, as well as the power to levy taxes and determine funding priorities to carry out these plans. Congressional committees oversee the executive branch to make sure that the president, cabinet departments, and all other federal agencies are implementing laws and administering programs as Congress intended and are not exceeding their authority or acting improperly.

The judicial branch—made up of the Supreme Court and the lower federal courts—settles legal disputes between individuals and federal, state, and local governments. Federal courts interpret the U.S. Constitution as well as other federal laws and treaties. The federal judiciary's authority to interpret laws (to say what a specific law actually means and how it should be applied to a particular set of facts) is the thrust of its power. For example, when the Supreme Court determines that a law is unconstitutional, that law is struck down and can only be resurrected if Congress decides to change it or amend the

President George W. Bush meets with members of his cabinet at the White House in September 2006. Left to right are Health and Human Services Secretary Mike Leavitt, Interior Secretary Dirk Kempthorne, and Secretary of State Condoleezza Rice.

AP Photo/Gerald Herbert

Constitution to allow it, or if a future Supreme Court reverses the decision.

The American people also play an important role in policy-making. By voicing an opinion, joining or supporting a special interest group, helping to fund an election campaign, and voting, citizens influence the direction of the country.

The twenty-first century has tested all three branches of government and the American people in new ways. The war on terror has led to proposed changes in the immigration system and controversial criminal investigative techniques. Increased concerns about the environment and health care costs are competing with worries about wages and the cost of education. Meanwhile, the increasing diversity of the country's ethnic, religious, and economic groups is testing the ability of the government to accommodate the needs and wants of all its people.

These and other challenges face Washington policymakers everyday. And, as always, complex debates will continue to arise as the government strives to provide for and protect all citizens while charting a course for the nation's future.

President Bush greets Supreme Court Justice Samuel Alito as he makes his way to the lectern to deliver his State of the Union speech in January 2006. This annual ritual—which takes place at the Capitol and is attended by nearly all members of the House, Senate, Supreme Court, and presidential cabinet—brings together the leaders of all three branches of the federal government in one room.

AP Photo/Pablo Martinez Monsivais, Pool

Race for the Presidency

The next U.S. presidential election does not take place until November 2008, so why were there dozens of presidential hopefuls already on the campaign trail by January 2007? This early start to the presidential race is due to a number of factors. Because President Bush cannot run for re-election, and Vice President Cheney decided not to run, large numbers of Republican and Democratic contenders seized the moment. The wide-open field made the race more competitive—and more expensive—than ever, and forced candidates to start raising money even earlier to have a chance at winning. Second, more than a dozen states moved up the dates for their presidential primaries, making early campaigning a necessity. Critics argue that this front-loaded process disadvantages lesser-known candidates and worsens the influence of money on the political process.

THE EXECUTIVE BRANCH

The executive branch of the federal government consists of the president, the cabinet departments, and all the federal agencies. In terms of size and scope, it is by far the largest of the three branches. This status is ironic given that the framers intended to create only a small and limited executive branch. But over the last 200 years, as the nation's size, population, and economy grew, the role of all three branches of the federal government grew, too.

Officials in the White House and the rest of the executive branch advise the president on how to decide on certain issues and then carry out the decisions once they are made. Although the president appoints many of the leaders of the executive branch—such as cabinet secretaries and agency directors—the vast majority of executive branch employees are career civil servants whose tenures are not affected by who controls the White House. In this way, the work of the federal government can continue even when the presidency changes hands.

According to the Constitution, the role of the executive branch is to carry out the laws passed by Congress by issuing

AP Photo/Susan Walsh

regulations or administering programs. But the president also relies on the executive branch to advance his or her policies, which may be at odds with those put forth by Congress. This push-and-pull between Congress and the executive branch illustrates the system of "checks and balances" laid out in the Constitution. At times, checks and balances can cause "Washington gridlock," a situation that arises when Congress and the president cannot agree and policy does not move forward. As President George W. Bush enters his final two years in office, he faces a Congress controlled by an opposing party and the possibility of persistent gridlock.

THE LEGISLATIVE BRANCH

The Work of Congress

According to the Constitution, Congress has the power to raise, print, spend, and borrow money; regulate interstate and foreign commerce; declare war and raise an army; ratify treaties and confirm presidential appointments; and make all laws necessary to execute these powers. This last power—the power to make laws—has become the main focus of Congress's work. Proposed legislation becomes law when the majorities of both the House of Representatives and Senate agree to its passage and the president signs it.

Making Laws. A member of Congress must introduce every piece of legislation. If outside interest groups, individual constituents, or the president want to propose legislation, they must first persuade a senator or representative to sponsor their proposal, called a bill. The road to passage is long and difficult; few bills ever become law.

Committees. After a bill is introduced, it is assigned a number and referred to the appropriate committee. If the committee chair thinks a bill is worthy of consideration, a subcommittee may hold public hearings in which witnesses testify for and against the proposed legislation. If the subcommittee approves the bill, it then gives the bill to the full committee. The full committee may or may not approve the bill. If approved, the bill may be sent to the House or Senate for debate.

The Debate and Vote. A powerful rules committee sets guidelines for debate in the House of Representatives. There is no equivalent committee in the Senate. Generally, House members are held to a strict time limit for debating a bill, while senators usually have unlimited time for debate. Bills are often amended during committee hearings and floor debates, and at some point a final vote is called or a bill is sent back to committee. No action is taken on the vast majority of bills.

If the House and Senate pass different versions of the same bill, a conference committee of representatives and senators works out the differences. The conference compromise bill is then returned to each chamber for final debate and a vote. If both the House and Senate pass the same version of the bill, it goes to the president. The president can sign the bill into law or veto it. If he vetoes, Congress may override the veto by securing a two-thirds majority vote in both houses.

In July 2006, President Bush issued the first veto of his presidency when he rejected legislation that would have permitted federal funds to support stem-cell research. Congress attempted, unsuccessfully, to secure enough votes to overturn the veto. In May 2007, the president vetoed an emergency war

Construction on the new underground Capitol Visitor Center is already several years late and hundreds of millions of dollars over budget. But the project's supporters say that when it is completed (estimates now say summer 2008) the center will provide additional security and a more welcoming experience for the millions of people who visit the Capitol each year.

AP Photo/Manuel Balce Ceneta

funding bill which required a specified date for U.S. troops to begin withdrawing from Iraq.

Hazards Along the Way. Some experts say it is easier to kill bills in Congress than to pass them. Powerful committee chairs can decline to consider bills, committees can completely change a bill's intent by adding amendments, or senators can hold up votes with filibusters or other delay tactics. Members' differing viewpoints, as well as party alliances, can stop a bill's progress through Congress.

Influencing Legislation. When considering so many complex bills, how do individual members of Congress make decisions? First, these officials have access to the world's best library as well as a research staff to help them learn about important policy issues. Constituents call, write letters, and send e-mail expressing their views. During hearings, committees seek the advice of outside experts. But there are other forces that affect legislation as well.

Comprised of individuals and corporate members, special interest groups—such as the oil industry and environmental conservation groups—often hire lobbyists who argue their case to members of Congress. Lobbyists try to persuade senators and representatives to vote a particular way on upcoming legislation and often give, and direct their clients to give, money to political campaigns to gain access to elected officials. In 2007, in response to several scandals involving lobbyists and members of Congress, House and Senate leaders adopted a number of changes to the congressional ethics rules. However, "sweeping reforms" to lobbying practices that were promised during the fall 2006 campaigns have yet to materialize.

Congress and President Bush

In January 2001, when President George W. Bush took office, Republicans held a majority in the House and, by virtue of Vice President Dick Cheney's tie-breaking vote, had a slight advantage in the deadlocked Senate. The president had campaigned on a pledge of bipartisanship, but many Democrats complained that the president and Republican leaders pushed through only conservative priorities. Notable early actions included the 2001 passage of a $1.35 trillion tax cut package and an education reform law called No Child Left Behind, both strongly supported by President Bush.

After the September 11, 2001, terrorist attacks, Democrats and Republicans united to support retaliatory military action, including the invasion of Afghanistan. Additionally, Congress and the president passed the USA Patriot Act, a far-reaching law that expanded the powers of law enforcement to track down and prosecute domestic and international terrorists. Billions of dollars were added to the budget for defense and for enhanced homeland security efforts.

In October 2002, after vigorous debate, Congress approved, by a vote of 296-133 in the House and 77-23 in the Senate, a resolution authorizing military force against Iraq. However, by 2004, when the U.S. military did not find weapons of mass destruction in Iraq and operations there began to falter, tensions between the parties increased.

Do Federal Judges Need a Raise?

By law, federal district court judges make about $165,000 a year. However, they could make thousands (sometimes millions) more by joining private law practices or working for corporations. This salary gap has caused many, including Supreme Court Chief Justice John Roberts, to ask Congress to give federal judges a raise. Roberts and others believe that only by increasing salaries will the best and brightest legal minds be attracted to the judicial branch. Opponents of higher judicial salaries argue that public service involves sacrifice and that the power and honor of a lifetime judicial appointment should be payment enough.

Congressional Republicans also began conforming less often to Bush administration policies. For example, even though the president was touting his plan to reform Social Security in a Republican Congress, his proposal failed to win a consensus among members.

Deteriorating public support for the war in Iraq and high-profile lobbying scandals led to a changeover in Congress in 2006. Republican candidates experienced major defeats in the midterm elections and Democrats regained control of the House and Senate for the first time in twelve years. Eager to exert their newfound influence, Democrats approved several legislative proposals in their first few weeks and embarked upon an aggressive plan to rein in the Bush administration. President Bush now faces dwindling popularity and a combative Congress, both of which may make it difficult for him to regain control of the public policy agenda during his last years in office.

THE JUDICIAL BRANCH

Article III of the U.S. Constitution, which establishes the Supreme Court and the lower federal courts, is the shortest of the constitutional articles describing the three branches of government, but its brevity contrasts greatly with the vast and

The Supreme Court Justices: Top row (left to right): Stephen Breyer, Clarence Thomas, Ruth Bader Ginsburg, and Samuel Alito. Bottom row (left to right): Anthony Kennedy, John Paul Stevens, John Roberts, Antonin Scalia, and David Souter.

Supreme Court Historical Society

powerful federal judiciary that exists today. The federal court system consists of the Supreme Court, thirteen regional circuit courts of appeals, and ninety-four federal district courts. Deciding which kinds of cases can be brought in federal court is often a complicated legal matter, but essentially, federal courts hear disputes involving federal law, between the citizens of two different states, or involving a local or state government, or the federal government. The district courts serve as trial courts, where disputes are initially heard. If litigants are unhappy with the outcome of their case there, they may be able to appeal to one of the thirteen circuit courts to review the decision.

The Supreme Court. Cases that come before the Supreme Court are mostly on appeal from lower federal or state courts and are chosen by the justices. Each year, the Court receives roughly 8,000 petitions, from which the justices select fewer than one hundred cases to hear, usually involving matters of great public importance or issues on which lower courts have offered differing decisions. The Supreme Court term typically runs from October through May, with many decisions being announced during the summer recess.

A Job for Life. In an example of how the Constitution's system of checks and balances works, the president appoints Supreme Court justices, but the Senate must approve the appointees. These justices serve for life, unless they resign or are impeached.

Court Trends. Decisions of the nation's highest court have greatly affected U.S. political and social life. During the 1950s and 1960s, the Supreme Court, led by Chief Justice Earl Warren, made sweeping changes regarding laws affecting individual rights. The Warren Court struck down racial segregation and government-sponsored prayer in public schools. During the 1980s and 1990s, the Court led by Chief Justice William Rehnquist scaled back some of these rulings in an attempt to reduce the size and scope of the federal government.

New Faces on the Court. The membership of the Supreme Court, which remained unchanged for more than a decade, was altered significantly in 2005 by the death of Chief Justice William Rehnquist and the retirement of Associate Justice Sandra Day O'Connor. These departures provided President Bush with the opportunity to try to reshape the ideological makeup of the Court by appointing new justices with conservative views. After withdrawing his heavily criticized nomination of White House counsel Harriet Miers, the president selected and the Senate confirmed Chief Justice John Roberts in September 2005 and Associate Justice Samuel Alito in January 2006.

The ideologies of the nine individual justices profoundly influence the Supreme Court's rulings and therefore have a lasting impact on the nation's laws and policies. Conservative justices generally favor a strict interpretation of the Constitution, while liberal justices often prefer a broader interpretation of the Constitution that suits changing circumstances. Justices Scalia, Thomas, Alito, and Roberts are generally thought of as conservative in their views, while Justices Ginsburg, Breyer, Stevens, and Souter are seen as more liberal. Justice Kennedy is considered a "swing vote" because his views vary by issue and are unpredictable. Although the current Supreme Court has not yet established a discernable pattern, experts believe that it is likely to hand down more conservative rulings in the years to come.

President Bush and the Democratic-controlled Congress battled throughout the spring of 2007 over how to conduct and pay for the war in Iraq. Here, the president visits U.S. troops in California in April 2007.

AP Photo/Gerald Herbert

HOW THE FEDERAL GOVERNMENT WORKS

Case Study: The War in Iraq

The three branches of government often act independently of one another, but where their paths cross, the major issues facing the United States usually are found. The war in Iraq is a good example of the convergence of the roles and responsibilities of the three branches around one policy challenge.

Presidential Authority. President Bush initiated the move toward war with guidance and assistance from his foreign policy, defense, security, and intelligence advisors. The work of these officials in their respective executive agencies and cabinet departments led to the joint conclusion that invading Iraq was necessary because Iraqi leader Saddam Hussein likely had weapons of mass destruction, and was assisting terrorist groups with their violent anti-American plans.

Congressional Approval. To gain authorization for the Iraq invasion, President Bush sought the approval of Congress, which debated the merits of the idea and ultimately decided to authorize the use of force to invade Iraq, rid the country of weapons of mass destruction, and depose Saddam Hussein. President Bush then exercised his role as commander in chief of the armed forces, directing the military campaign while Congress in turn provided the money necessary to fund the action.

Judicial Intervention. Once the war began, the judicial branch was drawn into the conflict as the Bush administration's anti-terrorism policies, which were linked to the war effort in Iraq, came under fire. To prevent terrorist attacks, federal law enforcement agencies rounded up terror suspects and "military combatants" who were suspected of aiding terrorist organizations or supporting insurgents in Iraq. These suspects were often denied access to legal counsel and other U.S. constitutional rights, leading to the filing of hundreds of court cases calling for their release, and forcing the federal judiciary to consider the constitutional rights of non-U.S. citizens detained during wartime.

Congress Weighs In. After several years in Iraq, with casualties mounting and public support for the war on the wane, the new Democratic-controlled Congress began holding hearings, making speeches, and passing resolutions designed to push President Bush to end the war. Although the president controls the armed forces, Congress controls the funding for the military; it can thus indirectly force an end to a war by exercising its "power of the purse." In May 2007, Congress approved $124 billion for the war and tied it to a timeline for U.S. troop withdrawal, but President Bush vetoed the bill because of the withdrawal requirement. Lacking enough votes to override the veto, Congress approved $100 billion without a troop-withdrawal date.

Whatever the outcome, the interaction of the three branches of government over the Iraq war provides an instructive blueprint for how the Constitution's system of checks and balances works.

KEY PLAYERS IN THE FEDERAL GOVERNMENT

THE BUSH ADMINISTRATION

President

George W. Bush, a Republican, is the nation's forty-third president. After his narrow election in 2000, Bush's popularity soared following the terrorist attacks of September 11, 2001, with his strong national security stance against terrorism. His re-election in 2004 was followed by an ambitious legislative agenda, but a series of missteps caused his popularity to diminish. Increasing opposition to the war in Iraq, growing scandals in Washington, and the mishandling of the rescue and relief efforts following Hurricane Katrina caused his and his party's approval ratings to plummet, and in the 2006 midterm elections Democrats took control of both the House and the Senate for the first time in twelve years. With a hostile Congress and decreasing public support, President Bush will have a tough time achieving his policy goals during the remainder of his presidency.

Vice President

Vice President **Richard (Dick) Cheney's** long career in public service includes working in the Nixon, Ford, and George H.W. Bush administrations and serving as a longtime member of the House of Representatives from Wyoming. Before being chosen as George W. Bush's running mate in 2000, Cheney worked in business for the defense and oil industries. Although he ultimately will be known as one of the most powerful vice presidents in American history, political scandals and the contentious war in Iraq (a policy with which he is strongly identified) decreased Cheney's influence near the end of the Bush presidency.

CABINET

There are fifteen cabinet departments, each headed by a presidential appointee who must be confirmed by the Senate. President George Washington's first cabinet was made up of only four departments: state, treasury, war (now defense), and the attorney general. The exponential growth of the executive branch over the last 200 years represents a fundamental change in the scope of the federal government's authority. Cabinet members are listed below in chronological order of their department's creation.

Secretary of State

Before succeeding Colin Powell as secretary of state in 2005, **Condoleezza Rice** served as President Bush's national security advisor. As the United States' top diplomat, Secretary Rice is the nation's most visible spokesperson for U.S. foreign policy and the nation's highest-ranking woman in government. Recently, Secretary Rice has focused on the Middle East, where the U.S.-led war in Iraq has divided national loyalties, and in the view of some critics, further destabilized the region.

Secretary of Treasury

Henry Paulson, a former chairman of a large Wall Street investment banking firm, became treasury secretary in July 2006. The Treasury Department manages the government's financial accounts and public debt and oversees all national banks and other financial institutions. The department also collects the nation's taxes through the Internal Revenue Service, prints U.S. currency and postage stamps, and oversees the minting of coins. Paulson provides key economic advice to President Bush on his fiscal policies and spending priorities.

Secretary of Defense

A former Central Intelligence Agency director in the administration of George H.W. Bush, **Robert M. Gates** was sworn in as defense secretary in December 2006 following the resignation of Donald Rumsfeld, who many blamed for the lack of progress in ending the violence in Iraq. Gates was brought in to appease these critics and to mend fences with members of the intelligence community, some of whom felt left out of wartime policy decisions. The Defense Department maintains the Army, Navy, Air Force, and Marine Corps; conducts research on military weapons and strategies; and oversees U.S. military bases around the world.

Attorney General

Alberto Gonzales became attorney general and the head of the Justice Department in 2005, replacing John Ashcroft. A former Texas Supreme Court judge and longtime confidant of President Bush, Gonzales served as White House counsel before taking on his current position. The Department of Justice is the chief law enforcement agency of the federal government and is responsible for enforcing federal laws, ensuring public safety, and preventing crime. In 2007, Attorney General Gonzales became embroiled in controversy when Congress began investigating whether he and his staff were involved in the improper firing of U.S. attorneys.

Secretary of the Interior

Dirk Kempthorne, a former governor of Idaho and U.S. senator, became secretary of the interior in May 2006. The Department of the Interior is in charge of protecting the nation's public lands, wildlife, fish, and other natural resources, as well as administering the Bureau of Indian Affairs. The Interior Department is often at the center of debates involving the environment, such as how the government should protect endangered species and where oil drilling should be allowed.

Secretary of Agriculture

The Department of Agriculture provides assistance to farmers, oversees the inspection of food processing plants, administers the food stamp and school lunch programs, and works to control crop and livestock diseases. Secretary **Mike Johanns** grew up on an Iowa dairy farm and later served two terms as governor of Nebraska. His priorities include expanding domestic and international markets for U.S. agricultural products and improving food safety.

Secretary of Commerce

The Department of Commerce advises the nation's business community and provides assistance to American industries, conducts the census, and issues patents and trademarks for inventions. **Carlos Gutierrez** became commerce secretary in February 2005. A powerful Latino businessman, Gutierrez was chief executive officer of the Kellogg Company before joining the federal government. He views the promotion of trade and the expansion of global markets for U.S. goods to be among his chief priorities.

Secretary of Labor

The Labor Department is responsible for enforcing federal labor laws, administering employment and training programs, and tracking and analyzing statistics on prices, inflation, and employment. Before becoming secretary of labor, **Elaine Chao** gained considerable administrative experience as director of the Peace Corps and the head of the United Way.

Secretary of Health and Human Services

The Department of Health and Human Services (HHS) is the largest civilian department in the federal government. Prior to being named HHS secretary, **Mike Leavitt** served as administrator of the Environmental Protection Agency, and before that spent eleven years as governor of Utah. One of his priorities has been to maximize the use of technology in improving health care and managing rising costs. His department is also responsible, through the Centers for Disease Prevention and Control, for overseeing the nation's response to epidemic health threats such as avian flu.

Secretary of Housing and Urban Development

Alphonso Jackson became secretary of Housing and Urban Development (HUD) in 2004. He had previously served as deputy secretary. HUD helps provide housing for low- and middle-income Americans and collaborates with state and local agencies to encourage community development and home ownership. Two major crises facing HUD in 2007 were the continued shortage of housing for Hurricane Katrina evacuees and the rise of mortgage foreclosures in the housing market.

Secretary of Transportation

Mary Peters became transportation secretary in September 2006. Peters was a former transportation consultant and director of the Federal Highway Administration. The Transportation Department oversees the safety and regulation of the nation's airways, roadways, and waterways.

Secretary of Energy

Samuel Bodman, a former deputy secretary in the treasury and commerce departments, became energy secretary in February 2005. The Department of Energy guards the nation's nuclear secrets, promotes the use and conservation of energy sources, works to develop new sources of energy, and regulates the nation's utilities. Reducing dependence on foreign oil is a priority of this department.

Secretary of Education

The Department of Education is responsible for providing assistance to the nation's elementary, secondary, and higher education programs; conducting research on educational practices; and promoting equal access to the nation's schools. Secretary **Margaret Spellings,** a longtime advisor to President Bush, was the architect of the No Child Left Behind federal education policy, which is up for congressional reauthorization in 2007.

Secretary of Veterans Affairs

The Department of Veterans Affairs, the second largest cabinet department, was created to administer medical, educational, and financial help to Americans who have served in the armed forces. Prior to becoming secretary in 2005, **Jim Nicholson** served as U.S. ambassador to the Vatican and chairman of the Republican National Committee. Recently, Nicholson has come under fire for the poor condition of medical care facilities serving veterans of the Iraq war, and for significant computer security lapses affecting the personal data of thousands of veterans.

Secretary of Homeland Security

The Department of Homeland Security (DHS) was created in the wake of the September 11, 2001, terrorist attacks and combined the security functions of several agencies into one cabinet department. DHS is responsible for terrorism prevention, and disaster preparedness and response. The Federal Emergency Management Agency and the Transportation Safety Administration are part of this department, as is the Coast Guard. **Michael Chertoff** was a federal appeals court judge and assistant attorney general before becoming DHS secretary.

KEY PRESIDENTIAL APPOINTEES

Director of National Intelligence

The position of director of national intelligence did not exist until 2005, when it was created in response to concerns that a lack of communication among members of the splintered intelligence community may have been a contributing factor in the September 11, 2001, terrorist attacks. The director serves as the head of the intelligence community and acts as the principal advisor to the president, the National Security Council, and the Homeland Security Council for intelligence matters related to national security. He also oversees and directs the implementation of the National Intelligence Program. **Mike McConnell,** a former National Security Agency director and security consultant, was sworn in as director in February 2007, taking over from John Negroponte, who was the first to hold this position.

National Security Advisor

National Security Advisor **Stephen Hadley** served in numerous policy advisory positions in the security and defense sectors of the federal government before taking on this role in January 2005. Hadley serves as head of the National Security Council, which is the president's principal forum for considering national security and foreign policy matters with his senior national security advisors and cabinet officials. The council also coordinates these policies among various government agencies.

KEY CONGRESSIONAL LEADERS

Speaker of the House

In her tenth term as a member of Congress, **Nancy Pelosi (D-Calif.)** is the first woman to serve as the Speaker of the House of Representatives, a position she assumed in January 2007 following Democratic victories in the midterm elections that ousted Republicans from control of the chamber for the first time in twelve years. Pelosi, who represents the San Francisco area, has struggled to unite the liberal, moderate, and conservative members of her party, particularly on the Democrats' top legislative priority of ending the war in Iraq.

House Majority Leader

Congressman **Steny Hoyer (D-Md.),** who represents suburban and rural areas of Maryland near the border with Washington, D.C., has served in Congress for more than twenty-five years. As majority leader, he is responsible for ensuring that Democratic policy proposals are supported by the party's members and receive enough votes to pass in the House.

House Minority Leader

A longtime member of the Republican leadership, **John Boehner (R-Ohio)** was elected to Congress in 1990. As House minority leader, Boehner attempts to unify members of the Republican delegation to amend or oppose Democratic legislative initiatives.

Senate Majority Leader

Senator **Harry Reid (D-Nev.)** is the Democratic leader in a closely divided Senate chamber. Due to the unique procedural rules of the Senate, many legislative initiatives require more than a simple majority to move forward. Reid and his fellow Democrats must therefore compromise more frequently than their House counterparts in order to win a sufficient number of Republican votes on key issues.

Senate Minority Leader

Senate Minority Leader **Mitch McConnell (R-Ky.)** has served in the Senate since 1984. A loyal conservative Republican, McConnell has the difficult job of pursuing Republican legislative victories while not appearing to align too closely with President Bush, whose popularity has recently declined.

THE SUPREME COURT

Chief Justice of the Supreme Court

Chief Justice **John Roberts** was nominated by President Bush and joined the Court in September 2005, following the death of former Chief Justice William Rehnquist who had served in that role for twenty years. A former White House advisor, Justice Department official, and federal appeals court judge, Roberts was approved by a wide margin in the Senate. He is generally viewed as a "strict constructionist" whose opinions are likely to shift the Court's decisions to the right.

DOMESTIC POLICY ISSUES

INTRODUCTION

"U.S. Economy Up 1.6 Percent." "President Talks Immigration Reform." Prominent headlines like these capture Americans' attention every day. They relate to events at home which affect the lives of people throughout the United States as well as their elected officials. Lawmakers' decisions about such domestic issues become public policy—laws, regulations, and other guidelines that help the nation run effectively. When formulating the nation's domestic policy, lawmakers adhere to a process laid out in the Constitution that sets forth the government's powers, defines its limits, and lists the rights of the people.

Over the years, U.S. citizens have grown accustomed to government support in their daily lives; many do not even notice it. They eat food inspected by government employees, receive protection from state and local police, drive on roads maintained with taxpayer dollars, and enjoy liberties such as the rights to worship, demonstrate, and speak freely. The policy that government makes—and how it balances protecting cherished rights with preserving order—deeply affects all Americans.

For the nation's first 150 years, the federal government was relatively uninvolved in people's daily activities. For example, in the nineteenth century, the government in Washington contributed little to the financial welfare of citizens. Poor people depended on family, friends, religious congregations, and perhaps local governments to help meet their needs.

The Great Depression of the 1930s redefined and increased the federal government's role. President Franklin Roosevelt and Congress established the first programs to help Americans who suffered from hunger and poverty. In the 1960s, President Lyndon Johnson expanded federal programs to provide low-income citizens with jobs, medical care, food, and housing. Congress also passed civil rights laws prohibiting discrimination in education, housing, public accommodations, and voting. Later, legislators confronted energy, environmental, and health issues.

Many American men and women believe that only the federal government has the resources and power needed to resolve national issues. They think that the president and Congress can best ensure that health care is accessible for all people, the environment is adequately protected from pollutants, and all children receive a first-rate education. To achieve such goals, many accept that the federal government must regulate certain aspects of society.

Other Americans think the federal government is far too involved in their lives, making decisions that states, communities, and individuals should make instead. They point to the concept of federalism, set out in the Constitution. Federalism binds states together into one country but allows them to retain certain powers separate from the government in Washington, D.C.

New domestic issues, such as the need for increased homeland security and economic concerns such as the recent housing slump continually force federal lawmakers to ask tough policy questions. Americans worry about how they will pay for health insurance and health care. Workers of all ages wonder whether Social Security funds will be available to assist them in their old age. Citizens across the country wrestle with what to do about those who wish to come to the United States of America. Hundreds of thousands arrive each year, many illegally. Who should be allowed in and how should the government balance the needs of these new arrivals with those of American citizens?

Every day, U.S. officials examine and debate an array of domestic issues, spending priorities, and policy proposals. Equally important is the job of all citizens: to read about, discuss, and share their views on these issues with lawmakers so that many voices are heard in the making of domestic policy.

THE FEDERAL BUDGET

The United States federal budget affects every American and, because of the country's influence, it often affects people around the world, too. This annual plan for how much money the government expects to receive and spend represents the nation's priorities. Money allocated by Congress funds salaries of government and military workers, medical and scientific research, foreign aid, highway construction, Social Security, border control, and many other programs and services.

KEY QUESTIONS

- Should Congress use its appropriations powers to affect Iraq policy?

- Should Congress follow a pay-as-you-go approach to control the budget deficit?

- Should President Bush's Social Security overhaul be enacted?

For most of the last forty years, the federal government has spent more money than it has taken in. Recently, some Americans have expressed anger at Congress's appetite for spending. Others worry that the $8 trillion national debt could someday undermine America's economic strength. The new Congress has pledged to rein in spending, but faces big challenges in doing so.

The war and nationbuilding efforts in Iraq and Afghanistan continue to drain the U.S. Treasury. Once projected to cost $100 billion, expenditures are now estimated to exceed $700 billion. As the public's disillusionment with the Iraq war grows, Congress may try to exercise its "power of the purse" to influence defense policies. Another big-ticket item is the Alternative Minimum Tax (AMT), which provides an important revenue stream but increasingly is raising taxes on middle-class families—leading some legislators to call for its reform or repeal. Meanwhile, spending threatens entitlement programs like Social Security and Medicare, which face shortfalls in the coming years as retiring baby boomers swell the ranks of eligible recipients. Together, these issues pose great challenges for economists, legislators, and budget conscious citizens.

BACKGROUND

Setting Priorities

The federal budget, revised every year, is a plan for how the U.S. government will take in money as well as how it will spend it. Developed by both the president and Congress, the budget outlines the nation's priorities for the coming year and describes how the government will reach those goals. For instance, if elected officials decide an important goal is to have more students achieve higher test scores in mathematics and reading, they may allocate more federal funds to programs that will help the nation reach that goal. Because it governs the collection and expenditure of billions of dollars every year, the federal budget plays an important role in the U.S. economy.

The Federal Budget Process

Each year, the president and Congress prepare a budget for the federal government. Together, they decide how much money the government will spend on defense and homeland security, health care, education, food stamps, national parks, space exploration, foreign aid, and hundreds of other federal programs. In addition, lawmakers must estimate how much tax revenue the Treasury can expect to receive.

The President Develops a Budget. In the executive branch, the Office of Management and Budget (OMB) is responsible for drawing up the president's budget for the coming fiscal year, which always begins on October 1 and ends the following September 30. The president relies on the OMB to produce a budget that reflects the administration's priorities. After compiling requests from the various agencies in the executive branch, the OMB submits a budget to the White House for approval. The president then sends the administration's budget to Congress no later than the first Monday in February.

Congress Takes Over. No federal agency or program can operate without receiving both approval and funding

The Federal Budget

In February 2007, President George W. Bush submitted a budget to Congress for fiscal year (FY) 2008 totaling $2.9 trillion. The budget also estimates spending for FY 2009.

	(outlays in billions of dollars)		
	FY07	**FY08**	**FY09**
National defense	$ 572	$ 607	$ 602
International affairs	35	36	36
General science, space, and technology	25	27	28
Energy	2	1	2
Natural resources and environment	35	33	31
Agriculture	20	20	20
Commerce and housing credit	.2	-2	.6
Transportation	75	79	73
Community and regional development	33	25	20
Education, training, employment, and social services	94	83	87
Health	269	281	298
Medicare	372	392	414
Income security	365	381	387
Social Security	587	613	645
Veterans benefits and services	72	83	86
Administration of justice	45	47	47
General government	19	21	24
Net interest	239	261	274
Allowances	7	2	1
Undistributed offsetting receipts (civilian retirement contributions and income earned from leasing or sale of government assets)	-82	-86	-89
TOTALS			
Budget Outlays	$ 2,784	$ 2,902	$ 2,985
Receipts	2,540	2,662	2,798
Deficits	-244	-239	-187

Note: Spending that is shown as a minus sign means that receipts exceed outlays. Numbers may not add to the totals because of rounding.

Source: Office of Management and Budget

from Congress. Congress grants approval for each program by passing an authorization bill, which states the program's goals, Congress's rules and regulations, and the requesting agency's spending limits. Then lawmakers must approve a separate appropriations bill, which actually gives the designated agency the money to run its program. This dual system—authorization, then appropriation—is designed to create a fiscal check by having programs discussed first on their merits and then on their costs.

Congress is also responsible for raising money, or revenue, for the federal government. Lawmakers raise money by collecting taxes and authorizing the U.S. Treasury to borrow more, if necessary, to make up for any difference in the amount of revenue collected and spent. The House and Senate approve a joint budget resolution by April of each year. The resolution sets guidelines for how much the government can spend and predicts how much revenue it will collect. Later in the year, the legislators pass a second budget resolution, which reflects any recent changes in the economy and in expected revenue. If appropriations bills already passed by Congress exceed the new limits, members draw up a reconciliation bill to bring spending within the limits set by the second budget resolution.

Breaking Down the Budget. The federal government will spend more than $2.9 trillion on hundreds of programs and dozens of agencies in fiscal year 2008. Revenue comes from individual income taxes (about 43 percent of the annual revenue), payroll taxes to fund Social Security (35 percent), corporate income taxes (15 percent), and various other sources.

Government spending is divided into four main categories: defense, nondefense discretionary, mandatory, and interest on the national debt. In 2008, defense spending will consume more than $600 billion, including monies for the wars in Iraq and Afghanistan. Nondefense discretionary spending—about $456 billion—pays for all of the budgetary programs for which funding is adjusted by the president and Congress every year. This includes such items as environmental protection, space exploration, education, highway construction, flu vaccines, and much more.

In his FY08 budget, President Bush announced a ten-year, $1 billion effort to enhance America's national parks including Yellowstone (right). In a new approach to funding federal efforts, the president also called for private investment and urged Congress to match it, dollar for dollar, up to $100 million a year for ten years.

W. Perry Conway/CORBIS

Mandatory, or entitlement, spending covers programs such as Social Security, Medicare, and Medicaid, which the government is obligated by law to fund. These programs are called entitlements because anyone who qualifies is entitled to receive benefits. Within the next ten years, entitlement spending could consume nearly half of the federal budget. The proportion of retirees will continue to grow so that by 2040, at least one in four Americans will be eligible for Social Security and Medicare benefits. That demographic shift will cause first Medicare and then Social Security to face shortfalls in the future.

The fourth main category of the budget is annual interest on the national debt. Interest for fiscal year 2008 is expected to be about $261 billion. This money buys nothing; it simply pays the interest on all of the money the government borrowed in past years to cover its deficits. If the national debt decreases, the federal government will owe less interest; if the debt increases, so will the interest owed.

A Government Beyond Its Means

Budget Deficits. Deficits are the amount by which spending exceeds revenue. To cover the government's debts, the U.S. Treasury must borrow money. Some economists worry about the effects of heavy government borrowing on the economy. When the government borrows, it competes for loans with other borrowers, such as individuals and businesses. Competition between the government and other borrowers can drive up interest rates, making it more expensive for Americans to borrow for private investment.

Federal deficits have been the norm rather than the exception since 1969. The deficit grew most dramatically in the 1980s and early 1990s—reaching a historical high of $290 billion in 1992. That pinnacle precipitated the Balanced Budget Act of 1997, which included significant spending cuts as well as tax increases. To the surprise of many, a balanced budget and the first surplus in thirty years followed in 1998—successes credited to the new policies but also to economic expansion and reduced defense spending (a "peace dividend") after the end of the Cold War.

Some budget experts predicted surpluses through 2010. However, 2001 defied all forecasts. The economy slid into recession and the stock market declined. To bolster the economy, President George W. Bush and Congress implemented tax cuts, which reduced government revenues. And after the

Spending a Tax Dollar

23¢	16¢	21¢	13¢	7¢	11¢	9¢
Defense	Non-security discretionary spending[1]	Social Security	Medicare	Medicaid	Other entitlements[2]	Interest on the debt

Source: Office of Management and Budget, FY08

[1] Such as education and foreign aid.
[2] Such as food stamps and farm aid.

AP Photo/Gerald Herbert

AP Photo/Gerald Herbert

Creating the national spending plan—and collecting the revenue to pay it—is one of the biggest tasks of the federal government. At right, people line up to receive copies of President Bush's proposed FY08 budget. Above, Sen. Sam Brownback (R-Kan.) speaks at a podium behind the large stack of books that make up the U.S. tax code. Like many, he believes the tax code is too complicated and cumbersome.

September 11, 2001, terrorist attacks, government spending skyrocketed to pay for increased homeland security and military operations in Afghanistan and Iraq. The budget deficit reached a record high of $412 billion in 2004.

In 2005 and 2006, actual deficits came in lower than projected, largely because of economic growth. However, the government continues to spend far more than it takes in. In fiscal year 2007, the White House predicted a deficit of $244 billion.

The National Debt. The national debt, currently more than $8.8 trillion, is the total sum of money borrowed by the government from the U.S. population, lending institutions, foreign banks, and the government's own holdings, most notably the Social Security trust fund. The debt—along with the amount of interest the government owes on it—is predicted to rise for the foreseeable future. Some economists fear that growing debt could dampen long-term investment and eventually lead to an economic depression—or worse. But others argue that the debt poses no problem for the strong and flexible U.S. economy.

Budget Challenges

Taxes. Currently, individuals pay taxes on the income they receive—salaries from employers, interest payments on investments, profits on sales of assets, and gifts. The current income tax system is progressive because generally people with lower incomes pay fewer taxes than people with higher incomes. The tax code features many exceptions and deductions that make calculating taxes complicated and time consuming and hinder the government's ability to find tax cheats. Americans paid about $1 trillion in federal income taxes in 2006.

Tax Cuts. In 2001, 2003, and 2006, Congress passed a range of temporary tax cuts championed by President Bush. The measures reduced income tax rates, offered breaks to families and businesses, and cut taxes on profits from investments and sales of assets such as real estate. Most of these tax cuts will expire in 2010. President Bush and others have called for making the cuts permanent, arguing that they reversed the recession and that allowing them to expire would crush economic expansion. Others argue that the tax breaks favor the wealthy and increase the national debt.

The Alternative Minimum Tax. To try to ensure that wealthy Americans pay their fair share of taxes, Congress passed the Alternative Minimum Tax (AMT) in 1969. Initially, this provision prevented rich Americans from using deductions and other tax shelters to avoid paying standard income taxes. However, Congress revised the deductions that trigger the AMT in 1986, and since then inflation has also risen. Combined, these factors have recently triggered the AMT for more and more middle-class Americans, often couples with children.

Officials predict that the AMT could force 25 million Americans to pay higher taxes after 2008 (and could cancel out benefits some might have received from the Bush tax cuts). In recent years, Congress has passed yearly stopgap measures to curtail the tax's reach. However, many legislators believe that the tax should be formally restructured to serve its original purpose or should be repealed altogether. Their dilemma: how to replace the current AMT's projected contribution to the Treasury over the next ten years—an estimated $1 trillion.

A Taxing Process

Many people criticize the U.S. income tax code, which runs thousands of pages, as unduly complicated. Some say this complexity also enables the wealthiest Americans to avoid paying their fair share of taxes and makes it easy for everyone, including businesses, to cheat. Almost $300 billion in taxes owed goes unpaid and uncollected nearly every year. But major tax code reform, often talked about, has proved difficult in practice. In 2005, a presidential panel recommended reducing the number of tax brackets. Some policymakers call for more dramatic changes, such as a flat tax that taxes all income at the same rate. Others want to ensure that tax reform does not disproportionately burden working class and poor Americans or hurt businesses.

Earmarks. When Congress writes spending bills, lawmakers have the opportunity to insert specific targeted spending provisions—for example, $166,000 for salmon quality standards. These provisions, known as earmarks, are often designed mainly to please a legislator's constituents and supporters. Increasingly, earmarks have been anonymously slipped into spending bills at the last minute with little or no debate. These earmarks, or "pork" to critics, came under fire recently. The cost of such provisions had tripled over twelve years to more than $64 billion annually and several members of Congress were accused of trading earmarks for cash or favors from special interests. To reduce the abuse of earmarks, in 2007, the newly elected House of Representatives voted to require lawmakers to attach their names to the provisions they initiate and to certify that they will gain no financial benefit from the programs.

Social Security. Social Security, the largest and most expensive federal program, has been called a "social contract" between generations. Established in 1935 to fight poverty, the program serves more than 47 million men, women, and children and is the main source of income for a majority of older

Americans. Social Security receives much of the credit for reducing the poverty rate among senior citizens from 50 percent in the 1930s to about 10 percent in recent years. Two-thirds of the program's beneficiaries are retirees; the rest are disabled workers, spouses and families of deceased workers, and children. The money taken out of today's workers' paychecks pays for current retirees' Social Security benefits. The benefits formula is complex, but generally, those who earn lower wages over their lifetimes (and have less to save) receive a higher percentage of their incomes in Social Security benefits than do higher earners.

Since 1983, the amount of taxes taken in has exceeded the amount of money needed to pay benefits. The federal government uses that extra money to pay for other programs and writes the equivalent of an IOU to the Social Security Trust Fund. However, the number of Americans approaching retirement is growing faster than the number of younger Americans replacing them in the workforce. By 2017, the government will be spending more on Social Security benefits than it receives in income payroll taxes. To provide full benefits to everyone eligible through 2041, the government will have to repay the money it borrowed from the Social Security program. After that, Social Security will continue to function, but will only be able to pay benefits from the revenues it collects from payroll taxes—covering an estimated 60 to 80 percent of benefits currently promised.

Identifying the coming shortfall as a crisis, in 2005 President Bush proposed allowing Americans to divert their Social Security payroll contributions to private investment accounts. However, many citizens and legislators rejected the idea.

Medicare. Americans over age 65 and people with disabilities are automatically eligible to receive government Medicare benefits. Medicare helps pay for hospital nursing care and other routine medical services. Like Social Security, Medicare operates with a trust fund, but unlike Social Security, the Medicare program is already spending more than it takes in. Medicare's trustees estimate that, because of skyrocketing

Reuters/Jim Hollander/Corbis

Since the September 11, 2001, terrorist attacks, defense spending increased dramatically. Among the costs are hundreds of billions of dollars to fight wars in Afghanistan (above) and Iraq.

health care costs and the increasing numbers of retirees, the trust fund will be exhausted by 2019.

CURRENT ISSUES

War Dollars. The Constitution designates the president the commander in chief of the U.S. armed forces. But it grants Congress the authority to approve federal spending. In the past, Congress has used its "power of the purse" to rein in war efforts. After years of the unpopular Vietnam War, Congress imposed a cap on troops, and in 1982, Congress denied President Ronald Reagan's request to fund the Contra rebels fighting in Nicaragua. Today, as public disillusionment with the war in Iraq grows, policymakers and others debate whether Congress should use its appropriations powers to influence or restrict President Bush's military policy in Iraq.

Those advocating that Congress use its power of the purse to change Iraq policy argue that the public has expressed clear dissatisfaction with the war. If the president refuses to change course, these critics argue, Congress's constitutional authority allows it to use fiscal policy to carry out the will of the people. They say the argument is simple: America's unending presence in Iraq is doing more harm than good. The president's policies have cost thousands of Americans lives and wasted billions of taxpayers' dollars and therefore must be changed. Some propose that Congress do this by denying additional funding for war efforts. Others suggest that Congress use its appropriations power to tie any military funding to certain conditions or benchmarks of progress.

The president—elected by the American people—is the commander in chief and has the sole power to decide how to conduct America's battles, insist those opposed to Congress's interference. According to these executive branch supporters, the president's administration is better equipped than Congress to determine and carry out military policies that will ensure victory. Congressional micromanagement, contend these opponents, will put the troops in harm's way and lead to greater loss of life. Finally, detractors assert, conflicting messages from the White House and Congress will embolden insurgents and terrorists and doom the war effort. To prevent this outcome, say critics, the president can and should veto any legislation constricting Iraq war policy.

Hitting the Pocketbook to Make Change

Many economists and other policy experts suggest that increasing the federal gas tax (currently 18.4 cents a gallon) would change consumer behavior, thus achieving important environmental, energy, and foreign policy goals. Higher fuel prices would encourage citizens to buy more fuel-efficient cars and use more public transportation. Costlier fuel would also likely lead to reduced pollution, increased interest in alternative fuels, and less reliance on anti-American sources of foreign oil. But politically, the idea is considered dead on arrival. Lawmakers and citizens alike loathe tax increases, and many people worry that a higher gas tax would most severely impact low-income Americans.

Spending What We Can Afford. Concerned about excessive congressional spending and the persistent budget deficit, Congress passed a pay-as-you-go budgeting measure in 2007. This rule, also known as "paygo," requires that any tax cuts or increases in entitlement spending be offset with spending reductions elsewhere. But the effort prompted debate on whether paygo is the right approach to current budget challenges.

Proponents say that pay-as-you-go is necessary to show that Congress understands that deficits matter and should be contained. Such supporters argue that paygo rightly responds to citizens' concerns about profligate spending and the rising national debt, which some fear could lead to economic catastrophe in the future. Paygo advocates contend that the rule will hold Congress to the same standard most families and businesses must already follow—spending only what you can pay for. Furthermore, supporters argue, by eliminating wasteful spending and collecting unpaid taxes, Congress can easily raise most of the funds needed to pay for its new initiatives, without going into further debt. Finally, proponents point out

that paygo can be suspended as necessary, such as in case of recession or crisis.

Opponents criticize paygo as the wrong approach to budget deficits. Some charge that rather than limiting spending, paygo will merely result in tax hikes to pay for new programs, which will hurt all Americans and the economy. These critics insist that budget deficits should be eliminated through economic growth rather than through the painful and stifling budget cuts or tax increases required by paygo. Some opponents worry that the constraints of paygo will prevent Congress from being able to reduce the growing reach of the Alternative Minimum Tax. Others contend that paygo unduly restricts Congress's ability to respond to national emergencies. Finally, although many believe the public wants Congress to be financially responsible, some fear that program cuts or tax increases required by paygo will anger voters.

Social Insecurity. The Social Security program, which will soon be spending more money than it takes in, needs to be fixed. But how to fix it, and how soon? Some people believe the system requires a serious overhaul. Since taking office, President Bush has proposed a number of significant changes, including private investment accounts. But others say that less dramatic adjustments will keep the system strong.

The Social Security system is going bankrupt and threatens the nation's economic health, say advocates for big changes. The system must be overhauled, they claim, because the nation has promised retirees more than it can afford without cutting other programs or raising taxes. Proponents of this view contend that the program was never intended to be the national retirement program into which it has evolved. They say major changes—like offering the private investment accounts the president favors or cutting benefits for everyone but those Americans truly in need—are required and must be implemented now to save the program.

Others argue that the system remains strong and that the future shortfalls can be easily averted without harming the economy. Those supporting this view contend that Social

Security has become a national retirement system that works—citizens pay into it and value the benefits they receive in return. These advocates stress that the program currently runs a surplus and successfully brings financial security to millions of people. Such supporters argue that the system can be shored up with modest fixes, such as raising the cap on earnings that can be taxed for Social Security (currently $90,000), and gradually raising the retirement age.

OUTLOOK

The annual budget process and ensuing back and forth between the president and Congress has been contentious throughout history—and will likely continue that way. Many members of Congress disagree with President Bush's approach to a number of domestic and foreign policy issues. While trying to keep an eye on the budget deficit and national debt, Congress may try to use its appropriations powers to steer a new course.

THE DEBATE: THE FEDERAL BUDGET

Congress should use its appropriations powers to affect Iraq policy.

PRO: Congress's "power of the purse," granted by the Constitution, can rightly be used to influence Iraq policy. More and more people argue that the unending U.S. presence in Iraq foments unrest and will lead to more lost lives and wasted money. If the president refuses to carry out the people's will, Congress should use its appropriations power to do so.

CON: The Constitution grants the president the sole power to make and conduct war. Furthermore, the president's administration has the best expertise in military policy. If Congress interferes, it will not only undermine the troops, but also doom the mission in Iraq and embolden terrorists everywhere—outcomes America cannot afford.

Congress should follow a pay-as-you-go approach to control the budget deficit.

PRO: The pay-as-you-go rule responds to Americans' concerns about persistent budget deficits and rising national debt. The rule will force Congress to balance spending with cuts and to curb the deficit. Congress can find money for social programs by reducing waste and collecting unpaid taxes, and can bypass paygo during emergencies.

CON: The best way to reduce the deficit and national debt is through policies like low taxes and targeted government spending policies that promote economic growth—not pay-as-you-go. Under paygo, Congress will not be able to pay for social programs without raising taxes. That kind of belt-tightening will anger the American people.

Social Security should be overhauled.

PRO: With the number of retirees swelling, the Social Security system is going bankrupt and threatens America's economy. Without major and immediate changes, Americans will face painful benefit cuts or tax increases. Congress should implement private investment accounts or reduce Social Security benefits for middle-income and wealthy Americans.

CON: Social Security is a strong national retirement program that runs a surplus. The system brings financial security to millions of people who are relying on it throughout their later years. Altering or dismantling it would cheat workers out of their contributions. With minor changes to the tax structure and retirement age, Social Security can be shored up for decades.

CONSTITUTIONAL DEBATES

The first ten amendments to the U.S. Constitution are known as the Bill of Rights. Added to the Constitution in 1791, these amendments were designed to protect individual freedoms and to limit the power of the federal government. The Bill of Rights guarantees Americans the freedoms of expression, religion, and association. It also establishes a fair process for people accused of crimes and shields them from "cruel and unusual punishment." Although the Bill of Rights lists many liberties, other sections of the Constitution also grant rights to the American people.

KEY QUESTIONS

• Should the government restrict access to abortion?

• Should the First Amendment's separation of church and state be absolute?

• Should habeas corpus be restored for Guantanamo Bay detainees?

Today, many controversial debates—such as those over abortion, religious expression, and civil liberties during a time of war—stem from conflicting interpretations over what rights are guaranteed to individuals under the Constitution. Much of the wording in the Constitution and its amendments is general; therefore, Americans often disagree on how this language applies to certain situations. Such conflicts often have to be resolved in court.

The nine justices of the U.S. Supreme Court decide which cases they will review each term based on a number of considerations, including whether lower courts have handed down conflicting opinions on the issues in each case, and whether the cases involve issues of significant interest to the American people. Based on these narrow criteria, the Court hears only a small fraction of the cases filed each term. The Court's decisions ultimately determine whether laws are constitutional. Some people believe that the Court should interpret the Constitution strictly according to the literal intentions of its authors. Others think that the Supreme Court should apply the spirit of the framers' ideas to modern-day situations. These conflicts help keep American democracy responsive to a changing society.

BACKGROUND

Guaranteeing Individual Rights

Written in 1787, the Constitution of the United States needed to be ratified by nine of the existing thirteen states to become law. Many states approved the document with the provision that Congress would add amendments listing individual rights. James Madison of Virginia, a member of the first Congress, wrote the proposals that formed the basis of these amendments. In December 1791, ten amendments collectively known as the Bill of Rights were ratified by the states and became part of the Constitution.

Although they are more than 200 years old, many of the ideas expressed in the Constitution and in the Bill of Rights are still relevant. In particular, the following issues have been at the center of many famous cases argued before the U.S. Supreme Court. They continue to provoke public debate today.

Freedom of Religion. Part of the First Amendment reads, "Congress shall make no law respecting an establishment of religion, or prohibiting the free exercise thereof." The courts have interpreted this to mean that government and religion should be separate. However, Americans often disagree on how to maintain this separation without interfering with a person's

The U.S. Constitution is on permanent public display at the National Archives in Washington, D.C. Millions of visitors each year come to the Archives to see firsthand the actual document that established the government of the United States.

right to practice religion. Some Americans, called "separationists," believe that to protect religious liberty, the line between religion and government should not be crossed. Others are "accommodationists" and think that the government should make allowances for the long religious tradition in U.S. society. Many Americans fall somewhere in between these two views.

Historically, the Supreme Court has ruled on both sides of this issue. Beginning in the mid-twentieth century, the Supreme Court began ruling more frequently against religious displays "in the public square," holding, for example, that public schools could not require students to say a prayer at the opening of the school day or at the beginning of a commencement ceremony. However, the Court has upheld some religious displays (such as nativity scenes, Christmas trees, and menorahs) near government buildings if their placement and context does not imply government endorsement of religion.

Freedom of Expression. The First Amendment also forbids Congress from making laws that prevent Americans from speaking or writing freely. The courts have ruled, however, that the right of free expression can be limited. For example,

Campaign Finance

Congress and some states are attempting to control political campaign spending, but their efforts may not get past the courts. In 2007, the Supreme Court reviewed parts of a 2002 federal campaign finance law known as McCain-Feingold that, like similar laws passed in a number of states, attempts to curb the influence of money in politics. At issue is whether these laws, which are designed to safeguard the political process from corruption, are infringing on individuals' rights to free speech. Supporters believe they help create a level playing field on which all voices, not just those of well-funded special interests, can be heard. Opponents say that keeping money from influencing elections is not a compelling enough interest to override the important First Amendment rights at stake, and remind critics that "special interests" speak on behalf of average voters with shared beliefs.

the First Amendment does not allow speech or writing that makes false statements about a private person's character, specifically plans the violent overthrow of the government, or incites a riot. However, the amendment does allow citizens to hold peaceful meetings and public protests asking the government to correct a perceived wrong.

The Supreme Court is sometimes asked to decide whether unpopular speech should be protected in the same manner as popular speech. For example, the Court has ruled that burning the American flag is a form of free speech protected by the First Amendment and that local governments cannot outlaw the display of racist symbols such as a Nazi swastika. People who support such rulings say that even offensive speech should be protected to ensure that the government does not censor citizens' views. Others argue that outlawing certain types of inflammatory or hurtful speech does not violate the First Amendment.

The Right to Bear Arms. The Second Amendment protects "the right of the people to keep and bear arms." After the American Revolution, the first Congress wanted to ensure that people could, if needed, form armed militias, such as the National Guard. The wording of this amendment has caused much debate about whether it gives individuals the right to own any gun for any reason. Currently, federal laws prohibit private ownership of certain types of firearms. Still, Americans own more than 200 million rifles, shotguns, and handguns. Individuals who collect guns, use them for sport, or keep them for self-defense often cite the Second Amendment when criticizing gun control laws. Lawmakers who support restrictions on the ownership of firearms say gun control laws are needed to stop gun violence in the United States and that the right to bear arms refers to state militias, not private individuals.

Protecting Suspected Criminals. The Bill of Rights states that the government should treat fairly any persons accused of crimes. Several amendments address the rights of suspected criminals.

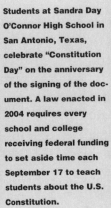

Students at Sandra Day O'Connor High School in San Antonio, Texas, celebrate "Constitution Day" on the anniversary of the signing of the document. A law enacted in 2004 requires every school and college receiving federal funding to set aside time each September 17 to teach students about the U.S. Constitution.

AP Photo/Eric Gay

- The Fourth Amendment protects persons from "unreasonable searches and seizures."
- The Fifth Amendment forbids forcing suspects to testify against themselves; protects defendants from double jeopardy (being retried for crimes for which they were previously found not guilty); and prevents the government from taking a person's life, property, or freedom except in ways specified by law.
- The Sixth Amendment guarantees the right to a "speedy and public trial" by jury, the right to an attorney, and the rights to confront adverse witnesses and obtain favorable ones.
- The Eighth Amendment forbids "excessive bail" and "cruel and unusual punishment."

Unspecified Rights. The Ninth Amendment acknowledges that no listing of rights can be truly complete. It states that rights not specifically mentioned are "retained by the people." In other words, the government must honor rights that are defined in the future. For example, the Supreme Court has recognized the right to privacy, the right to vote, and the right to travel, even though they are not specifically mentioned in the Constitution. However, the Court has most often based such rights on the Fourteenth Amendment, rather than the Ninth Amendment.

Federalism. In a federalist system like that of the United States, national and state governments share power. The Tenth Amendment says that powers not given to the federal government, nor prohibited to the states by the Constitution, are reserved for the states or the people. This amendment is often cited when making cases for increasing states' rights and decreasing the power of the federal government.

The Fourteenth Amendment. Originally, the Bill of Rights applied only to the federal government, but the Fourteenth Amendment extended most of those protections to the actions of state and local governments as well. Section one of the Fourteenth Amendment reads in part, "No state shall make or enforce any law which shall abridge the privileges or immunities of citizens of the United States; nor shall any state deprive any person of life, liberty, or property, without due process of law; nor deny to any person within its jurisdiction the equal protection of the laws." Ratified after the Civil War, this amendment was intended specifically to guarantee former slaves the same rights and protections enjoyed by other Americans.

Although the Fourteenth Amendment is not part of the Bill of Rights, it is often cited to protect the rights of individuals. It forms the basis for civil rights laws and the Supreme Court also has ruled that the amendment, despite its general wording, supports voting rights, prohibits discrimination on the basis of sexual orientation, and protects a woman's right to have an abortion.

Abortion. In its 1973 landmark decision in *Roe v. Wade,* the Supreme Court ruled that a woman has a constitutional right to an abortion (a medical procedure in which a fetus is removed from a woman's body, thus ending her pregnancy). The Court based its ruling on two findings. First, the justices held that the right to privacy allows a woman to end a pregnancy. Second, the Court said that a fetus is not a person and thus is not protected under the Fourteenth Amendment's guarantee that "no person" can be deprived of life without a fair trial.

CURRENT ISSUES

Restrictions on Abortion. The Supreme Court's 1973 ruling in *Roe v. Wade* held that the Constitution protects a woman's right to decide whether to terminate her pregnancy. *Roe* further decided that the number and type of restrictions a state could impose on a woman's access to abortion should be determined by how long she had been pregnant. In practice, this "trimester" framework prohibited most state restrictions on abortion during the early months of pregnancy, but allowed restrictions to be imposed later in pregnancy unless the abortion was necessary to protect the life or health of the mother.

In the years since *Roe,* many states have attempted to impose additional restrictions on the circumstances in which a woman can have an abortion. In *Planned Parenthood v. Casey* (1992), the Supreme Court upheld the right to an abortion but abandoned the trimester framework, instead holding that state restrictions on abortion were permissible as long as they did not impose an "undue burden" on the woman seeking the procedure. Since this new standard was adopted, the issue of what constitutes an "undue burden" has been the focus of many Supreme Court cases. Not surprisingly, determining whether a law imposes an "undue burden" often depends on who is evaluating the law.

A number of state legislatures are currently considering various laws restricting abortion access. In 2007, the Supreme Court upheld a federal ban on partial-birth abortions. And in recent years, the arguments fueling the abortion debate have spread to other issues like stem cell research. Some scientists and health care advocates believe that cells harvested from embryos can help researchers devise new cures for debilitating diseases. But opponents say that this method of stem cell harvesting is, like abortion, the taking of human life.

Opponents of abortion believe that there is no constitutional right to kill a fetus, which they see as an unborn child, and that in time the Supreme Court will see that *Roe* was wrongly decided and vote to overturn it. They believe that states have an interest in protecting fetuses and that it is not an "undue burden" to impose regulations on the serious matter of

Citizens share their opinions about a 2006 law passed by the South Dakota Legislature that would have banned abortion in almost all cases. Voters later rejected that law as too extreme, but in February 2007, the legislature proposed a new abortion ban which includes exceptions for rape and incest, in the hope of gaining more support.

choosing to have or perform an abortion. They believe, for example, that public funding should not be used to pay for abortion services and that abortion should not be allowed even when the mother's health or the viability of the fetus are at issue. Many opposed to abortion believe, and have successfully lobbied states to require, that women seeking an abortion must tell their parents or husbands before they have the procedure.

Supporters of abortion rights believe that a fetus is not a child and that the Constitution, as interpreted in *Roe v. Wade*, protects a woman's right to choose whether to terminate her pregnancy. They contend that states should not be allowed to infringe on this right by setting mandatory waiting periods, passing laws that limit counseling about abortion options, or imposing excessive regulations on abortion providers. Some argue that notification laws might force young women to confide in parents who will abandon them or force wives to tell abusive husbands who might further hurt them. Ultimately, contend abortion rights supporters, restrictions like these are "undue burdens" because their existence often prevents a woman from exercising her constitutional right to end a pregnancy.

Separation of Church and State. The First Amendment provides both freedom of and freedom from religion. These two fundamental rights—to be free to practice one's own religion and to be free from having to practice another's religion—are central to the American ideal of democracy. Indeed, pursuit of religious freedom was one of the main reasons that British and other European citizens came to the original American colonies. However, although these early Americans sought to escape religious persecution in their homelands, they did not intend to abandon religion altogether. Religion has always been an important part of American life and is reflected in many traditions sanctioned by government. For example, the phrase "In God We Trust" appears on all U.S. currency and the U.S. Congress opens its sessions with a prayer. Many of the nation's "founding fathers" were themselves religious men who often quoted scripture in support of their views on how to shape the republic.

But such religious traditions compete with equally long-established beliefs that government and religion should remain separate. It was Thomas Jefferson who first described the Establishment Clause of the Constitution as necessary to erect "a wall of separation between church and state" and warned against the entanglement of religion and government, for fear it would lead to tyranny. But defining what constitutes an appropriate separation has become more challenging in recent years as politics and religion have become more intertwined. The increased political participation of organized religious groups, such as Christian Evangelicals, has influenced candidates for political office and sparked intensified public debate on morality, faith, and religion. In addition, the ongoing conflicts in Iraq and Afghanistan and the war on terror, have brought the Islamic religion into the spotlight. These developments have tested the American ideal of religious tolerance and prompted a re-examination of the First Amendment's purpose and reach. How the country balances competing individual and government interests surrounding religious freedom has been a central focus of constitutional debate for centuries.

Supporters of a strict separation of church and state argue that allowing religious beliefs to inform government policy or practice, even if well-intentioned, can lead to disastrous consequences. By introducing religious practices into a government context, such as when public schools encourage prayer in the classroom, the government may exclude or discriminate against those with unpopular religious beliefs or no religious beliefs at all. If a government building posts quotes from the Bible (a Christian text) but not the Koran (an Islamic text), these advocates believe, then government is endorsing both the practice of religion as well as a specific religion. Separationists also worry that allowing religious organizations to provide federally funded social services (such as drug treatment or job training) amounts to government support of those organizations' religious beliefs and practices. Overall, advocates of strict separation believe that allowing government to impose religious choices is exactly the kind of activity that the First Amendment was designed to guard against and that allowing such activity is harmful to both religious and nonreligious citizens.

But not everyone believes that the wall between church and state must be "absolute." Such critics say that the pendulum has swung too far and that reading the First Amendment as a literal ban on religion in government denies the religious traditions and values on which the United States was founded and in which many Americans still deeply believe. The desire to keep religion and government separate has become too extreme, these Americans argue, and now actively discriminates against religious believers. Many feel that certain government traditions—such as invoking God in the Pledge of

A Student's Right to Free Speech?

Do students at school-supervised events have the right to display messages about illegal drug use? No, said the Supreme Court in 2007 in *Morse v. Frederick*—the most important student free-speech case in nearly forty years. In 2002, at an off-campus high school event, senior Joseph Frederick held up a banner saying, "Bong Hits 4 Jesus." Principal Deborah Morse confiscated the banner and suspended Frederick for ten days, citing the school's responsibility to protect students from harmful messages—in this case, a reference to smoking marijuana. Frederick however, claimed his message was a meaningless act of free speech. But the Court ruled 5-4 that while the message on Frederick's banner was cryptic, it was reasonable to believe the words advocated illegal drug use and thus to disallow it.

Allegiance—use religious symbols and words only in a ceremonial way, and are not meant to endorse a specific religion. They contend that outlawing all religion from the public square for fear of offending some is a violation of the constitutional right to practice one's religion freely.

In a Holding Pattern. In 2002, the United States established a high-security detention facility at the Guantanamo Bay Naval Base, Cuba, for foreign terror suspects considered threats to U.S. national security. Over the last five years, about 775 people have been detained in the camp; as of April 2007, almost 400 remained. "Gitmo" as it is often called, is controversial for many reasons. Critics are especially concerned about the fact that the suspects—who are not U.S. citizens—have faced a legal labyrinth and yet still cannot challenge their status as "enemy combatants." Since 2002, only 10 detainees have been charged with a crime. Detainees' rights have been vigorously debated since the camp first opened and many detainees have brought—or tried to bring—suit against the U.S. government over a number of issues.

One such claim involves the concept of habeas corpus, or wrongful imprisonment. Many detained suspects have filed petitions with U.S. federal courts for habeas corpus, a writ that allows a prisoner to go before a judge and argue that he or she has been held illegally. This writ, first recognized centuries ago in English law, is a central tenet of the American justice system and is enshrined in Article I, Section 9 of the Constitution. In a 2004 victory for the detainees, the Supreme Court ruled in *Rasul v. Bush* that although Gitmo detainees are not U.S. citizens, federal civilian courts had the jurisdiction to consider their habeas corpus appeals since the Guantanamo Bay detainment facility is controlled by the United States.

Further court cases in 2005 and 2006 challenged the legality of the U.S. government's plan for handling and trying the Guantanamo Bay terror suspects. When the Supreme Court ruled against the military hearings implemented by the Bush administration in 2006, Congress and President Bush came together to sign into law the Military Commissions Act (MCA), which legalized a new military tribunal system. Among its many provisions, the law also suspends detainees' right to file habeas corpus petitions with U.S. federal courts and was applied retroactively, so that pending habeas corpus appeals were thrown out. The constitutionality of the law's habeas corpus clause was challenged in February 2007 and upheld in a case in a U.S. district court. When asked, the Supreme Court chose not to review the case, and thus the MCA stands. Critics are calling for Congress to reinstate habeas corpus for the Gitmo detainees.

Those who favor restoring habeas corpus for the detainees say that denying a prisoner the opportunity to go before an independent body and contest his incarceration and status as an enemy combatant goes against the principles of democratic government. Further, they say, the current commissions will not be fair or transparent since only military officers conduct the proceedings and the MCA permits the use of classified evidence against defendants. (U.S. law has long held that defendants and their counsel should have access to the evidence against them to prepare their defense.) In some cases, critics also point out, Gitmo prisoners have already been held for five years without any charges being filed against them.

Without being able to petition for habeas corpus, their detainment could continue indefinitely. If the detainees are truly threatening, critics argue, habeas corpus proceedings will confirm the allegations against them and prove that the U.S. government has good reason to keep them locked up.

Enemy combatants should not be permitted to petition for the writ of habeas corpus in civilian courts, say supporters of the MCA. Military tribunals, they argue, are proper and fair venues for trying the Guantanamo Bay suspects, many of whom are exceedingly dangerous and have demonstrated their plans to make war on the United States. Each prisoner's detention status, supporters point out, is reviewed annually by a formal board which has indicated that many prisoners will be released as soon as their home countries agree to accept them and not torture them. The Guantanamo Bay facility has been instrumental in fighting the war on terror, say supporters. And the nature of terrorist acts, they argue, means that classified information must be used to protect and save American lives; therefore, it is also necessary in trials concerning terror suspects. The MCA, advocates assert, follows a long tradition of military courts established during the Revolutionary War, Civil War, and World War II for trying enemy combatants and is useful—and lawful—today.

OUTLOOK

The Constitution is a living document, amendable by the American people and interpreted by the courts. However, the modern era has posed challenges to defining Americans' rights that the framers could never have anticipated. The current debates over abortion, religious expression, and war time policies are rooted in Americans' differing interpretations of what rights the Constitution does and does not protect and to whom they should be applied. Thus, Americans have an ongoing responsibility to understand their constitutional rights and to monitor the government and other citizen's actions to ensure that those rights are honored.

THE DEBATE: CONSTITUTIONAL DEBATES

The government should restrict access to abortion.

PRO: *Roe v. Wade* was wrongly decided and eventually will be overturned by the Supreme Court. In the meantime, state governments should do all that they can to make it more difficult for women to seek out abortions and for physicians and hospitals to provide them. A woman's constitutional right to privacy is outweighed by the state's interest in protecting the lives of unborn children.

CON: The Supreme Court has held that abortion is legal and that governments cannot impose an "undue burden" on women seeking to have the procedure. Restricting access to abortion violates a woman's constitutional right to make decisions about her body and her medical care. Forcing a woman to tell her parents or her spouse about her pregnancy may cause her harm and thus imposes an undue burden.

The First Amendment's separation of church and state should be absolute.

PRO: The First Amendment protects an individual's right to be free from religion imposed by the government. Even well-meaning attempts to introduce or allow religious practice or traditions into government-sponsored activities can be harmful because they are exclusionary and can impose a particular set of beliefs. The right to practice a religion is an individual, not a governmental, choice.

CON: Religious beliefs and traditions have always had a place in U.S. society. The separation of church and state should not be read so literally as to be extreme. The First Amendment guarantees citizens the right to freely practice their religion. Using religious symbols and words in official ceremonies and government traditions is constitutional because it does not endorse a specific religion.

Habeas corpus should be restored for Guantanamo Bay detainees.

PRO: Democracies recognize individuals' rights; the habeas corpus suspension under the Military Commissions Act is contrary to American values and is forcing detainees into prolonged imprisonments without opportunity to defend themselves. Habeas corpus proceedings will ensure that innocent people are not being held illegally. If the suspects are all terrorists, as accused, then the evidence against them should be made known.

CON: Military tribunals have been used fairly and correctly over many centuries to try enemy combatants. The Guantanamo Bay detainees are not average suspects; many have fought against the United States or shown plans to do so. Currently, a formal board ensures that each prisoner is detained for good reason, so an opportunity to petition for habeas corpus in a civilian court is not necessary.

CRIME AND SECURITY

Violent crime in the United States was in decline for many years but according to the U.S. Justice Department, it increased by 2.3 percent in 2005 and preliminary reports show a further increase in 2006. Some state and local officials believe that violent crime, or "street crime" as it is sometimes called, is on the rise because law enforcement agencies are more focused on preventing crimes with potentially catastrophic effects on large numbers of people, such as terrorism, at the expense of anti-street crime initiatives.

KEY QUESTIONS

- Is expanded government surveillance of citizens necessary for public safety?

- Should big cities receive more federal homeland security funding?

- Should anti-drug efforts focus on rehabilitation over punishment?

This new emphasis on homeland security has also led to controversies about how best to protect the nation from terrorism. Some see increased government surveillance as a necessary and effective security measure, while others believe it represents an encroachment on individual constitutional rights. Debates over how to pay for anti-terrorism measures and who should get federal funding continue as the war on terror goes on.

And the threat of terrorism is only one of the many challenges facing law enforcement. Officials are also struggling to determine the best method—rehabilitation or punishment—to combat a rising tide of drug-related crimes that are filling the nation's prisons with convicted criminals. Some believe that only strong punishment will deter future offenders. Others say that unless drug addicts receive treatment, the streets will not be safer. The discussion and resolution of these debates likely will shape the nation's approach to crime and security issues in the coming years.

BACKGROUND

Crime in America

Crime On the Rise. According to the Federal Bureau of Investigation's (FBI) Uniform Crime Report, about 11.55 million crimes were documented in the United States in 2005. Crimes against property, such as burglary or car theft, accounted for more than 90 percent of these crimes; the rest were violent crimes—murder, rape, robbery, and aggravated assault. In 2005, there were 16,692 murders in the country—about one murder per 18,000 residents—an increase of 3.4 percent from the previous year. And overall, violent crime increased by 2.3 percent, leaving many to wonder whether the dramatic decreases of the past ten years are over, and if so, why?

Crime Fighting in the 1990s. An increase in violent crime in the 1980s, spurred in large part by illegal drugs, led citizens and policymakers to demand more get-tough-on-crime programs. In 1994, Congress passed the Violent Crime Control and Law Enforcement Act, which provided $30 billion over six years for crime control. Major provisions of the law included funding to add 100,000 police officers nationwide; a ten-year ban on certain semiautomatic assault weapons; an expansion of the death penalty to cover additional federal crimes; and approval to impose a mandatory life sentence on any criminal convicted of three felonies for violent crimes.

Crowded Prisons. This "get tough" approach did help bring about significant decreases in crime throughout the last decade, but it also led to other problems. In 2005, U.S. prisons and jails held more than 2.32 million people, a 1.9 percent increase from the previous year. Many legal experts argue that the nation's mandatory minimum sentencing guidelines unfairly imprison people for excessively long periods of time and waste taxpayer money. States and the federal government are debating the issue presently.

What Causes Crime? Many experts say the roots of crime are poverty, drug abuse, and lack of employment and education opportunities. Others blame easy access to firearms. Some believe the "culture"—especially violent video games, music, and movies—is lowering people's moral standards and is the engine behind many crimes. Some also criticize the judicial system for failing to rehabilitate convicted offenders or failing to keep such criminals off the streets.

Millions of Guns. Many law enforcement officials cite the availability of guns and the willingness of people to use them as major factors in the high crime rate. Americans own more than 200 million handguns, rifles, and shotguns. Although legal purchases are regulated, people can buy guns illegally with relative ease. Gun control advocates suffered a setback when the 1994 Assault Weapons Ban—which prohibited sales of certain semiautomatic weapons and ammunition—expired in September 2004.

The Role of Drugs. Most experts say that the sale and use of illegal drugs, particularly heroin, cocaine, and methamphetamine, contributes greatly to violent crime. The U.S. Department of Health and Human Services researches drug use annually in its National Survey on Drug Use and Health. The 2005 survey found that about 19.1 million Americans—7.9 percent of the population age 12 and over—were users of some sort of illicit drug. Ten percent of 12- to 17-year-olds admitted to using illegal drugs in the month

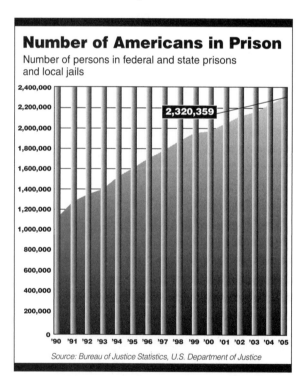

Number of Americans in Prison

Number of persons in federal and state prisons
and local jails

2,320,359

Source: Bureau of Justice Statistics, U.S. Department of Justice

According to the Sentencing Project, a criminal justice think tank, the United States imprisons a higher percentage of its population than any other country.

preceding the survey. Marijuana use is the most commonly reported, with 14.6 million users in the preceding month, or 6.1 percent of the population. A much smaller number—0.8 percent—are current cocaine users. Many Americans are also concerned about the increasing popularity of methamphetamine, or "crystal meth," a powerful drug produced from various chemical ingredients.

New Challenges and Boundaries in Law Enforcement

The Role of the Federal Government. The Preamble to the U.S. Constitution mandates that the government must "ensure domestic tranquility"—a responsibility that has been shared throughout the years by local, state, and federal governments. Basic crime prevention and law enforcement has traditionally been considered a "local issue." Therefore, state and local governments generally provide about 95 percent of all funding for law enforcement while the federal government complements these efforts by providing technical and strategic assistance and limited funding.

In the early twentieth century, the federal government began involving itself in the prosecution of treason, espionage, mail fraud, antitrust, and banking offenses. Since the 1970s, Congress has added more and more crimes to the federal statute. Many observers call this trend the "federalization" of law enforcement and criticize what they see as a seizure of authority from state and local control.

The terrorist attacks of September 11, 2001, demonstrated the existence of significant threats to domestic, or "homeland," security. The USA Patriot Act, passed by Congress six weeks after the attacks, granted law enforcement agencies sweeping new powers to conduct expanded telephone and Internet surveillance and to monitor, without "probable cause," some religious and political groups. The Patriot Act also authorized the FBI and the Central Intelligence Agency (CIA) to cooperate and share information more closely and to provide local law enforcement with much more information than they had previously received.

The result is a more concentrated, integrated system, connecting not only federal agencies but also local governments. Many Americans are concerned that to meet the demands of this partnership with the federal government, local law enforcement officials have become intelligence-gathering officers, possibly at the expense of their more traditional crime-fighting responsibilities. Others say they feel safer with the new changes, but nonetheless are worried about the federal government's expanded and piercing eye, trained on their neighborhoods and communities.

CURRENT ISSUES

The "Surveillance Society." With powers provided to it by the USA Patriot Act, the U.S. Justice Department began an overhaul of the nation's intelligence-gathering operations in 2002, lifting many restrictions on domestic surveillance. Then-Attorney General John Ashcroft described the actions as essential to the "new mission of preventing future terrorist activities."

While a majority of the American public applauded these measures, many advocacy groups, including the American Civil Liberties Union, the American Library Association, and Gun Owners of America, warn that the merging of intelligence collection and the ability of the government to carry out wiretaps, electronic and computer eavesdropping, searches,

A sign indicating the use of closed-circuit cameras is mounted to a traffic light post at an intersection in Philadelphia. Surveillance cameras are being installed in some city neighborhoods across the country to combat crime and terrorism.

AP Photo/Matt Rourke

video surveillance in public places, and a wide range of other information-gathering techniques will lead to dangerous, unchecked power.

These concerns were heightened in December 2005 with the revelation that President George W. Bush had authorized the National Security Agency (NSA) to monitor telephone and Internet communication of American citizens without first obtaining warrants. The White House admitted that it did not abide by the Foreign Intelligence Surveillance Act of 1978, which requires the government to obtain a court order before carrying out electronic surveillance. The president argued that he had the inherent authority under the Constitution, as commander in chief, to approve this type of operation.

In February 2006, it was revealed that several large telecommunications companies were asked to give the NSA access to the phone records of millions of Americans, making those communications available for "data mining," whereby a computer scans messages for terms that could indicate terrorist plots. Using these techniques, it is estimated that the NSA has identified and further reviewed the conversations and e-mail messages of thousands of Americans. This revelation prompted widespread criticism from civil liberties groups and some lawmakers. Throughout 2006, President Bush attempted to get congressional approval for the NSA program, but lawmakers were reluctant to pass such legislation without knowing more about how the program works.

In early 2007, Attorney General Alberto Gonzales announced that the Bush administration would now submit its requests for domestic surveillance to the Foreign Intelligence Surveillance Court for approval. This move appeased some citizens and members of Congress, but many others still worry that citizens' rights are being violated, often without their knowledge. The Democratic-controlled Congress has pledged to continue challenging the administration on the issue.

For such critics of the administration, the mere existence of a warrantless eavesdropping program confirms their fear that the federal government is exercising dangerous, unchecked authority to monitor the American people, creating what some call a "surveillance society." These critics concede that surveillance can be an essential tool to prevent major crimes from being committed. However, they argue that the increase and centralization of surveillance poses a great danger to citizens' civil liberties, especially since potentially vast amounts of information are being collected on people who have not been accused of wrongdoing. Opponents point out that many Americans are also being "spied" on by video cameras constantly recording public space—a tactic more popular since the bombing of London's mass transit system in the summer of 2005. A 2005 New York Civil Liberties Union study counted more than 4,600 cameras in just three neighborhoods in New York City, up from less than 1,000 there in 1998. The Fourth Amendment to the U.S. Constitution states that people, their houses, papers, and other personal items are protected against "unreasonable searches and seizures." Using video cameras to watch public places, say opponents of such surveillance techniques, constitutes an unreasonable search.

Proponents of the government's new policies contend that civil libertarians ignore the potential of aggressive investigative techniques to help prevent the commission of major crimes. The federal government has a duty in times of uncertainty and extreme danger to protect the public and minimize threats. Advocates of the policies argue that surveillance is a valid use of the state's power to protect its citizens. Supporters liken continuous video surveillance, for example, to a mechanical police officer: it does not intrude upon an individual's zone of privacy, but rather impartially records events occurring in public space, where individuals do not have reasonable expectations of privacy to begin with. Ultimately, say proponents of the government's new efforts, the only people who should fear aggressive surveillance are those planning or committing crimes.

Who's More at Risk? The terrorist attacks of 2001 forced the federal government, as well as cities and towns across the United States, to take a long, hard look at security, disaster preparedness, and emergency response plans. The Department of Homeland Security (DHS) is responsible for coordinating the federal government's anti-terrorism efforts and overseeing the distribution of federal funds to states and localities for this purpose. Originally, DHS calculated funding based mostly on population and a desire to spread equitably the funds among many cities, without necessarily considering their likelihood as terrorist targets. This formula was roundly criticized.

In January 2006, DHS revised its formula to focus more on "relative risk" when determining how to distribute the nearly $800 million in homeland security grants. Relative risk was

A Transportation Security Administration (TSA) worker fills a garbage can with confiscated items at a security checkpoint in the Denver International Airport in August 2006. The TSA banned all liquids and gels from carry-on luggage after a terror plot in Britain was discovered. The ban has since been modified, but passengers are still inconvenienced by the restrictions.

AP Photo/David Zalubowski

Identity Theft

One of the fastest-growing crimes is "identity theft," when someone's personal information, such as a social security or credit card number, is used without permission by another. In 2004, the Department of Justice estimated that 1 in 33 households (about 3.6 million) had experienced an identity theft in the previous six months, causing $3.2 billion in losses. Victims of identity theft often discover the crime only after they are contacted by debt collectors or credit card companies seeking payment for fraudulent charges. To prevent identity theft, consumers are urged to keep personal information secure and review credit reports and bank statements regularly.

calculated by examining a combination of factors including the locality's number of critical infrastructure facilities and large financial institutions, population density, proximity to international borders, and recent suspicious incidents. However, the results of this revised formula were also sharply criticized when it became clear that cities with the highest profile targets—such as New York City and Washington, D.C.—would see fewer federal homeland security dollars while some mid-sized—and seemingly safer—cities, such as Omaha, Charlotte, and Louisville, would receive more than the previous year. Meanwhile, the DHS list of identified potential terrorist targets has grown exponentially—from 160 in 2003 to 77,069 in 2006—causing many to wonder whether the department's priorities need to be re-examined once again.

Some experts believe that the bulk of federal homeland security dollars should be given to large metropolitan areas since they are more likely to be the targets of terrorist attacks than are rural areas or small cities far from the country's economic and population centers. It is not fair, observers say, to expect cities like Washington, D.C., New York, and Chicago, to foot the bill for first responders and emergency preparedness equipment when the threat of terrorism is a national problem and when attacks in these cities would devastate the national economy. The desire of individual lawmakers to steer homeland security funds back to their home states and districts should not take precedence over the logical concentration of federal homeland security spending on the nation's most vulnerable areas.

Critics of concentrating homeland security spending on big cities say that the government should not underestimate the possibility that terrorists will try to attack an unexpected target, as domestic terrorists did in Oklahoma City in 1995. These proponents of the revised funding formulas point out that rural areas and small cities are often home to some of the nation's most important infrastructure such as oil and gas fields, major agricultural farms, ports, and nuclear power plants. Moreover, they contend, big cities already have much of the equipment and expertise needed to respond to a terrorist attack while rural areas and small cities need federal dollars to develop these initiatives.

Rehabilitation or Imprisonment? Since the 1970s, the federal government has waged a "War on Drugs." In the ensuing decades, as drug use and drug-related crimes have soared, federal, state, and local governments have attempted to solve these problems mainly through anti-drug law enforcement efforts and mandatory minimum prison sentences for drug offenders. As a result of these policies, the number of drug offenders in federal and state prisons has skyrocketed.

According to the Department of Justice (DOJ), in 2003, 55 percent of federal prisoners and 20 percent of state prisoners were incarcerated due to drug-related charges. In 2005, DOJ estimated that 1 in 136 U.S. citizens were imprisoned and that federal prisons were holding about 34 percent more prisoners than they were intended to house. As prison overcrowding reaches crisis proportions, many lawmakers are wondering whether it is time to shift the focus away from punishment and toward rehabilitation of drug users.

Proponents of continuing a punishment-focused drug policy contend that stringent and consistent prison sentences are the best way to deter illegal drug use. Adults who choose to use or sell illegal drugs should be held accountable for their actions and governments should build more prisons if more space is needed to hold these criminals. While chronic addiction needs to be addressed, drug dealers and potential drug users (especially children) get the wrong message if those who break the law are not appropriately punished. Proponents of punishment say that President Bush's 2006 National Drug Control Strategy, which acknowledges the need to focus on rehabilitation but not at the expense of law enforcement, demonstrates the right set of priorities.

Supporters of increased funding for rehabilitation believe that automatic imprisonment for drug offenders—even those who have no prior convictions and who are not guilty of drug distribution or related violent crimes—only leads to prison overcrowding and does not address the root cause of the drug problem—drug addiction. States and localities that have experimented with increased funding for drug rehabilitation have had success: in California, a rehabilitation program for drug offenders begun in 2000 is saving about $173 million per year on prison costs; a similar initiative in New York City is partly responsible for that city's recent dramatic crime decrease and prison population decrease. Funding rehabilitation efforts for drug addicts in and out of prison is the best way to treat the illness that causes drug offenders to commit and repeat their crimes.

OUTLOOK

After decades of decline, the violent crime rate in the United States is on the rise again. Some lawmakers believe that the goal of combating street crime is being shortchanged by new priorities including the prevention of terrorism. As homeland security needs compete for law enforcement officials' time and money, many worry that crime may continue to increase in the coming years. The high proportion of crimes related to illegal drug use is also fueling the debate over whether rehabilitation or punishment is the best means of dealing with this problem.

THE DEBATE: CRIME AND SECURITY

Expanded government surveillance of citizens is necessary for public safety.

PRO: In the past, the United States has curtailed civil liberties to ensure greater protection of the nation and its citizens. These measures were usually temporary but absolutely necessary. With new threats facing Americans at home, it is important for the federal government to have far-reaching domestic surveillance powers to identify threats before attacks occur. A concentration of intelligence gathering will improve communication and collaboration and make everyone safer.

CON: While the threats to public safety are real, the answer does not lie in providing virtually unchecked surveillance powers to the federal government. Multiple abuses of this authority have been reported. Through increased monitoring by video camera, telephone, and Internet surveillance, ordinary citizens are now unfairly treated like would-be criminals. Strengthening intelligence-gathering and -sharing operations requires sensible reforms, not a blank check for the government to dismantle civil liberties.

Big cities should receive more federal homeland security funding.

PRO: Large metropolitan areas like Washington, D.C., and New York City should receive the majority of federal homeland security funds because they are the most likely targets of terrorist attacks. Combating terrorism is a national problem that should be supported by the federal government. Lawmakers should not steer homeland security funds to small cities and rural areas to win political favor, especially if those areas have only a remote chance of being attacked.

CON: Small cities and rural areas should receive a fair share of federal homeland security funds. Although these areas are not the nation's most prominent population centers, they are crucial to our nation's energy and food supply. Big cities have always been terrorist targets and have spent years developing infrastructure to prepare for attacks. In this new post-September 11 world, small cities and rural areas need federal help to catch up.

Anti-drug efforts should focus on rehabilitation over punishment.

PRO: Continuing to fill America's prisons with nonviolent drug offenders is only causing prison overcrowding, not solving the illegal drug use problem. Arresting more drug offenders and building more prisons is expensive and is not decreasing the number of drug users. Funding rehabilitation programs to address the underlying problem of drug addiction is the best way to combat drug crimes.

CON: The only way to deter and prevent drug crimes is to ensure that drug criminals receive and serve harsh prison sentences. Holding people accountable for their actions sends a message that illegal drug use will not be tolerated. While the problem of drug addiction should be addressed, it should not come at the expense of punishment and deterrence efforts.

THE ECONOMY

The state of the economy plays a large role in determining not only the strength of the United States, but also the mood of its people. The economy affects everyone. It governs how much money workers earn and what they can afford to buy. Consequently, the economy is an important issue to most Americans—and one likely to influence the way they vote. Economists measure growth in terms of wages, productivity, job creation, and the cost of living. These indicators show policymakers, investors, and the public the latest trends.

Sometimes, average citizens can be hit hard by economic problems. For example, beginning in 2006, many areas of the United States saw a rapid decline in the once booming housing market. As mortgage interest rates rose, home values stagnated or decreased. Many buyers who took on adjustable rate mortgages defaulted when their payments increased, some Americans lost their homes to foreclosure, and loan companies nationwide declared bankruptcy.

The American economy also relies on a complex system of global finance and trade. Low-wage labor in other countries affects the number and kinds of U.S. jobs—as well as wages and benefits. At the same time, worldwide industrialization has brought about global climate change—a trend that will probably affect the economies of the United States and many other countries. Decisions that citizens and governments make now will likely determine the extent of global warming and its long-term economic effects. Citizens and policymakers must ask: Who should bear the costs of addressing climate threats? Is it possible simultaneously to stem global warming and promote economic growth?

Ultimately, policymakers and economists must consider all these trends as they debate what the federal government should do to ensure that the great majority of Americans prosper.

KEY QUESTIONS

- Should the federal government do more to protect domestic jobs?

- Are "green" energy policies good for the economy?

- Should lawmakers increase regulation of mortgage lenders?

BACKGROUND

Economic Policy Basics

Government's Role. The American economy encompasses the production, distribution, and consumption of goods and services. For decades, U.S. lawmakers have struggled to determine the best way to regulate the economy. Economists and lawmakers alike have difficulty anticipating the economy's ups and downs, so they look to recent trends. They rely on statistics—issued by government agencies and private organizations—to make important policy decisions. When officials need to influence the economy, they use three major tools—fiscal policy, monetary policy, and trade policy.

Fiscal Policy. Congress and the president aim to promote steady economic growth, full employment, and stable prices through fiscal policy—the use of the federal government's taxing and spending powers. In addition to raising or lowering taxes, the government bolsters the economy by spending taxpayer dollars on specific programs—such as those that provide additional jobs—and on subsidies for important industries, like agriculture.

Monetary Policy. The federal government tries to promote steady growth without inflation or unemployment. It does so by controlling the amount of money in circulation. This function, called monetary policy, is entrusted to the Federal Reserve, which is the central bank of the United States. In 1913, Congress created the Federal Reserve, commonly called the Fed, to provide the nation with a safe, flexible, and stable financial system. The Fed issues U.S. currency and regulates short-term interest rates to banks. A board of governors, selected by the president and confirmed by the Senate, runs the Fed; board members serve fourteen-year terms.

Federal Reserve Board Chairman Ben Bernanke, shown here testifying before Congress in 2007, is the nation's chief of monetary policy.

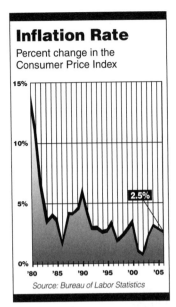

Inflation Rate

Percent change in the Consumer Price Index

2.5%

'80   '85   '90   '95   '00   '05

Source: Bureau of Labor Statistics

The rate of inflation measures how fast the prices of goods and services increase. The Consumer Price Index (CPI) was 2.5 percent higher at the end of 2006 than at the end of 2005.

Trade Policy. Trade—the exchange of goods and services among nations—typically increases a country's overall standard of living. Trade policy includes promoting exports, restricting imports when necessary, and pursuing agreements that boost trade benefits.

Measuring the Economy

Statistics form the heart of economics, providing a snapshot of the relative health of the economy. Consumers often make decisions about big purchases, such as homes and cars, when they feel secure about their jobs and the economy. Bankers use statistics to monitor the performance of American companies and other factors that help them decide where to invest. This data also enables policymakers to steer the economy toward growth.

Inflation. Inflation is the continuing rise in prices for goods and services. The higher the rate of inflation, the faster prices go up. Unless accompanied by a comparable increase in wages, inflation lowers the standard of living. In other words, people can afford to buy less. Inflation particularly hurts people living on fixed incomes, such as retired Americans. A high rate of inflation also induces people to buy on credit and to forgo saving money. The economy suffers when individuals do not save because banks then have less money to lend for investments. Inflation has been low in recent years—between 1 and 4 percent since the early 1990s, and most recently, 2.5 percent in 2006.

The government can control inflation in a variety of ways, but the most common method is through monetary policy. The Federal Reserve Board can reduce, or tighten, the money supply by raising interest rates. When interest rates go up, consumer spending decreases, and prices level off or go down, thus reducing inflation. When the Fed reduces interest rates, it increases the money supply, and consumer spending increases.

Unemployment. The rate of unemployment refers to the percentage of men and women who want to work but cannot find jobs. Because there are always people between jobs, the unemployment rate is never zero. According to many economists, full employment occurs when 4 percent or less of the employable population is looking for work. The average unemployment rate for 2006 dropped to 4.6 percent from 5.1 percent in 2005. Traditionally, unemployment hits groups such as minorities, women, and out-of-school teens harder than others.

Unemployment also affects federal, state, and local government treasuries. When men and women are out of work, they pay less or no taxes. As a result, the government takes in less revenue but has to pay out more in unemployment compensation and other social services. In times of high unemployment, the government works to create new jobs—usually by lowering taxes and interest rates to encourage businesses to expand their operations and hire more workers.

Recession. A recession is a period of economic decline marked by rising unemployment and reduced production, spending, and consumer demand. To stimulate economic growth and pull the economy out of a recession, the Fed can make more money available to banks for lending by lowering the interest rate it charges them. The government can combat recession through fiscal policies, such as funding programs to create jobs or reducing taxes to leave consumers and businesses with more cash to spend. Historically, the U.S. economy has gone through cycles of recession and recovery. The most dramatic downturn began in 1929 when the stock market collapse led to the Great Depression of the 1930s. The latest recession occurred in 2001; it was considered mild by many economists and officially lasted eight months, although the economy was slow to recover for several years thereafter.

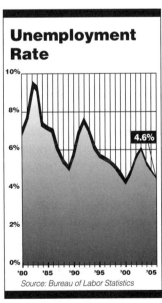

Unemployment Rate

10%

8%

6% — 4.6%

4%

2%

0%

'80 '85 '90 '95 '00 '05

Source: Bureau of Labor Statistics

The rate of unemployment measures the percentage of workers that cannot find jobs. The average unemployment rate for 2006 fell to 4.6 percent from 5.1 percent in 2005.

Productivity. The rate of labor productivity refers to the amount of goods and services produced per person per hour. A rising rate of productivity usually leads to higher wages and profits, and lower prices. Although high productivity and modernization are generally considered good for the economy, they can change the nature of the workforce and sometimes increase unemployment. For example, new machines and computers can increase output, but also reduce the need for workers. In 2006, business productivity rose 1.7 percent over that of 2005, marking a slip from increases of more than 2 percent from 2000 through 2005. Despite these productivity boosts, U.S. wages have not kept pace. Some analysts cite growing competition from cheap labor in foreign countries as an explanation.

Other Economic Factors

International Interdependence. Increasing trade among the world's nations has made them more interdependent than ever before. For example, as the world's largest importer, the United States creates jobs overseas. Similarly, the strength of the U.S. economy depends largely on how well American products sell in foreign markets. Furthermore, the U.S. economy can be adversely affected by rising costs of certain imports, like oil, a necessity to fuel transportation and industry.

To coordinate policies for worldwide economic issues, the world's leading industrial nations meet annually at the Group of Eight (G-8) summit. The G-8 countries—Canada, France, Germany, Italy, Japan, Russia, the United Kingdom, and the United States—discuss trade agreements, unemployment problems, exchange rates, and economic difficulties, and try to develop cooperative solutions. European Union (EU) representatives also participate in these summits, although the EU is not an official member of the G-8.

The Stock Market. People invest in the stock market by buying shares of ownership, called stocks, in companies. If businesses make profits, their stocks generally go up in value. In recent years, millions of working citizens began buying stocks through mutual investment funds and employer retirement

Personal Savings in Decline

The rate of personal savings, or the difference between earnings and spending, in the United States has been dropping since the mid-1980s, when it was about 10 percent. The Commerce Department announced that in 2006, the personal savings rate was -1 percent, the worst since the Great Depression. A negative savings rate means that Americans spent more than they earned. In some cases, consumers have dipped into their savings accounts, the equity of their homes, or charged purchases on credit cards. Experts say such practices might be the result of poor budgeting habits or stagnating wages, which force people to spend beyond their means to survive. For comparison, China's estimated personal savings rate is 30 percent.

plans—enabling more Americans to profit from the market's highs, but also making them more vulnerable to its lows. In April 2007, the Dow Jones Industrial Average (a measure of stock market activity and company performance) closed at a record 13,000, a high that surpassed the previous milestone of 12,000 set in October 2006.

Recent Economic Developments

Economic Expansion and Recession. From 1992 to 2000, the economy went through the largest expansion in postwar American history, fueled by technological innovation and the rising stock market. Many of the stocks that increased most in value in the 1990s were in telecommunications and technology—Internet, telephone, computer, and fiber-optics companies. However, many of these stock prices were based on projected rather than previously reported profits. By 2001, many projected profits failed to materialize, which caused the values of many technology stocks to plummet. Meanwhile, recession set in as retail sales and manufacturing decreased, and unemployment and bankruptcies increased.

AP Photo/ Paul Sakuma

The American economy is bolstered by innovation and success in high technology industries. In November 2006, Apple released the iPod Shuffle, its smallest mp3 player.

Throughout the recession and the start of the recovery, the Fed tried to stimulate consumer and business spending by lowering interest rates thirteen consecutive times starting in 2001. In 2003, the rate was dropped to 1 percent, the lowest since 1959. The resulting low mortgage rates helped spur demand for housing and led to skyrocketing home prices in and around many cities. Between June 2004 and June 2006, the Fed raised the interest rate sixteen times to discourage inflation. The increase in rates led to a bust of the housing "bubble" beginning in 2006, ushering in a period of devaluing home prices, mortgage foreclosures, and lender bankruptcies.

Tax Cuts. In 2001 and 2003, Congress passed $1.7 trillion in tax cuts at the urging of President George W. Bush. The 2001 legislation reduced income taxes, expanded retirement and savings programs, and repealed the estate tax. Those cuts were based on budget surpluses projected to occur over the next decade. However, rather than surpluses, the government began running deficits in 2002. Policymakers blamed the recession, war spending, and reduced tax revenues. The 2003 tax cuts—intended to help spur economic growth— further reduced income taxes and cut rates on capital gains and dividends. Most of these tax cuts will expire in 2011 unless Congress votes to extend them or make them permanent. Supporters argue that tax cuts have contributed to increased consumer spending, higher productivity, and business growth. However, detractors counter that these tax-cutting policies have overwhelmingly favored the richest Americans, contributing to a widening divide between lower-income citizens and the ultra-wealthy.

Jobs in the Global Economy. In spite of signs of economic recovery in 2003 and 2004, unemployment remained problematic, with some geographic regions hit much harder than others.

Policymakers differ over the causes. Some point out that job creation typically lags behind the resumption of economic growth. Others suggest that the economy is in a natural process of restructuring to become more efficient and profitable. After several years near 6 percent, the unemployment rate had improved to 4.5 percent by April 2007.

Nevertheless, some Americans remained concerned about job prospects. A number of manufacturers have closed factories in the United States and moved them to nations like Mexico and China, where labor costs are lower. Certain industries have eliminated white-collar jobs—such as those in software development—and hired skilled workers in places like India, Russia, and the Philippines for a fraction of the cost. Other companies need fewer workers thanks to higher productivity and modernization. Finally, some businesses have hired free-lancers and consultants rather than full-time employees, for whom companies would have to pay benefits and payroll taxes.

Energy and the Global Environment. Economic growth usually entails increasing energy consumption. Factories need more fuel to make more products, and consumers use more energy as they prosper. In recent years, however, scientists and policymakers in the international community have acknowledged that burning fossil fuels has produced global warming. This gradual increase in temperature causes oceans to warm, polar ice to melt, sea levels to rise, and extreme weather events—including hurricanes, tsunamis, and drought—all of which can lead to devastating environmental and economic problems. As they consider solutions, industry leaders seek to balance the costs of transitioning to "green" technologies against the possible economic calamity of inaction.

CURRENT ISSUES

Offshore Outsourcing. In recent years, a number of American companies have hired foreign companies or laborers to do work once performed within U.S. borders. The U.S. job losses affect both low and highly skilled workers, such as those in software development, accounting, and medical radiology. Many refer to this practice as "offshore outsourcing." Some Americans want the federal government to raise trade barriers to limit outsourcing. Others think that the government should provide incentives for companies to keep jobs in the United States.

Those who support government action to keep American jobs at home argue that the health of the economy depends on keeping citizens employed in good jobs. If jobs are sent offshore, Americans are left with fewer employment options. Meanwhile, increased competition for the remaining domestic jobs, supporters say, will keep unemployment high and wages low—conditions that ultimately restrict the American economy. Although supporters of protections agree that free trade practices that allow companies to relocate and outsource often work well, they insist that the government must intervene to ensure that trade is also fair to U.S. workers.

As the economic growth continues, opponents contend, new jobs will be created and unemployment will drop automatically. Such free trade proponents acknowledge that a small percentage of jobs do get lost as companies pursue ways to operate efficiently at the most profit. But, they say, such efficiency saves consumers money and increases companies' profits, thus providing money that goes into the domestic economy and creates jobs in other sectors. The best course of action, say opponents, is to recognize that some people will lose jobs, and to provide better safety nets to help such people survive until they gain the skills they need to find new work.

"Green" Energy and Economic Growth. In April 2007, the United Nations and more than 200 scientists issued a 1,500-page report detailing the status and probable outcomes of global warming, concluding that human activity is driving dangerous climate change. Consequently, there is a growing consensus that governments must reduce the buildup of carbon dioxide in the atmosphere. Such news has spurred environmentalists, policymakers, and even some industry leaders to recommend a broad range of solutions, including imposing

new regulations (such as caps and taxes on emissions) and offering incentives that encourage investment in technology and greater efficiency.

Supporters of "green" energy policies point out that severe storms like Hurricane Katrina are already straining the insurance industry and costing the U.S. government billions of dollars. To avoid such environmentally based economic woes, government, industry, and individuals must change how they consume fossil fuels. Public awareness campaigns and Al Gore's popular documentary *An Inconvenient Truth* have helped increase consumer demand for green products, such as Toyota's popular hybrid car the Prius. Therefore, proponents of new energy policies argue that there are big profits to be made in the green market. They also say that corporations will save money through energy conservation and that investments in green technologies will create jobs. Advocates of environmentally sound energy policies recommend that various changes be implemented across economic sectors over time, so that industries avoid big costs all at once and the nation averts any serious economic disruption.

Blogging Their Way Out of Debt

America is sometimes called a "credit card nation," reflecting the amount of debt U.S. consumers rack up using plastic. In 2006, the average American household carried about $7,000 in credit card debt. Because most credit cards charge interest of more than 20 percent, that kind of debt is very expensive—and very difficult to pay off. Some desperate consumers have started "debt blogs" to confess their financial sins, rein in their spending, and focus on paying off their debt. With a blog, hundreds of people can oversee the consumer's progress; the consumer thus has great incentive to change. Although credit cards often get a bad rap, banks are quick to point out that credit cards do serve useful economic functions. They simplify transactions, and available lines of credit can help people get through temporary financial crunches.

Critics of green energy regulations counter that the responsibility for implementing energy policies will be overwhelmingly borne by the utility and transportation sectors, which produce the most greenhouse gases. They say that strengthening emissions rules will hamper economic growth, cause inflation, and result in job losses. Furthermore, opponents argue, these policies might not even effectively reduce carbon dioxide emissions in the long run. Unless China and other developing nations cooperate, U.S. energy regulations might have no measurable effect—and will surely hurt U.S. economic competitiveness. Finally, many critics question predictions about the long-term effects of global warming, which they say are alarmist and unrealistic. They argue that society will be able to adapt to changing environmental conditions, as will the Earth.

Regulating Lenders. When the real estate bubble collapsed in 2006 and 2007, the first mortgage lenders to suffer were those who provide loans to people with bad or little credit history. These sub-prime lenders charge borrowers higher interest rates, and sometimes offer adjustable interest rates, to offset their increased risk. As the Fed increased interest rates from 2004 to 2006, many people saw their house payments increase dramatically. At the same time, falling demand decreased home values. Many people were "stuck" with homes they could not sell and loans they could not afford. Rates of delinquency (late payments) and defaults rose; lenders foreclosed on loans; people lost their homes; and some sub-prime lenders even declared bankruptcy.

Senator Charles E. Schumer (D-N.Y.) said, "This is a terrible instance where a lack of oversight has led to a Wild West mentality among unscrupulous lenders and, frankly, the exploitation of large numbers of financially unsophisticated borrowers." Consequently, lawmakers are considering a number of proposals to regulate the mortgage business. Some advocates want lenders to be clearer on the mortgage terms, so that borrowers better understand their loan commitments. Others want lenders to ensure that loans better suit customers' ability to repay them. Supporters of such regulation argue that these policies will "clean up" predatory and fraudulent lending, which they say led to real estate speculation and over-valued properties. Proponents say that greater federal oversight will shore up the lackluster housing market, reassure investors, and help borrowers and homeowners.

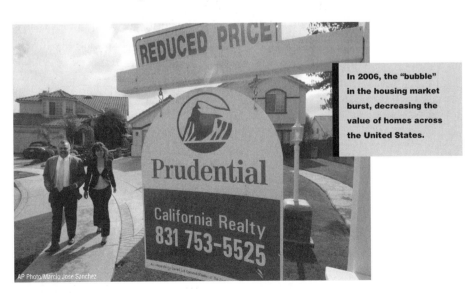

In 2006, the "bubble" in the housing market burst, decreasing the value of homes across the United States.

Opponents of greater regulation point out that new types of loans, combined with historically low interest rates, have led to record rates of homeownership—69 percent of American households in 2006. This statistic represents a great financial achievement for millions of American families. At the same time, the mortgage business has become bigger and more competitive. Fees are much lower than those imposed twenty years ago. Additional regulation, critics contend, will make loans more expensive and stifle innovation. Moreover, they point out that risky mortgages ultimately are bad for people who invest in banks and lending companies, and say the current crisis has already prompted lenders to reassess and improve their lending procedures.

OUTLOOK

The well-being of every American depends on the health of the economy. Even as the U.S. economy shows signs of growth and the unemployment rate falls, global warming creates economic vulnerability. Policymakers, industry leaders, and consumers debate the merits of "green" energy policies, as Americans grapple with a complex irony—that economic growth is powered by energy consumption, which could eventually harm the U.S. economy if it is not managed properly. Other forces, such as instability in the housing market and job outsourcing continue to cause concern. These and other issues will confront officials as they try to cultivate prosperity for all Americans.

THE DEBATE: THE ECONOMY

The federal government should do more to protect domestic jobs.

PRO: Nations like China and India have been stealing jobs away from American workers. The federal government must use trade barriers and incentives to keep domestic jobs at home. If American workers, both in manufacturing and service sectors, must compete with foreign workers, they will face increasingly lower wages and reduced standards of living, thus harming the economy.

CON: Companies will always seek to operate in ways that reduce costs and increase profits. This might result in some job losses, but the federal government should not interfere with this natural move toward economic efficiency. When companies bring profits home, they inject money into the U.S. economy, boosting job creation in other areas. The net effect is to strengthen the nation's economy.

"Green" energy policies are good for the economy.

PRO: Unfettered global warming will lead to devastating economic effects similar to those resulting from Hurricane Katrina. The U.S. government must impose new regulations and incentives to discourage greenhouse gas emissions. Market demand for green products and technological investment will yield corporate profits and domestic job gains. Such benefits of "going green," along with avoiding drought and flood, are good for the economy.

CON: The effects of global warming are exaggerated, and the economic costs of transitioning to green energy sources are underestimated. Utilities and car companies will bear the brunt of the costs for new energy regulations, expenses that will ultimately weaken their competitiveness, and force them to cut jobs and raise prices. Emissions caps in the United States will not make significant reductions in global carbon dioxide if China, India, and others do not change, too.

Lawmakers should increase regulation of mortgage lenders.

PRO: Lax lending standards promoted real estate speculation and fraud, causing serious problems in the housing market, issues that threaten to spill over into the economy at large. Mortgage lenders need greater federal oversight to ensure that borrowers understand their loan agreements and have the financial means to pay for their homes. Regulations will help stabilize home values and protect consumers.

CON: New types of mortgage loans and other innovations in lending have increased rates of homeownership—an indicator of economic well-being—to record-high levels. American families have benefited from reduced loan fees as well. Increasing federal regulation of mortgage lenders threatens to overturn these advances. Sound loans yield profits; lenders have already revised their procedures to ensure their success.

EDUCATION

To serve its citizens and help the country prosper, the United States provides a free public education to all students from kindergarten through twelfth grade. The nation does not offer free postsecondary education—the rising costs of which are an issue of great debate—but the government and private organizations do offer scholarship, grant, and loan programs for some students.

The public education system strives to prepare students for productive citizenship, work, and adult life. But people have long worried that public schooling fails many students. This view has led to frequent efforts to improve the system.

KEY QUESTIONS

- Will increased funding make the No Child Left Behind law more effective?

- Should the federal government encourage states to adopt national content standards?

- Should the federal government do more to help students pay for college?

The most recent reform efforts began in the 1980s. States, which are primarily responsible for education, began adopting standards of learning for all academic subjects. They also implemented regular tests. Building on the momentum for change, the No Child Left Behind (NCLB) law of 2001 put the federal government firmly behind the push to improve education. The sweeping law requires regular standardized tests and school accountability in an effort to lift overall achievement and close achievement gaps between white students and students from some ethnic minorities.

In recent years, policymakers and others have closely followed test scores, the implementation of NCLB, and the rising costs of college tuition. Among the many reform proposals on the table are raising teachers' salaries, creating a national curriculum, offering more school choice, increasing school funding, giving schools greater flexibility, and allowing private companies and organizations to run schools. Many people believe that more can be done to improve education, but disagree on how to best ensure a high-quality education for all students.

BACKGROUND

Public Education in the United States

Americans have always valued education. The Puritans viewed education as an important means of passing on religious teachings. Many Americans hoped that publicly supported schools would wipe out the legacy of the British system, in which the ability to read and write separated the economic classes. Since its inception in the mid-1800s, the nation's public school system has also helped millions of immigrant children learn the English language and the skills necessary to succeed in their new country.

The U.S. public school system is highly decentralized. Traditionally, local and state governments have had primary responsibility for running the schools, with local school districts determining programs of study, selecting books, and hiring teachers. A superintendent heads an administration that manages each school district, while a board of education, usually elected by the people, makes budget and policy decisions. Some Americans say that a major problem with the education system is that schools are often funded unequally because local real estate taxes, commonly used to finance education, vary widely. Wealthy districts in which land, homes, and buildings have a higher market value take in more taxes and thus can afford more modern schools and higher teacher salaries than can districts with lower property values.

State governments commonly distribute funds to local schools, set accreditation standards, certify teachers, and provide other guidelines for public schools. The federal government was generally not involved in education until the 1950s. Although it is taking an ever-larger role in directing policies today, the federal government gives U.S. schools just over 8 percent of total school expenditures. State and local governments pay the rest.

Most U.S. students take advantage of free public education. Today, more than 48 million attend public schools, including nearly 1 million students who attend charter schools, publicly funded schools that operate independently. More than 6 million students pay tuition to attend private schools, which are often run by religious groups. More than 1 million students are schooled at home.

Twentieth-Century Turning Points in Public Education

School Desegregation. In the landmark case of *Brown v. Board of Education of Topeka, Kansas* (1954), the U.S. Supreme Court ruled that racially segregated public schools were unconstitutional. Later court decisions ordered schools to desegregate. To comply, many school districts began busing students to schools outside their neighborhoods to bring together children of different races and ethnic backgrounds. In 1991, the Supreme Court ruled that districts could be released from court-ordered busing plans if they could show that they had done their best to eliminate the effects of segregation.

The Great Society. In the 1960s, President Lyndon Johnson tried to address the problem of poverty through his Great Society programs. Among them, he proposed three new federal education programs: the Economic Opportunity Act (1964), the Elementary and Secondary Education Act (1965), and the Higher Education Act (1965). Included in these laws were provisions funding Project Head Start for disadvantaged preschool-aged children and establishing college loan programs.

In a major turning point for U.S. public education, the Supreme Court ruled in 1954 that segregated schools were unconstitutional. Afterward, schools like the one to the right in Ft. Myer, Virginia, took steps to racially integrate.

Bettmann/CORBIS

Recent Reform Efforts

School Choice. Traditionally, public school students could only attend a public school in their neighborhood. Arguing that such a system confined some students to failing schools, policymakers and advocates began proposing school choice or school voucher programs. In these programs, which first appeared about twenty years ago, parents receive state or federal government coupons to help them pay for their children's education at private, often religious (parochial) schools of their choosing. In 2002, the Supreme Court ruled that school voucher programs that allow taxpayer money to underwrite private or parochial school tuition do not infringe on the constitutional separation of church and state as long as parents' choices include some nonreligious schools.

Despite some public misgivings and occasional court challenges, major voucher programs exist in Arizona, Maine, Ohio, Wisconsin, Vermont, and the District of Columbia. Furthermore, federal law now mandates a school choice plan among public schools, requiring failing schools to allow parents to send their children to a better-performing or safer public school. However, so far, less than 1 percent of eligible students have chosen this option.

Standards and Accountability. In the 1980s, states began developing standards of learning, defining what students should be learning statewide, and holding teachers, school administrators, and school districts more accountable for students' achievement. Many states began to link standards-related testing with promotion, graduation, school funding, and accreditation.

No Child Left Behind. In 2001, Congress created the most sweeping education reform legislation in more than three decades when it passed the No Child Left Behind law (NCLB). The law reflects many of President George W. Bush's education initiatives, and aims to close achievement gaps among students from different ethnic and socioeconomic backgrounds, as well as among those with special needs or learning disabilities. It mandates nationwide improvements,

Evolving Controversy on Teaching Evolution

The scientific theory of evolution forms the basis of modern biology and has been taught in public schools for decades—but not without controversy. In the past, some public schools tried to teach creationism—the biblically based perspective that Earth and man were created by God. The courts ruled against this. The latest controversy involves an idea known as "intelligent design," which seeks to cast doubt on evolution's singular role in the expansion of life. Intelligent design (ID) proposes that life is too complex to have developed solely from random genetic mutations and natural selection, and thus an unnamed intelligent designer must be involved. In recent years, some school districts mandated that the "controversy" over evolution and the idea of intelligent design be presented in school science classes—prompting court challenges and national debates.

saying that all students should be proficient in reading and mathematics by 2014.

The law requires accountability for students' academic achievement. Among its requirements, NCLB mandates that states test students annually in reading and mathematics from third grade through eighth grade and once in high school. Federal funding is tied to those results. Testing in science was added in 2007. States that do not adhere to the law's requirements risk losing federal education money.

Highly Qualified Teachers. Improving teaching is a major goal of NCLB, which requires all states to have a highly qualified teacher in every classroom. To be highly qualified according to NCLB, a teacher must have a college degree, a state license, and competency in subjects taught. Meeting the NCLB teaching requirement presented a challenge to states, which had to be given an extension on the original deadline for compliance. Rural areas in particular criticize the requirement as impractical for situations in which a single teacher may have to teach multiple subjects. Some leaders have called the requirement unreasonable because it focuses more on teachers' paper credentials than on effective teaching skills. Some policymakers want greater flexibility and propose changing the NCLB provision from "highly qualified" to "highly effective" teachers.

CURRENT ISSUES

Making NCLB Work. More than five years after NCLB was signed into law, results remain mixed. Scores from the 2005 national assessments show that the gap in scores between white students and black students narrowed for fourth-grade mathematics. However, for fourth-grade reading and eighth-grade reading and math, the gap remained unchanged. Other studies of state results confirm that gaps remained despite general overall improvement in scores. Some blame the lack of progress on insufficient federal funding, which has been an ongoing complaint from many states since the law's inception. Although the federal government gives the states money, many say the funding does not cover the full costs of changes required by NCLB, including increased testing and tutoring programs and the adoption of new curricula and textbooks. Some say that to close the achievement gap by 2014, funding must be increased.

Those who favor increasing funding for NCLB argue that the law has placed an unfunded mandate on states by requiring

AP Photo/The Gazette, Jim Slosiarek

The NCLB law requires high schools receiving federal funding to give military recruiters the same access to students on school grounds as those schools give to college and corporate recruiters. The law also requires schools to provide students' contact information to recruiters, but parents can opt not to share their children's information.

changes without providing enough money to implement them. Funding supporters claim that the government underfunded NCLB programs by tens of billions of dollars and thus handicapped states' efforts to close the achievement gap. As long as this situation continues, these critics contend, the NCLB goals cannot be achieved. Furthermore, they argue that even more funding should be directed to measures that will directly benefit low-performing students, like programs to attract high-quality teachers to poor schools and for early childhood education.

Others say that the government already spends generous amounts on NCLB initiatives and gives states more flexibility than ever before on how to spend the money. They emphasize that funding for programs authorized by NCLB has increased 41 percent since the law passed. They also caution against rushing to judgment against the law and note that many states just fully implemented it in 2005. These NCLB supporters argue that the nation should wait to evaluate progress before spending more money. Many reason that rather than ask for more funds, schools should improve their strategies for meeting the needs of low-performing students.

Answering to Higher Standards. The NCLB law requires schools to show annual yearly progress in assessments of mathematics and reading, but allows the individual states to set their own standards and develop the tests. Some critics worry that states are "dumbing down" their standards to allow students to pass and thus maintain the flow of federal education dollars. They point to comparisons of state test results and results from the federally funded National Assessment of Education Progress (NAEP), a test conducted nationwide to measure long-term national trends. One study in 2006 noted that states reported 68 percent of their fourth-grade students as proficient in reading, whereas NAEP results deemed only 31 percent of fourth-graders proficient.

Worried that this trend could undermine the goals of NCLB, some legislators and education leaders have argued that national content standards are the only sure-fire way to guarantee that all students are encouraged and able to reach rigorous benchmarks. In 2007, some members of Congress introduced legislation that would, if enacted, offer incentives to states to voluntarily adopt national content standards created by a national board. But the idea of national standards has

Charters for Success?

Are charter schools the way to successful education reform in the United States? Since the 1990s, charter schools have been favored by some reformers and legislators despite the protests of many public school advocates. Currently, about 4,000 charter schools exist in forty states and serve about 1 million students. Nonprofit groups or for-profit companies run the schools, which are funded with taxpayer dollars but are free from school board regulation and other traditional rules. Charter schools must, however, comply with the requirements of the NCLB law. Some charter schools have shown great success in educating students, but one small national study in 2006 reported that when students' race and socioeconomic status were factored in, students in public schools generally outperformed their peers in charter schools. More research is under way.

been rejected before. In the 1990s, critics shot down the idea when President Bill Clinton and others raised it. Despite some growth in support since then, establishing national content standards remains controversial.

Those calling for voluntary national content standards argue that the current patchwork of state standards fails students and the nation by allowing too many students to receive substandard educations. Supporters cite the concerns of business leaders who worry that weak state standards threaten America's economic competitiveness by producing students unable to succeed in the adult world. Proponents say the proof that national standards work lies abroad; several of the nations that outscore the United States on international education assessments have national curricula. Supporters discount concerns about federal interference with states' rights, arguing that any national standards would be optional. Finally, proponents insist that federal involvement would be restricted to establishing benchmarks and that the states would still make the decisions about how students are taught.

Critics contend that national content standards run counter to the long tradition—established by the U.S. Constitution—of local control of schools. They argue that local leaders know what's best for their students and should be making the curriculum decisions, not the federal government. Critics further contend that standards cannot be considered "voluntary" if states must follow them to receive critical federal

New regulations issued by the federal government in 2006 will enable school districts to expand the number of single-sex classes and schools. Some research suggests that under certain circumstances, students learn better when separated by gender. However, critics charge that same-sex education is discriminatory.

AP Photo/Charleston Daily Mail/Bob Wojcieszak

Photo Courtesy of The University of Virginia. Dan Addison

Higher education costs have increased dramatically over the past decade. In 1998, it cost $4,866 per year for an in-state student to attend the University of Virginia in Charlottesville (left). In 2007, the annual tuition was $8,005, a 65% increase. Experts say infrastructure and technology costs along with decreased state contributions and increased health care and utilities expenses are to blame.

funding. Opponents of national standards also argue that the nation would find it difficult if not impossible to reach agreement on what the specific standards should be, as evidenced by recent controversies over the teaching of evolution in science classrooms. Some opponents reject the notion that U.S. education faces a "crisis" requiring a federal solution, asserting instead that U.S. economic strength shows that the decentralized education system works.

Paying for College. For more than a decade, the average cost of college tuition has grown faster than the rate of inflation. Accordingly, between 2001 and 2006, student loan balances rose 16 percent, to an average of more than $14,000 per student. Many members of Congress and others believe that the government should do more to ensure that college remains financially accessible and that students do not graduate overburdened by debt. In January 2007, the House of Representatives passed a measure that would, if enacted, cut the current federally subsidized student loan interest rate in half. Senators and representatives also proposed measures that would increase the dollar value of Pell Grants (federal grants to low-income students that do not need to be paid back), provide higher tax credits for student debt, and offer more flexible loan repayment options. However, not everyone agrees that such measures would allow greater access to college.

Those who advocate increased financial support argue that higher education leads to higher lifetime earnings and better overall well-being, and that the more educated the citizenry, the stronger America's economic competitiveness. Thus, the federal government makes a wise investment when it makes college accessible to more students. Such proponents also stress that students need relief; some graduate from college with such heavy debt burdens that they must postpone buying homes, starting families, and saving for retirement, all of which could have adverse effects on society. Advocates contend that halving interest rates could save students with $20,000 in loans about $4,000 overall. Supporters also say that the federal government can pay for measures like interest rate reductions and larger grants by raising fees on lenders, many of whom are growing rich off student debt.

Opponents counter that federal student financial aid, which has doubled since 2001, is already generous enough. They argue that taxpayers should not be asked to subsidize college-goers who will eventually earn good incomes. Furthermore, they contend that loan and grant initiatives fail to address the real issue—the rising costs of college. According to these critics, there is evidence that increased federal subsidies for loans and grants actually prompt further increases in tuition, thus worsening the problem. Instead of lowering rates, the federal government should confront colleges about this trend. Finally, opponents point out that halving student loan interest rates would cost the government $18 billion over five years and hinder efforts to reduce the budget deficit.

OUTLOOK

Education policy involves many complex issues, such as what to teach and how to teach it, and how to establish and pay for schools that provide equal opportunities for students and raise their achievement. Citizens, policymakers, educators, and others disagree about how to resolve these issues. However, most agree that the trend of increased federal involvement in the schools is likely to continue.

THE DEBATE: EDUCATION

Increased funding will make the No Child Left Behind law more effective.

PRO: Without increased funding, states cannot meet NCLB achievement goals by 2014. So far, the law has burdened states with unfunded mandates. States have struggled to make progress, as evidenced by the persistent achievement gap. When programs are fully funded, achievement will increase and NCLB will be a success.

CON: Achievement may be lagging because many of the provisions of NCLB were just implemented in 2005. It is certainly not due to lack of funds—the federal government is spending more on education than ever before. The law needs time to work, and schools need to refine their strategies to reach achievement goals.

The federal government should encourage states to adopt national content standards.

PRO: Differing state content standards mean that students nationwide receive unequal educations. National standards would ensure equal opportunities for students and allow the nation to truly measure students' progress. Voluntary standards would not violate states' rights and would help the nation achieve the important goals of NCLB.

CON: National standards would create new federal bureaucracy and be counterproductive to the nation's education goals. States and local school boards know better than the government in Washington what is best for their students. Furthermore, it would be nearly impossible to come to a national consensus on specific standards.

The federal government should do more to help students pay for college.

PRO: America benefits from a college-educated citizenry. The federal government should increase efforts to help students afford college and graduate without punishing debt burdens. Measures like reducing interest rates will save students thousands of dollars, and can be paid for by raising fees on lenders.

CON: Increasing federal subsidies is not the right approach to making college more accessible. The federal government already gives generous amounts of aid. Increasing aid will cost billions and add to the budget deficit. Rather than spending more money, the government should investigate rising tuition costs.

HEALTH CARE

Illness strikes people of all ages and incomes, and Americans spend more than people in any other nation on medical treatment—about $2 trillion in 2005. This figure translates into an average of $6,697 for every man, woman, and child. Health care spending now comprises one-sixth of the nation's economy. Many policymakers and citizens agree that soaring medical costs have contributed to a crisis in the health care system.

In the United States, most people pay for medical expenses through insurance—often provided through employers or government programs. Insurance can pay for up to 90 percent of certain medical fees. However, the price of insurance has risen dramatically with the cost of medical services. Some companies can no longer afford to provide insurance, so many working people go without it. Americans over the age of 65 are eligible for Medicare, the government's program to insure older and disabled men and women. Another government program, Medicaid, assists the lowest-income citizens with medical bills. Despite these safety nets, some people fall through the cracks. According to the U.S. Census Bureau, 16 percent of the population—almost 47 million people—had no health insurance in 2005. Many more are underinsured, meaning their coverage is inadequate.

There are many problems facing U.S. health care. The rising cost of Medicare is, according to many, unsustainable. How can policymakers rein in those costs and improve patient care? Also, recent years have seen a number of cases of food poisoning, raising serious food safety concerns. How can the country better monitor its agricultural and food products to protect citizens' health?

KEY QUESTIONS

- Should health care reform be comprehensive or incremental?

- Should lawmakers impose quality standards for Medicare doctors?

- Should the government reform its food safety regulations?

BACKGROUND

The U.S. Health Care System

American hospitals and doctors are among the best in the world. Medical students from foreign countries vie to train and conduct research in the United States. Yet many Americans cannot afford to visit a doctor, or they cannot afford health insurance that can help pay for such care. Many Americans believe that the government should guarantee adequate medical care for all citizens. Over the years, lawmakers have taken steps toward achieving that goal.

Making Health Care Accessible

Since the early 1900s, a number of U.S. leaders have recommended that the federal government make health care accessible and affordable for all Americans. During that time, plans have varied, but, in general, most have sought government funding for health insurance programs intended to help the neediest citizens.

Medicare. Today, more than 42 million Americans age 65 or older or who have disabilities receive Medicare benefits. One part of Medicare helps pay for hospital nursing care. Medicare beneficiaries must first pay a certain amount—called a deductible—out of their own pockets, and then Medicare covers the remaining hospital expenses. Each working person in the United States pays a special payroll tax to fund this hospital insurance. The second part of Medicare, supplemental medical insurance, covers 80 percent of doctors' fees, laboratory tests, and other medical expenses for each beneficiary. Participation in this plan is optional and requires additional fees.

In 2003, President George W. Bush and Congress passed an enhancement to Medicare called "Part D," which provides optional coverage for prescription drugs. Medicare recipients can choose from among dozens of insurance plans in their area, and the program pays for some of their drug costs. After participants pay an annual premium and a deductible, their drug prices are reduced by 75 percent. This new benefit

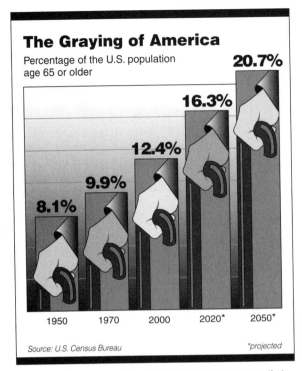

The Graying of America

Percentage of the U.S. population age 65 or older

20.7%

16.3%

12.4%

9.9%

8.1%

| 1950 | 1970 | 2000 | 2020* | 2050* |

Source: U.S. Census Bureau   *projected

As the baby boom generation begins to retire, many worry that the government will not be able to afford Medicare in its present form.

has increased government Medicare expenditures significantly.

Medicaid. Medicaid is a joint federal-state program that helps more than 38 million men and women with low incomes pay for health care. The federal government matches state funds for Medicaid. Each state establishes its own eligibility requirements based on income and administers its own program. States follow federal regulations when paying for hospital care, long-term nursing care, doctors' fees, laboratory tests, and X-ray examinations. Medicaid also covers the fees and premiums for Medicare recipients who are near the poverty level.

As medical costs have risen, Medicaid spending has consumed an ever-increasing portion of state budgets. According to a 2004 report by the National Governor's Association, Medicaid was the largest component in the budgets of twenty-two states, where it outpaced spending on K-12 education for the first time. Many policymakers admit both Medicare and Medicaid must be changed—and costs trimmed—to keep these programs viable.

Paying for Good Health

A National Expense. For almost forty years, health care expenses have increased much faster than the overall cost of living. In 2005, annual health expenditures reached about

$2 trillion. Federal, state, and local governments paid almost half of that total.

Most experts agree that three major developments have fueled the increase in health care costs:

- the expansion of a system in which government and insurance companies, rather than patients, pay medical bills
- the introduction of expensive new medical technologies and drugs
- the rapid growth of America's older population

How Insurance Works. Private insurance companies and federal and state governments—not patients—pay for most health care services. About 60 percent of Americans receive health insurance through their employers. Commonly, workers pay monthly premiums to participate in their employer's insurance programs, and employers pay additional costs. Self-employed workers must buy their own coverage and sometimes band together to receive group discounts. Generally, insurers pay a percentage of patients' doctors' and hospital fees. Until the 1990s, most insurers used an "after-the-fact,

HIV Testing for Teens?

Each year about 40,000 Americans become newly infected with the Human Immunodeficiency Virus (HIV), the virus that causes Acquired Immune Deficiency Syndrome (AIDS). Unfortunately, many of those victims do not learn they have the virus until years later, during which time they have likely infected others. To combat this problem, in 2006 the Centers for Disease Control, a federal government agency, recommended that all people ages 13 to 64 get tested for HIV at least once. According to this proposal, testing would be voluntary, but to administer the test more efficiently, the current requirements for consent forms and counseling would be removed. For several reasons, civil liberties groups oppose the policy changes. In the short term, they fear that without counseling, many Americans, and particularly teens, would not understand the seriousness of a positive result.

fee-for-service" payment policy. Under this system, hospitals and doctors submit bills directly to insurance companies and are reimbursed for most of their charges. Depending on the insurance plan, patients sometimes pay a deductible of hundreds of dollars before receiving benefits. In many plans, patients are also responsible for paying up to 20 percent of the cost of some services.

Most analysts agree that "after-the-fact" payment results in a "cost screen." Consumers rarely know in advance the total costs involved in their medical care and treatment. Without this information, patients are unable to comparison shop, and providers don't have to compete for patients by offering lower prices. Because third parties pay large portions of the bills, many policymakers assert that the health care industry has been able to raise prices above that which consumers—and now even employers and the government—can bear.

Managed Care. Beginning in 1990, many employers began to move employees from traditional fee-for-service plans into less expensive, managed care plans. In 2005, almost 70 million American workers were enrolled in managed care plans, such as preferred provider organizations (PPOs) and health maintenance organizations (HMOs). PPOs and HMOs

offer consumers a range of medical services for a set monthly fee. These plans control costs by promoting illness prevention, monitoring decisions of health care professionals, requiring preauthorization for hospital visits, and limiting access to expensive specialists. Managed care has both proponents and critics; some believe it is helping to keep costs down and promoting better health, while others argue that it denies patients access to important diagnostic tools and medical specialists.

Expensive Technology and Medication. The development of new technologies has also increased health care bills. New medical equipment is often expensive and requires highly trained and well-paid technicians to operate effectively. Today, organ transplants are commonplace; dialysis is available for kidney failures; respirators keep people breathing when their lungs fail; and machines assist diseased hearts. Doctors go to great lengths to give patients the best treatments possible and to prolong life, but these efforts are costly.

Prescription drugs are another factor in rising health care bills. For the most part, drug companies fund the research and trials necessary to develop drugs and ensure their safety. Once these medications reach the market, pharmaceutical companies charge consumers hefty sums to offset those research and development expenses. From 1993 to 2003, the cost of prescription drugs climbed an average of 14 percent per year, a greater increase than any other type of health care expense.

An Older Population. The size of America's older and retired population will dramatically increase as members of the "baby boom" generation (people born between 1946 and 1964) enter their sixties. Some experts believe that by 2020, men and women over age 65 will account for about 16 percent of the U.S. population. As a result, the nation's medical bills will soar.

Each older American consumes nearly four times as much in health services as a young adult. Because of Medicare, less than 1 percent of people over the age of 65 do not have health insurance. However, older Americans still have to pay monthly insurance premiums and a deductible before Medicare will cover any expenses. Then the government picks up the tab for most medical services. Moreover, elderly men and women tend to use more prescription drugs than do younger people. The steady increase of medication costs and the new Medicare drug benefit, combined with the aging population, will likely force lawmakers to change both Medicare and the U.S. health care system as a whole.

Efforts to Improve Health Care and Lower Costs

Expanding Coverage. "New" ideas about health care are not really new. In response to the growing concern about the rising cost of health care, Washington lawmakers have proposed a number of reform initiatives over the years. More recently, in 1993, President Bill Clinton and First Lady Hillary Rodham Clinton championed sweeping health care reform in the hope of achieving health care coverage for all Americans. However, the insurance and drug industries opposed the plan, and the initiative was defeated. Thereafter, the Clinton administration pursued more modest reforms.

In 1996, Congress passed the Health Insurance Portability and Accountability Act (HIPAA), making it easier for people to keep their health insurance even if they change jobs or have a preexisting medical condition. In 1997, federal legislators instituted the State Children's Health Insurance Program (SCHIP), the largest expansion of health insurance coverage to children since Medicaid. The program primarily offers insurance to children in families with incomes too great to qualify for Medicaid, but without enough money to afford private insurance. Like Medicaid, SCHIP is jointly funded by federal and state governments, but the states administer the program within federal guidelines.

State-Level Efforts. In early 2007, leaders in California, Maryland, New Jersey, and Pennsylvania called for expanded health care coverage in their states. Plans for each state vary, but California's version is the most aggressive, partly because it has the greatest number of uninsured people (20 percent of its population, or 6.5 million people) and because Governor Arnold Schwarzenegger eventually hopes to offer universal coverage. If such measures pass the four states' legislatures, the states will join Maine, Massachusetts, and Vermont in working to address the issue of uninsured Americans.

Reining-in Medicare Costs. The government spent about $420 billion on Medicare in 2006—an increase of 25 percent over the previous year. Many experts agree that because of increasing costs and the beginning of the "baby boom" retirement wave, the program will run out of money early this century unless reforms are implemented. To avoid this crisis, lawmakers in Washington, D.C., have debated ways to preserve Medicare.

In January 2007, California governor Arnold Schwarzenegger unveiled his plan to create statewide universal health care coverage. His plan is ambitious because the state has 6.5 million uninsured people, and it is controversial in its aim to insure illegal immigrants.

In 1997, to postpone the program's insolvency and help balance the budget, President Bill Clinton and Congress agreed to cut Medicare spending by almost $120 billion over the following five years. They also restructured the program by raising monthly premiums and encouraging older Americans to join managed care organizations.

In 2006, a new prescription drug benefit for Medicare went into effect. To participate in the program, insurance companies must keep prices at certain levels, but are ensured a steady supply of customers. Competition for enrollees has helped keep some anticipated costs at bay. Nevertheless, in early 2007, Democrats in Congress proposed legislation allowing the federal government to negotiate lower drug prices for Medicare participants. Many Republicans oppose the plan because they believe the government should not be involved in setting market prices for drugs.

Health Savings Accounts. The legislation that instituted the new Medicare drug benefit also created a way for people to save money tax free for medical expenses. To qualify for a Health Savings Account, a person must have a high-deductible insurance plan. The individual can then save money tax free for certain health care expenses. Health Savings Accounts are intended to encourage cost reduction by making consumers

Mental Workouts Keep Aging Minds Agile

Cognitive exercises, such as memory games, can help slow the decline of mental abilities in middle-aged and elderly people. In late 2006, researchers published these findings in the Journal of the American Medical Association after a study of more than 2,800 people who were, on average, age 73. With a growing older population that will be at risk for Alzheimer's disease, dementia, and related illnesses, U.S. health experts are anxious to spread the word to the public. They expect that the challenges in implementing mental exercises will be similar to those regarding physical exercise. The benefits are motivating at first, but making the commitment to perform "brain workouts" regularly, and over the long term, will be difficult.

more conscious of the price of their medical care and by rewarding them with tax benefits for selecting and using services carefully.

CURRENT ISSUES

Comprehensive vs. Incremental Health Care Reform.
In 2007, consensus emerged across the political spectrum and at all levels of government that the nation's system for financing health care must be reformed. New proposals from several state governors, the Bush administration, and contenders for the 2008 presidential race, such as New York Senator Hillary Rodham Clinton, headlined the news. Experts characterize the vast range of proposals, which differ significantly in details, in two general ways—first, those that involve comprehensive changes (usually focusing on universal coverage) and second, those that use incremental adjustments to expand existing programs to reduce the number of uninsured people.

Supporters of providing universal health care argue that the best way to ensure equal access to medical care is to overhaul the financing of the nation's health care system. They say that decades of government programs such as Medicare and Medicaid have fueled the increase in medical costs; created an enormous and wasteful bureaucracy; and failed to provide an adequate safety net for the uninsured. As the population ages, these programs will become unsustainable, and comprehensive reform of health care will be necessary. Many advocates for universal health care coverage say that the federal government could become a single purchaser, acting on behalf of all patients. In that way, the government could force health care providers to rein in charges and hold them accountable for the quality of care. Another proposal for comprehensive reform relies on mandating government subsidies in which the poor receive tax credits or money that enables them to purchase insurance. Finally, some policymakers favor a hybrid system of universal health care vouchers that includes government funding for basic health care, plus elements of choice and competition. Basic care would be universal, and there would be no means-testing for eligibility. However, participants could choose from competing plans and opt to purchase additional coverage.

Critics of comprehensive reform do not oppose the idea of health care for all. Instead, they disagree with the means to achieve that goal. In particular, they contend that a government-sponsored medical program would result in less competition among providers and would ultimately produce poor care. Opponents cite the universal coverage systems

AP Photo/Stew Milne

In 2006 and 2007, several state and local governments—including New York City, Los Angeles, Rhode Island, and Michigan—moved to ban the use of trans fatty acids, or "trans fats," in restaurants and eateries. Trans fats, found in partially hydrogenated vegetable oil, cause heart disease and increase risk for diabetes. Shown here is a restaurant manager in Rhode Island displaying a pizza made with olive oil, which does not contain trans fats.

in Canada and the United Kingdom, where long waiting periods are commonplace for surgeries. Furthermore, they believe that government oversight would add to bureaucracy, inefficiency, and soaring costs—not alleviate such problems. In addition, critics argue that the health care industry is a vital part of the American economy and that state-sponsored health care would leave thousands of insurance and medical industry workers unemployed. Consequently, they favor making incremental changes, such as enhancing tax-free Health Savings Accounts and offering tax deductions for people who buy their own health insurance. In general, detractors of universal coverage favor empowering consumers with greater information on medical costs and quality. By making consumers pay greater shares of health care insurance and medical expenses from their own pockets, these policymakers believe that the market will naturally rein in medical costs.

Ensuring Quality Care for Medicare Patients. Most policymakers agree that Medicare must be reformed if it is to remain solvent. As of 2008, doctors who treat Medicare patients will face cuts of 5 to 10 percent in their reimbursements

Drug Safety and FDA Reform

In 2004, drug safety grabbed headlines as Vioxx, a popular arthritis drug, was withdrawn from pharmacies due to heart attack risks. About the same time, controversy arose regarding antidepressants, which caused some teens to consider suicide. The rash of safety concerns prompted the Food and Drug Administration (FDA) and policymakers to examine the approval process for medication. Critics charged that the present arrangement, whereby drug companies pay fees to support the FDA's clinical trials, creates a conflict of interest. Supporters of the system countered that the process was created so that lifesaving medications could reach consumers faster. After a report by the independent Institute of Medicine issued a critique and recommendations, the FDA responded in January 2007. The FDA now wants to monitor new drugs for up to eighteen months after they are introduced.

from the federal government. Moreover, President Bush's budget for fiscal year 2008 proposed savings of $70 billion on Medicare and Medicaid over the next five years.

With drastic cuts seemingly imminent, some policymakers have devised a plan to reduce Medicare expenditures while ensuring that Medicare patients still have access to quality services. As Medicare is presently set up, doctors get paid based on their quantity of services rather than quality. For example, if a physician misdiagnoses a patient, he or she actually gets more Medicare reimbursements for repeat patient visits to correct the mistake.

In late 2006, legislators approved a new "pay-for-performance" system that will allow Medicare to pay doctors a 1.5 percent bonus for providing information about the type and quality of their services. For example, physicians can report the kinds of treatments and drugs they prescribe to reduce blood pressure or help diabetes patients. This voluntary program is set to begin in July 2007. With the help of statistical data gathered in the reporting phase, program administrators plan to work with medical experts to set clinical guidelines for quality care. Over the long term, supporters of this legislation want Medicare to reward superior doctors and hospitals that provide quality, cost-effective treatment for Medicare beneficiaries.

Supporters of "pay-for-performance" for Medicare physicians cite a three-year pilot project that involved hospitals around the country. In that program, Medicare found that participating hospitals steadily improved their quality of care under a pay-for-performance system. Those hospitals, for example, had 1,300 fewer deaths in heart attack patients than in previous years. Proponents claim that detailed clinical guidelines promote better communication among health professionals about the best treatments. With benchmarks, medical care is also more consistent. Medicare bonuses, they believe, will help win recognition for the best hospitals and doctors and thus attract more patients to them. Finally, advocates for pay-for-performance programs point out that similar, successful quality-assurance programs already exist, particularly among insurance companies and medical associations.

Opponents of government-led pay-for-performance medical programs deride what they think will become "cookbook medicine." Representative Pete Stark (D-Calif.) said, federal officials "do not have the capability, the understanding, the knowledge, or the training" to set standards for the quality of medical care. Detractors argue that, in setting proscriptive guidelines, the government undermines doctors' autonomy and judgment. They liken the proposed program to paying for "compliance," rather than performance. Furthermore, critics say that the reporting phase alone places a severe burden on doctors' offices, and that a 1.5 percent bonus will not justify the resources necessary to participate. Finally, some opponents decry pay-for-performance in medicine altogether. They assert that doctors are expected to provide "quality care" at all times, and should not be paid extra for doing so.

Safe to Eat? In 2006, several highly publicized cases of food-borne illnesses called attention to the nation's process for ensuring the safety of fresh fruit and vegetables. An outbreak of food poisoning from the dangerous bacteria E. coli O157:H7 was traced to bagged spinach; the incident sickened more than 200 people and killed three. Testing revealed that this case originated at a California farm, where feral pigs had spread E. coli from cow manure into spinach fields. Similar incidents followed, causing more people to become ill.

In September 2006, spinach tainted with E. coli caused illness in about 200 people and the deaths of three. Here, a farmer inspects his spinach field with a California Farm Bureau agent. As a result of these and other food poisoning incidents, some Americans want increased regulation to ensure the safety of fruit and vegetables.

AP Photo/The Californian, Richard Green

Experts offer several reasons for increased food-borne illnesses. First, Americans are consuming greater amounts of fresh produce in an attempt to eat more healthfully. Unlike meat, fresh produce is often consumed raw. (Cooking usually kills off harmful microorganisms.) The large aging population is also at greater risk for getting sick from these toxins. In addition, agriculture has become centralized. Growers in California and Arizona account for half of the nation's produce. Finally, processing and distribution take place on large scales, so outbreaks affect larger numbers of people.

With these factors in mind, many consumer advocates have called for new safety regulations for the nation's supply of fruit and vegetables. Current safety standards are limited in number and broadly written. Whereas meat and poultry are highly regulated by the Department of Agriculture, fruit and vegetables fall under the purview of the Food and Drug Administration (FDA) and the states. Thus far, the government has relied primarily on self-regulation by the industry and farmers. After the events of late 2006, trade groups such as Western Growers, the Food Marketing Institute, and the National Restaurant Association began developing their own standards to restore consumer confidence.

For many observers, however, self-regulation is no longer sufficient. Consumer advocates argue that there should be just one agency responsible for ensuring the safety of the U.S. food supply. They assert that a single food-safety agency could issue specific, mandatory guidelines for growing, handling, and processing the nation's produce. Supporters of greater regulation note that recent outbreaks coincide with a 37 percent reduction in the budget (from 2003 to 2006) of the FDA's Center for Food Safety and Applied Nutrition, which now employs only 2,000 inspectors to monitor more than 12,000 facilities nationwide. Proponents urge greater funding for the FDA, or another food-regulatory body, so that it can hire more inspectors to enforce safety mandates. Advocates also cite the need for greater funding of scientific research in methods of preventing and identifying contaminated food. For example, E. coli cannot be "washed off," so experts need to test other destruction methods such as irradiation.

Opponents of greater government regulation claim that the growers, distributors, and restaurants are responding rigorously and effectively to recent events because their businesses are at stake. After the spinach scare, sales of bagged leafy vegetables dropped 60 percent below those of the previous year, and agribusiness knows that it must win back consumers' trust. Critics of government regulation point out that the industry can respond faster and more effectively than any federal agency. Greater federal regulation will also increase the cost of producing fruit and vegetables, an expense that will be passed along to consumers. Regulation detractors assert that more expensive produce will hurt agribusiness and reverse recent public health efforts to get Americans to eat more healthfully.

OUTLOOK

Health care expenses continue to increase dramatically in the United States. Despite decades of federal programs, 16 percent of the U.S. population still goes without health insurance. Should the country offer medical coverage to this group, and if so, who will pay for it? As the size of the elderly population grows, Medicare faces big budget cuts. How can the government trim these costs while preserving quality care? And should the United States do more to protect the safety of its produce? These and other health issues will occupy policymakers in the years ahead.

THE DEBATE: HEALTH CARE

Health care reform should be comprehensive, not incremental.

PRO: The federal government should offer health care to every American by instituting comprehensive reform. Medicare and Medicaid do not provide coverage for all citizens, yet they consume huge percentages of state and federal budgets. These expensive, ineffective programs must be replaced by a form of universal health care coverage that is better equipped to handle the aging population.

CON: Universal health care is not practical given the country's complex medical system. A government-sponsored service would provide inferior care at dramatically increased cost. Besides, cutting insurance companies out of the health care business would disrupt the economy. A better plan involves incremental changes, such as offering tax-free Health Savings Accounts and tax deductions for insurance costs.

Lawmakers should impose quality standards for Medicare doctors.

PRO: Medicare is currently set up to reward quantity of service over quality. Developing standards of quality with experts would provide benchmarks to measure a physician's quality of care. This plan would save Medicare money while encouraging doctors and hospitals to give those patients a high degree of service. Similar sets of standards have already been used successfully by insurance companies and medical associations.

CON: The federal government lacks the expertise to tell doctors how to do their jobs. Imposing quality standards and a "pay-for-performance" system would undermine the judgment of medical professionals. Instead of paying attention to patients, physicians would have to comply with regulations, thereby diminishing the quality of their care. Doctors must give all patients good service, and should not be paid extra for doing so.

The government should reform its food safety regulations.

PRO: Americans are consuming more fresh fruit and vegetables, yet the Food and Drug Administration does not adequately regulate the industry. One federal agency should be charged with overseeing all of the nation's agricultural products, including meat, poultry, fruit and vegetables. That single agency needs better funding to research produce safety issues and to enforce compliance with stepped-up regulations.

CON: Industry groups and the big agricultural states have already begun to develop regulations that proscribe improved procedures for food growing, handling, and distribution. Those groups can better set and enforce standards than can a federal agency. Increased federal regulation would also increase the cost of produce, harming agribusiness and challenging the healthy eating habits of many Americans.

IMMIGRATION

The United States, a "nation of immigrants," has welcomed new arrivals throughout its history. Many people credit America's immigrant tradition with building the nation's economic superiority and cultural diversity. To ensure that levels and patterns of immigration serve the nation's best interests, the federal government creates immigration policies. These rules affect immigration limits, border control, visa distribution, and the citizenship application process.

In recent years, immigration policy has come under fire. The terrorist attacks of September 11, 2001—carried out by nineteen foreign-born men who were in the country illegally—focused national attention on the security aspects of immigration. That led to immigration reforms aimed at hindering terrorism, like stricter border control, increased visitor tracking, and standardization of driver's licenses. But some say these changes have not been fast or thorough enough. Also in recent years, Americans have been alarmed at rampant illegal immigration, mostly across the U.S. border with Mexico. Officials estimate that 12 million illegal immigrants now live in the United States—and thousands more arrive each year.

Nearly everyone agrees that immigration policy requires major reform, but they disagree about what measures to take. Some believe illegal immigration harms the economy and threatens America's security and culture. They favor law enforcement measures like a fortified border and increased deportations and penalties. Others argue that immigrants help meet important economic needs and some have proposed temporary worker programs and new paths to citizenship. Congress and the president must balance all these concerns as they try to revamp immigration laws.

KEY QUESTIONS

- Should the United States build a fence along the southern border?

- Should the federal government create a new temporary worker program?

- Should the United States allow some illegal immigrants to become citizens?

BACKGROUND

Managing Immigration

The United States was built by immigrants, many of whom were seeking a new life in a new land. That opportunity attracted many people, and at first, anyone could move to the United States. After 1882, however, the swelling population prompted the federal government to begin making laws to control immigration and preserve the racial, religious, and cultural makeup of the United States. At times, quotas limited the number of entrants of certain nationalities, including Asians, Europeans from southern and eastern Europe, and Latin Americans.

Immigration Policy. Goods and people constantly flow in and out of the United States. Immigration policy spells out which people can enter, how long they can stay, and whether or not they can apply for permanent residence or citizenship. Post-September 11 reforms placed enforcement of immigration and border control policies set forth by Congress and the White House mainly under the control of the Department of Homeland Security. U.S. government policy specifies several categories of immigrants.

Legal immigrants come to the United States seeking to establish permanent residence. They may choose to apply for permanent resident status (popularly known as "getting a green card"). These residents receive protection under U.S. law, but do not hold all the rights and responsibilities of U.S. citizens. Permanent residents may apply for U.S. citizenship after living in the country for five years; a majority of those who apply become citizens.

Refugees and asylees come to the United States seeking protection from persecution in their home countries. The federal government limits the number of asylees. After one year of U.S. residence, these immigrants can apply for permanent resident status.

Illegal or undocumented immigrants, by law, can be deported—forcibly returned to their home countries. About

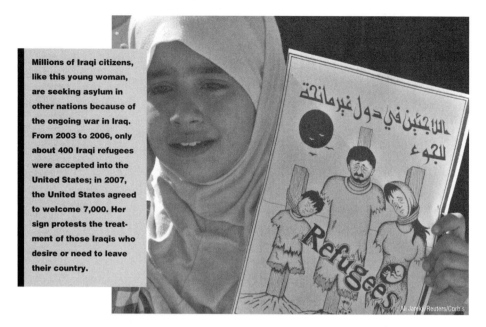

Millions of Iraqi citizens, like this young woman, are seeking asylum in other nations because of the ongoing war in Iraq. From 2003 to 2006, only about 400 Iraqi refugees were accepted into the United States; in 2007, the United States agreed to welcome 7,000. Her sign protests the treatment of those Iraqis who desire or need to leave their country.

Ali Jarekji/Reuters/Corbis

60 percent of illegal immigrants enter the country by crossing a U.S. border illegally or by misrepresenting themselves. The other 40 percent enter the country legally but stay beyond the limits of their visas, or authorizations, to visit the United States.

Nonimmigrants enter and exit the country legally with temporary visas that specify the purpose and length of their visits. These men and women are typically foreign government officers, guest workers, tourists, businesspeople, or students.

The Growing Immigrant Population. In 2005, the United States admitted more than 1 million legal immigrants. More than 40 percent came from seven countries—Mexico, India, China, the Philippines, Cuba, Vietnam, and the Dominican Republic. In addition, an estimated 500,000 people entered the country illegally. Officials estimate that about 12 million illegal immigrants currently live in the United States. More than half of that population comes from Mexico, and about another one-quarter is from Latin America. Many are poor and unskilled. They risk deadly border crossings hoping to find better-paying work in the United States, despite laws that forbid employers from hiring illegal immigrants.

Illegal Immigration and the Economy. American citizens disagree about the impact of illegal immigration on the economy. Some citizens worry that poor, low-skilled immigrants depress wages for everyone because immigrants will often work for lower pay than native-born Americans. Furthermore, some people argue that illegal immigrants harm the economy because they pay few or no taxes, and strain public services, such as schools and hospitals. But others insist that illegal immigrants work at jobs that are essential to the U.S. economy, particularly in the agricultural, construction, manufacturing, and service industries. Such advocates argue that immigrants do jobs Americans will not do, and that many illegal workers do pay income, Social Security, and property taxes, thus strengthening the economy and the nation.

Dealing with Illegal Immigration. The southern border states—California, Arizona, New Mexico, and Texas—have always experienced the most challenges in dealing with illegal immigration, including environmental damage from crossings, rising crime rates, and strains on local law enforcement and social services. As illegal immigration has increased in severity there, volunteer citizen border patrols have organized to monitor and protest illegal immigration.

In recent years, however, illegal immigrants have dispersed more widely across the country looking for jobs. As a

The Changing Faces of America

The presence of large numbers of both legal and illegal immigrants has contributed to dramatic changes in the racial, ethnic, and cultural composition of the United States. In 2005, the Census Bureau estimated that nearly one in eight U.S. residents was foreign-born—the greatest proportion since the 1930s. This group's demographic impact is amplified by the fact that it is growing at a rate six times faster than the U.S. population as a whole. Already, non-Hispanic white Americans—once the majority—make up less than half of the populations of California and Texas. The Census Bureau projects that by 2050, residents of Hispanic origin will represent 25 percent of the total U.S. population.

result, states and communities nationwide have had to decide what to do about illegal immigrants and their families. Local communities have argued over overcrowded immigrant housing and whether to permit illegal immigrants to gather in so-called "day laborer" sites to seek work. Some cities have declared English the official language and made it a crime to rent apartments or houses to illegal immigrants. And many state legislatures have debated controversial measures such as whether to deny medical care, school lunches, or tuition discounts to illegal immigrants and their children.

Immigration and Terrorism

Foreigners were responsible for two major acts of terrorism on U.S. soil—the 1993 bombing of the World Trade Center and the September 11, 2001, terrorist attacks. All of the 9/11 hijackers entered the United States through U.S. airports. Three stayed in the United States longer than their visas allowed, eight carried fraudulent passports, and some possessed U.S. driver's licenses. The war on terror and the effort

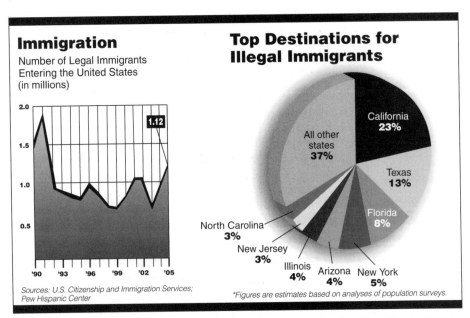

Immigration

Number of Legal Immigrants Entering the United States (in millions)

Sources: U.S. Citizenship and Immigration Services; Pew Hispanic Center

Top Destinations for Illegal Immigrants

California 23%
All other states 37%
Texas 13%
Florida 8%
North Carolina 3%
New Jersey 3%
Illinois 4%
Arizona 4%
New York 5%

Figures are estimates based on analyses of population surveys.

Following a decline after the September 11, 2001, terrorist attacks, both legal and illegal immigration to the United States have increased.

to strengthen homeland security has led to new immigration regulations and procedures.

Tightening Restrictions on Visas. Since the terror attacks of 2001, many foreigners trying to immigrate to the United States have faced longer waits and extensive FBI background checks—and more are being denied legal entry. In addition, workers, students, and vacationers have faced increased scrutiny and delays.

Identification. "For terrorists, travel documents are as important as weapons," noted the 9/11 Commission in its final report in 2004. Among its many recommendations, the commission called for the federal government to set national standards for important identification documents such as birth certificates and driver's licenses. Driver's licenses have, in practice, become national identification cards, giving holders privileges such as the ability to open bank accounts and board airplanes. In some states, undocumented immigrants could legally obtain driver's licenses. In 2005, Congress passed the Real ID Act, requiring states to guarantee that all people granted driver's licenses are legal residents. However, some states have protested that it will be too costly to begin complying with the law by the 2009 deadline.

Border Control. The United States shares a 2,000-mile border with Mexico and a 5,500-mile border with Canada, the latter of which is the world's longest open border. Thanks to the North American Free Trade Agreement, Canada and Mexico are two of the United States' biggest trading partners, which means that there is a constant flow of goods and people across the northern and southern borders. In addition, every day hundreds of people attempt to illegally cross both borders, although the southern border bears the brunt. Many Americans worry that the largely open borders make it easy for terrorists to enter the United States, even as it becomes harder for them to use airports.

To reduce illegal border crossings, the federal government has begun to implement sensor and tracking technology, and

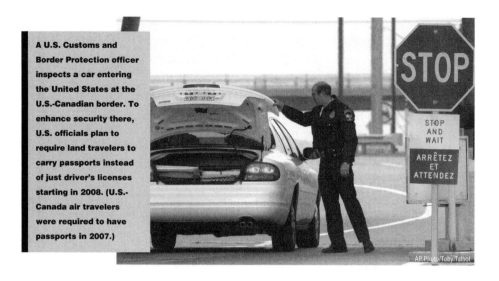

A U.S. Customs and Border Protection officer inspects a car entering the United States at the U.S.-Canadian border. To enhance security there, U.S. officials plan to require land travelers to carry passports instead of just driver's licenses starting in 2008. (U.S.-Canada air travelers were required to have passports in 2007.)

AP Photo/Toby Talbot

has sent out more patrols and built fences along some sections of the southern border. But rather than deter illegal migrants from Mexico, such efforts have prompted them to cross at more remote and dangerous places, and spread the impact of illegal immigration to more communities. In response, the governors of Arizona and New Mexico declared states of emergency in 2005, and the next year, President George W. Bush deployed thousands of National Guard troops to the southern border.

Tracking. Beginning in 2003, colleges and universities were required to use a national database to track foreign students. In January 2004, the Department of Homeland Security implemented the first phase of US-VISIT, a new program that will eventually track foreign arrivals and departures at borders, airports, and seaports. By taking fingerprints and photographs of nearly all visitors and using databases to identify people on watch lists, officials hope to deter terrorists and ensure visa compliance. The program currently monitors arrivals only; the ability to monitor departures remains five to ten years away.

Revising Immigration Policy

In 2006, Congress struggled to revise the nation's immigration policy. President Bush and others have called for comprehensive reform that includes increased border security and a new temporary worker program. Congress also considered measures for increasing penalties on illegal immigrants and on those who help them, and for designating English as the national language.

Debates over immigration policy broke out nationwide on talk shows and in editorial columns, and to the surprise of many, in the streets. Hundreds of thousands of men, women, and children—many of them illegal immigrants themselves—marched in Los Angeles, Washington, D.C., Phoenix, and other cities to protest the punitive aspects of the proposals and to call for Congress to offer legal status and citizenship to millions of illegal immigrants. With strong emotions and arguments coming from all sides, Congress was not able to agree on comprehensive immigration reform that year.

The new Congress again took up the issue in 2007. In the spring, a bipartisan group of legislators proposed a new immigration policy for the nation. As of May, the fragile coalition was fighting attacks on the bill from both sides, even as the public reiterated its desire for a new immigration strategy. Some Republicans argued that the proposed law's citizenship option for illegal residents was unfair. Many Democrats rejected the plan's revised methods for choosing who is allowed to enter the country legally. Congress was expected to continue contentious debate throughout the year.

CURRENT ISSUES

Fenced In. Many Americans are angry that, even after September 11 and with so many concerns about the illegal immigrant population, tens of thousands of people still sneak across the 2,000-mile U.S.-Mexico border each year. Currently, only about 5 percent of the southern border is fenced. In 2006, Congress and President Bush approved plans to build 700 miles of new fence along the border through parts of California, Arizona, New Mexico, and Texas. However, not everyone agrees that partial or even complete fencing is the best way to curb illegal immigration.

STOP The INVASION

100% Enforcement
No Guest Worker
Amnesty
No Excuses

AP Photo/Seth Wenig

IMMIGRATION NOW!

Mexican Pride

AP Photo/Elaine Thompson

In 2006, hundreds of thousands of people marched in cities around the United States protesting punitive immigration policies and calling for citizenship for illegal immigrants (right). Opponents of immigration held their own smaller rallies (above).

Those who advocate more fencing contend that the United States needs a physical barrier to stop illegal immigrants and terrorists from entering the country. Only after the border is secure, they say, can the nation determine what to do about the illegal immigrants already here. Fence proponents argue that the border can be sealed with a combination of fencing, barriers, and sensors and point to other nations, like Israel, with effective border fences. Such advocates claim that given Mexico's apparent reluctance to control illegal immigration from its side of the border, the United States has no other choice but to build a barrier. Finally, fence supporters contend that a fence is a wise investment that would restore order to border areas and reduce the economic burden of dealing with detentions, deportations, and mass numbers of poor immigrants.

Opponents to a fence counter that it will be expensive and ineffective. They contend that the rugged and environmentally sensitive border terrain would make fence construction difficult and costly. Once built, such opponents continue, the fence would require heavy maintenance and monitoring as illegal migrants try new entry methods, such as ladders and tunnels. Furthermore, opponents argue that a fence will not stop illegal immigration because as long as America has more jobs than workers, migrants will find a way in. Meanwhile, a land barrier does little to thwart terrorism, say critics who note that a fence would not have kept out the 9/11 hijackers, all of whom entered the country with documentation. Finally, critics argue that a fence would antagonize Mexico, a U.S. ally and trading partner whose support is needed in solving this problem.

Be Our Guest? The U.S. government currently offers two guest worker visas, H-2A and H-2B, which enable nearly 100,000 low-skilled workers to enter the country legally and work temporarily for one to three years. But tens of thousands more migrants come—illegally—and many U.S. employers break the law by hiring them. Some say that the flood of illegal immigrants proves that the current guest worker program is inadequate to meet the needs of America's businesses. To manage the situation, President Bush and some members of Congress have proposed creating a new temporary—or guest—worker program. Under these proposals, people could

Many immigrants to the United States become accomplished citizens and leaders. India-born Indra Nooyi became PepsiCo's president and CEO in 2006, making her one of the highest-ranking leaders in corporate America.

AP Photo/Manish Swarup

Legal Help Wanted

For years, U.S. businesses have hired illegal immigrants—knowingly or unwittingly—in violation of federal law and with almost no penalties. As national attention turned to this aspect of the immigration problem, the federal government launched several high-profile raids in 2006. The raid on Swift & Co., one of the nation's largest meat processors, netted about 1,300 illegal workers from six plants nationwide. As of February 2007, most had been charged with administrative immigration violations, and 270 faced criminal charges related to identity theft and fraud. No charges had been filed against the company. Since 1998, the company has been voluntarily participating in the federal Basic Pilot Employment Verification Program, which checks workers' employment papers against the Social Security Administration's database. Swift & Co. stated that all of its employees had been authorized to work by the program.

apply to work legally for three to five years, after which they would have to leave or pay to renew their work visas.

Opponents argue that a new temporary worker program will not resolve the problem of illegal immigration because guest workers will simply stay on illegally when their permits expire. Critics contend that guest worker programs will continue to depress wages for low-skilled jobs and thus harm native-born Americans. Furthermore, they argue that indulging businesses' addiction to cheap labor harms the long-term economy by allowing businesses to rely on low-wage (but inefficient) manpower rather than encouraging them to innovate. Finally, critics argue that guest worker programs harm immigrants by making them second-class citizens beholden to their employers for their legal status.

To the contrary, supporters contend that a new temporary worker program would deal compassionately with illegal migrants by making them legal members of society. In addition, proponents argue that such a program will make the border more secure by allowing those seeking work to enter the country in a safe, orderly, and legal way. That process will free up border agents to pursue the real security threats—terrorists, drug smugglers, and other criminals. Ultimately, say proponents, guest worker programs help the economy by ensuring that American businesses have enough workers and by reducing the need for expensive law enforcement efforts.

The Citizenship Club. In 1986, the United States granted amnesty (a government pardon) to about 3 million illegal immigrants and allowed them to apply for citizenship. At the time, officials hoped the move would curb illegal immigration. However, immigrants have continued to come illegally. As policymakers struggle with what to do about the sizeable illegal population today, some advocates and officials are proposing an "earned legalization." This process, different from amnesty, would allow certain people who reside in the United States illegally to apply for legal residence. Only workers with no criminal record would be eligible, and they would have to pay back taxes and fines, learn English, and wait in line for citizenship behind applicants who immigrated legally. But even the possibility of granting citizenship to people who broke the law angers many Americans.

Those who support a path to citizenship believe deporting 12 million people is impractical and undesirable, especially when the U.S. economy depends on their labor. Hard-working immigrants and their families deserve a chance at earning citizenship, say proponents. They argue that citizenship is more humane and efficient than a guest worker program that would require intense monitoring for compliance and uproot people repeatedly. Without citizenship, say supporters, the United States will soon have a huge and poor underclass without voting rights or full legal protection—a situation that conflicts with America's democratic values and strong immigrant tradition. Finally, many proponents insist that to ensure that this legalization program will truly be the last one necessary, the border must be secured at the same time.

Rewarding illegal behavior will only encourage more of it, counter opponents to citizenship for illegal immigrants. Such critics stress that although the United States is a nation of immigrants, it is foremost a nation of laws that must be respected. Some opponents call for zero-tolerance of illegal immigrants and advocate aggressive deportations as well as fines and denial of social services. Furthermore, opponents cite the impracticality of a citizenship program, pointing out that already-overwhelmed U.S. immigration services lack the technology and resources to process millions of applications. Finally, critics say that the nation simply cannot absorb massive numbers of poor, unskilled men, women, and children without increasing poverty and overburdening public services like health care and education.

OUTLOOK

Almost everyone agrees that federal immigration policies need to be revised. However, Americans passionately disagree on what changes the nation should make. Because immigration touches on economic, security, and cultural concerns, Congress and the president face long debates and difficult policy choices in the years ahead.

THE DEBATE: IMMIGRATION

The United States should build a fence along the southern border.

PRO: The first step in immigration reform is securing and enforcing the nation's borders. A closed border will stem the flow of illegal immigrants and prevent entry by terrorists and other criminals. A fence is a necessary and wise investment that will restore law and order and relieve the economic burden on law enforcement officials. Other countries have done it successfully and so must the United States.

CON: A fence will be impractical and expensive, and furthermore, will fail to curb illegal immigration. The border terrain will make building such a fence nearly impossible. And as long as America has more jobs than workers, foreign-born workers seeking employment will find a way in. A fence will only spur them to try new places or to use ladders and tunnels, and will require just as many resources to patrol.

The federal government should create a new temporary worker program.

PRO: Establishing a legal way to connect workers with the employers who want to hire them would drastically reduce illegal immigration, secure the border, and boost the economy. Furthermore, a new temporary worker program would deal compassionately with hard-working illegal immigrants by allowing them to come out of the shadows.

CON: A new guest worker program will only worsen illegal immigration because "temporary" workers will never return home. The program will harm native citizens by depressing wages and discouraging technological innovation. Finally, such a program would not help immigrants because they would be relegated to second-class citizenship.

The United States should allow some illegal immigrants to become citizens.

PRO: Earned legalization—especially if paired with a secured border—is the most practical way to deal with illegal immigrants already in the United States and contributing to the economy. Allowing them to toil without rights and legal protections compromises America's democratic ideals and is contributing to the growth of a poor underclass in the country.

CON: Forgiving illegal behavior will only encourage more of it, from both immigrants and the employers eager to exploit their labor. Instead of giving illegal immigrants the reward of citizenship, the U.S. government should deport or penalize them. The nation simply cannot afford to absorb millions of low-skilled, poor people; they will severely strain social services and the economy.

JOBS AND WELFARE

Jobs keep America's market-based economy running strong. People work for outside employers or start and run their own businesses and in return receive a financial reward for their work—which then creates wealth for the economy. The U.S. federal government plays a relatively small role in the world of work, collecting taxes on companies' profits and workers' incomes and regulating businesses to protect the common good.

This capitalist system has made the American economy the strongest in the world and has made the nation a leader in technological innovation as well as in creative industries like movies and software. The standard of living for average citizens has risen over time. Since 1947, inflation-adjusted hourly wages have increased more than 200 percent.

Over the last thirty years, the job market has undergone great changes due to growing international trade, advancing technologies, and the spread of high-speed Internet access. Some Americans have seen great financial success, but others have lost jobs or faced stagnant wages. Some policymakers and citizens have begun to worry about the growing gap between America's wealthiest citizens and the middle class. Meanwhile, how to help the poor remains an ongoing concern. Many people believe jobs lift people out of poverty, and recent welfare reform has required those receiving assistance to work. However, poverty persists, with about one in eight Americans living below the poverty line.

Dealing with issues of poverty and inequality and balancing business and worker interests presents many challenges. Policymakers, experts, and others disagree on how involved the government should be and what measures it should take.

KEY QUESTIONS

- Should the U.S. government do more to address income inequality?

- Will raising the federal minimum wage help workers?

- Is welfare reform working?

BACKGROUND

The Business of Work

Employers and Employees. Before the early 1980s, goods-producing industries (like manufacturing and construction) employed a significant portion of the working population. However, over the past few decades, service sectors (such as education, health services, retail, and information-related industries like computers and the Internet) have outgrown manufacturing industries and now employ more Americans—a trend expected to continue. Some of the fastest-growing occupations are computer and software engineers, postsecondary teachers, physical therapists, and veterinarians.

Today, total employment in the United States is about 150 million workers. The federal government employs nearly 2 million civilian workers, and through the Department of Defense, another nearly 4 million people in the armed forces. That makes the government the nation's largest employer. Wal-Mart Stores, Inc., is the nation's largest private employer, with more than 1 million people on its payroll. Other types of employers include large and small businesses, state and local governments, non-profit and charitable organizations, and professional practices like law or medicine.

AP Photo/Marcio Jose Sanchez

AP Photo/From the Collection of the Henry Ford & Greenfield Village

From Henry Ford (left), founder of Ford Motor Company in 1903, to Jerry Yang and David Filo (above), the founders of Yahoo in 1994, Americans with ingenuity and ambition have helped drive the U.S. economy. The Ford Company earned more than $160 billion in sales and revenue in 2006; Yahoo, now the world's largest online network, took in more than $6 billion.

Work and the Government. The U.S. federal government generally tries to minimize its interaction with the market economy. For example, Congress taxes corporate and small business income but often strives to keep those taxes relatively low. Many believe that allowing businesses to keep more profit fosters innovation and expansion that creates jobs and wealth for the American people. To protect workers, investors, and the public, the federal government regulates various business practices—such as on-the-job safety and financial reporting— while avoiding placing costly burdens on businesses.

Salaries. Salaries vary according to many factors, such as occupational field, job position, experience, and location. Besides an annual salary, full-time employment often confers valuable benefits like health care coverage. The average annual salary for someone in management is $88,000; for someone in education, $43,000; and in farm work, $21,000. But salaries can range far wider. In 2006, Citigroup Inc. paid its chief executive officer (CEO) nearly $26 million (including bonuses and stock options), while a full-time fast food worker earning the minimum wage made about $11,000. Some have criticized recent CEO pay packages as excessive.

Labor Unions. Organizations of workers called labor unions developed to protect the rights of workers, especially in large industries like manufacturing. Unions could use their strength in numbers to negotiate good wages, overtime pay, health care benefits, and job protections for all the employees in the industry. In recent decades, union membership has declined to about 12 percent of the workforce due in part to the loss of manufacturing industries. Unions have tried to expand in service industries, but contend that anti-union employers have blocked them. In 2007, Congress considered legislation that would enable unions to form more easily by allowing employees to choose union representation in public rather than by secret ballot—a move business advocates opposed.

Global Competition. Starting in the 1980s, technological innovation and globalization (greater global economic integration fostered by free trade) created enormous prosperity for many American businesses and workers but imperiled others. Many firms struggled to compete with lower-cost operations abroad, and some closed their doors. Other companies "outsourced" jobs in customer service and electronics assembly to other countries where they could be done more cheaply, thus increasing corporate profits. Policymakers disagree on how to maintain the advantages of globalization for businesses while helping domestic workers who have lost jobs to outsourcing. Some policymakers propose penalizing companies that take operations overseas or rewarding firms that keep jobs at home. Others favor retraining workers in new fields and providing a stronger safety net.

Poverty in America

Not everyone in the United States earns enough money to live comfortably. According to the federal government's definition of poverty, any U.S. family of four whose annual income in 2006 was less than $20,444 was considered poor. In 2005, 12.6 percent of Americans—about 37 million people—lived below the poverty line. For a significant number of the poor, the condition is temporary, resulting from job loss, divorce, or unexpected and dramatic changes in living circumstances. But for some Americans, poverty is a chronic condition.

More Flexibility for the Workforce

What might help American workers to thrive as they face pressures from globalization? Some say that American workers need the freedom to change jobs in response to the shifting job market, but that concerns over losing health care and retirement benefits often hold workers back. To address this, some have proposed "detaching" such benefits so that they would travel with a worker from job to job. Other policymakers want to develop better ways to help individuals who lose jobs because of globalization and must take lower-paying jobs to stay in the workforce. They suggest expanding federal wage insurance programs to cover income loss for a limited time when displaced workers must take lower-paying jobs.

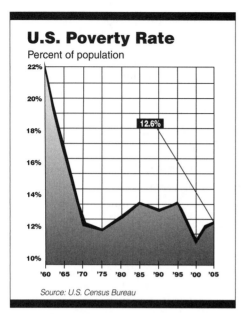

U.S. Poverty Rate

Percent of population

12.6%

'60 '65 '70 '75 '80 '85 '90 '95 '00 '05

Source: U.S. Census Bureau

In 1960, the poverty rate was 22.2 percent. Since then, the rate has fallen and remained between 11 and 15 percent. In 2005, 12.6 percent of Americans—about 37 million men, women, and children—lived below the poverty line.

Who Are the Poor? Poverty affects certain groups more than others. More than 17 percent of America's children are poor, as are about one in four African Americans and American Indians and one in five Hispanic Americans. Although many poor people are unemployed or employed only part-time, nearly 3 million full-time workers also live in poverty. Low-skilled legal and illegal immigrants, whose numbers have increased in recent years, also are often among the poorest residents.

Anti-Poverty Initiatives

Poverty in America reached an historical high during the Great Depression in the 1930s. From that time forward, the federal government implemented different programs to alleviate poverty.

Social Security, Medicaid, and Medicare. When it was created in 1935, Social Security aimed to give financial assistance to low-income, elderly Americans. Today, all citizens over age 65, regardless of income, are eligible to receive varying levels of Social Security benefits.

Created in 1965, Medicaid serves as a federal-state partnership to provide free or subsidized medical care for low-income Americans of any age. Medicare, also instituted in 1965, pays health care benefits to about 40 million older and disabled Americans, regardless of income. Combined, these three programs make up more than one-third of the federal budget.

Wage Assistance. Several anti-poverty programs aim to help workers.

Unemployment Insurance provides temporary financial help to workers who do not have jobs but are looking for work. It aims to lessen the hardship of temporary job loss as well as help the economy by allowing unemployed men and women to continue to buy products and services.

The *Earned Income Tax Credit (EITC)* is a refundable tax credit that supplements the wages of low-income workers by reducing the amount of taxes they owe.

The *Federal Minimum Wage* establishes a wage floor to ensure workers earn enough money to live on.

The Food Stamp Program. Needy individuals and families with incomes below certain levels can receive credits, in the form of cards, to exchange for food at authorized stores. Currently, no time limit exists for how long a person can receive assistance from the food stamp program. In 2006, nearly 27 million Americans received food stamp benefits each month.

Welfare. Aid to Families with Dependent Children (AFDC), created under the Social Security Act, was the program most often associated with the term "welfare." AFDC offered direct cash payments to low-income families with children under 18, in which one or both parents were deceased, incapacitated, absent, or unemployed. In practice, most payments went to single mothers.

In 1996, after years of criticism that AFDC inadvertently created a culture of dependence and provided incentives for recipients to stay unemployed, the program was renamed Temporary Assistance for Needy Families (TANF) and transformed into a federally funded but state-run program with more time limits and work requirements. Lawmakers believed that requiring recipients to find work within two years, and limiting them to five years of assistance during their lifetimes, would help needy families while encouraging them to find jobs and become self-sufficient. In 2005, about 5.1 million people received TANF benefits, 60 percent fewer than received those benefits in 1996 before the new law went into effect.

CURRENT ISSUES

All Things Being Unequal. Between 1979 and 2004, the share of national income going to the wealthiest 20 percent of households increased from 45.4 percent to 53.5 percent, while the share for the bottom 20 percent decreased from 5.8 percent to 4.1 percent. Today, the distance between top earners and the middle class also appears to be growing, as middle class workers face nearly stagnant wages and higher costs for health care, energy, child care, food, education, and retirement. Economists and policymakers cite different factors for this growing income divide, including globalization, technology, education, and tax policy. Members of Congress, President George W. Bush, and others have begun talking about income inequality and especially its impact on the middle class. But few agree on what, if anything, the government should do.

Although they agree that some inequality benefits the economy by offering increasing incentives for hard work, advocates for government efforts to reduce income inequality say that the current gap is unfairly wide. The federal government should impose restrictions on trade and outsourcing, say such supporters, to protect domestic jobs and maintain salary levels. Proponents also argue that the government should

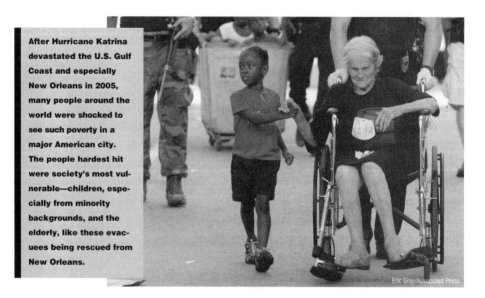

After Hurricane Katrina devastated the U.S. Gulf Coast and especially New Orleans in 2005, many people around the world were shocked to see such poverty in a major American city. The people hardest hit were society's most vulnerable—children, especially from minority backgrounds, and the elderly, like these evacuees being rescued from New Orleans.

Eric Gray/Associated Press

increase taxes on the wealthiest Americans and reduce taxes on middle-class and low-income workers to more fairly redistribute the nation's wealth. Finally, these advocates argue for expanding the social safety net with additional job retraining programs, wage insurance, and unemployment benefits to help workers harmed by globalization.

Those opposed to targeted government efforts to reduce income disparities say interventions like job protection and trade barriers would reduce business profits and leave less to distribute to employees—hardly an outcome that benefits workers. Such critics further contend that raising taxes would stifle economic growth and thus hurt all workers. Some opponents also say that with federal spending on entitlement programs and other social safety net efforts already consuming nearly half of the federal budget, the nation cannot afford new social programs. Ultimately, say free-market supporters, the forces of supply and demand, if left alone, will eventually—and more effectively—reduce income inequality.

Boosting the Minimum. Angry that the minimum wage had not been raised in more than ten years, many voters supported Democratic efforts in Congress to hike the wage from $5.15 an hour to $7.25 an hour. The increase would raise the take-home pay of millions of Americans, allowing full-time workers earning the minimum wage—and with the assistance of food stamps and the Earned Income Tax Credit (EITC)—to rise above the poverty threshold. In May 2007, Congress passed and President Bush signed a large Iraq war funding bill which included domestic spending provisions raising the wage and providing $4.8 billion in small business tax breaks. Despite the new law, debate over the minimum wage continues.

It's a moral outrage that a full-time worker earning the minimum wage would still live below the poverty line, protest those who support the minimum wage increase. They argue that the wage hike will positively affect the lives of millions of American workers, including single mothers, a group at high risk of severe and ongoing poverty. More people with more money to spend will boost the economy and counter any negative effect from businesses raising prices to cover increased

That's the Ticket

Education raises incomes, makes workers more competitive, and breaks the cycle of poverty. Most people agree, education is the ticket to greater individual and national prosperity. The federal government employs education in its fight against poverty by funding programs like Project Head Start and preschool programs that help children from low-income families start elementary school with the right tools for learning. Some advocates for the poor argue that expanding such programs is the best way to lift more people out of poverty for good. Business leaders, too, see education as essential for keeping the economy strong in the face of global competition. Many have joined together to call for more rigorous elementary, secondary, and postsecondary education programs.

wages, say supporters. Finally, some proponents say that new tax cuts should not have been tied to the increase in the minimum wage because businesses have already received generous tax cuts in recent years. They fear the additional tax cuts will remove needed revenues from government coffers.

Raising the minimum wage is counterproductive, declare opponents to the increase. These critics argue that the minimum wage is a weak weapon for fighting poverty because it affects only a small percentage of the workforce, and nearly half of workers receiving the minimum wage are teenagers, not people living in poverty. Raising the costs of doing business, opponents continue, will lead to higher prices and job cuts, which will hurt businesses and low-income workers alike. Critics insist that the market works best for the economy when the laws of supply and demand determine wages. Finally, many opponents suggest that a better way to help the working poor would be to expand the EITC, which rewards work without interfering in the market.

Putting Welfare to Work. After more than ten years of welfare reform and decreasing numbers of TANF cases, few people would argue for going back to the old no-strings-attached cash assistance program. But the picture of poverty today is full of complexity. The number of people receiving welfare benefits has plummeted. More poor single mothers are working. Child support collections have increased. Yet poverty persists. In 2005, 43 percent of those living in poverty took in income equal to half or less of $19,350—the government's definition of poverty for a family of four. This figure represents the highest percentage of people in deep poverty since the government began tracking it in 1975. Policymakers and citizens have reached different conclusions about the success of welfare reform.

About 2.5 million families have left the welfare program, and by getting many of them into the labor force, TANF has successfully moved them toward long-term self-sufficiency, say champions of the 1996 welfare changes. These advocates point out that child poverty today is lower than it was before the new law. Proponents insist that most people who left the welfare program found work, much of it full-time. While admitting that the jobs are often low-paying, advocates stress that as workers gain skills and experience, their earnings will increase. Supporters acknowledge that some people, especially

single mothers, have fallen through the cracks. That's why, they say, the government should enact stricter work requirements and encourage marriage for those with children through efforts such as funding marriage skills courses and divorce reduction programs.

Critics say that fewer TANF cases alone cannot be considered a measure of success, and that persistent poverty—and growing deep poverty—show that changes in the welfare program have failed America's most vulnerable citizens. Opponents suggest that time limits force families off the program even when they cannot support themselves, and merely shift the government's financial burden to other forms of public assistance like food stamps and Medicaid—currently being used by higher proportions of the population than ever before. Furthermore, opponents point out that poor, low-skilled Americans who do find full-time jobs frequently fail to earn enough to escape poverty. Critics say the government must increase funding for job training, child care for working parents, and early childhood education programs for the poor.

OUTLOOK

As globalization and technology march forward, policymakers will continue to argue about jobs, prosperity, and poverty. Should income be redistributed to help more Americans? Should trade policies be changed to protect domestic jobs and help ensure employment for lower-skilled workers? What strategies will best help all Americans prosper?

THE DEBATE: JOBS AND WELFARE

The U.S. government should do more to address income inequality.

PRO: Today's income inequality punishes middle class families and pushes them further behind. The U.S. government should intervene to protect jobs and wages against the encroachments of free trade and globalization, and change the tax structure to help middle-class workers. Furthermore, the nation must increase spending on social programs to help workers.

CON: Government limits on trade and outsourcing would hurt the economy, reduce profits, and do more harm than good for all workers. Raising taxes hurts business owners. The nation already spends generously on social safety net programs and cannot afford to implement new ones. If the forces of supply and demand are left alone, the income gap will narrow over time.

Raising the federal minimum wage will help workers.

PRO: The wage hike will give millions of hard-working Americans a much-needed and long-overdue pay raise. More earned income will lift some of society's most vulnerable citizens, like single mothers, out of poverty. Furthermore, the economy and all workers will benefit when more Americans have more money to spend. Companion tax cuts for small businesses, however, are unneeded and wasteful.

CON: Raising the minimum wage will be counterproductive. Many minimum wage earners are teenagers, not poor people. Increased costs will force small businesses to lay off workers and raise prices, circumstances that harm the economy and especially low-income workers. A better approach overall would be to expand the EITC, which rewards work without meddling in the market.

Welfare reform is working.

PRO: Millions of Americans have moved off welfare and into jobs, increasing their skills, incomes, and self-sufficiency in the process. Out-of-wedlock births have slowed and child support collections have increased. To reinforce the welfare program, the government should encourage stricter work requirements and marriage for those with children.

CON: Even as the number of TANF cases decreases, poverty persists, and more Americans than ever rely on forms of government assistance like food stamps. Low-skilled people who do find work often still cannot rise above poverty. Welfare reform has failed. America's poor need more job training, child care support, and other help to permanently escape poverty.

MINORITIES AND WOMEN

Americans value equality and liberty. However, putting those principles into practice has taken decades of debate and effort. When the Constitution was first written in 1787, it gave the right to vote only to white male property owners. Gradually, legislators amended the Constitution to extend voting rights to non-landowners, racial minorities, and women. But it became clear that overcoming discrimination and guaranteeing all Americans civil rights—equal participation in politics, education, and public affairs—would require more effort.

Thanks to the modern civil rights movement that began in the 1950s, the federal government outlawed discrimination based on race and gender and passed laws to protect the rights of minorities and women. It also enacted programs such as affirmative action, designed to help minorities and women overcome disadvantages they faced because of past discrimination. Some Americans believe the playing field has now been leveled. Others, however, argue that minorities—especially people of African-American, Native-American, and Hispanic descent—still lack equal access to social services and economic opportunities.

Other demographic groups who have faced discrimination—such as older Americans, people with disabilities, religious minorities, and homosexuals—also have called for equality and protection. Some issues, such as whether gay people should have the right to marry, have divided the nation. Citizens and legislators face the ongoing challenge of evaluating whether discrimination is depriving Americans of their constitutional rights, and, if so, what should be done about it.

KEY QUESTIONS

- Should the U.S. Constitution be amended to ban same-sex marriage?

- Is race-based affirmative action still needed for college and university admissions?

- Are racial balancing plans in public schools constitutional?

BACKGROUND

Overcoming Discrimination

Race—particularly the relationship between white Americans and black Americans—has always been a volatile issue in the United States. Following the Civil War, three constitutional amendments gave former slaves certain rights of citizenship: the Thirteenth Amendment abolished slavery; the Fourteenth Amendment guaranteed civil rights; and the Fifteenth Amendment granted black men the right to vote. However, racial prejudice could not be legislated away easily. After Reconstruction ended in 1877, southern states implemented "Jim Crow" laws, which segregated public facilities by race. In 1896, the Supreme Court upheld such laws in the case of *Plessy v. Ferguson,* writing that segregation was legal as long as "separate but equal" facilities were provided.

Civil Rights Reforms. Change came slowly at first. More than fifty years after *Plessy v. Ferguson,* in 1948, President Harry Truman extended some civil rights by ordering the U.S. military to desegregate its units. He also proposed bills to protect citizens' voting rights, to prohibit lynching, and to end discrimination on trains and other interstate

Associated Press

In 1939, the Daughters of the American Revolution (DAR) refused to allow operatic singer Marian Anderson to perform in Constitution Hall due to the organization's "white artists only" policy. Then-First Lady Eleanor Roosevelt resigned from the DAR in protest, and Ms. Anderson was invited to sing at the Lincoln Memorial on Easter Sunday, April 9. Her concert, attended by 75,000 and broadcast on radio nationwide, turned a spotlight on racial discrimination.

U.S. Army Sergeant Isaac Reyes-Mejia of Lima, Peru, is sworn in as a U.S. citizen in July 2004. Reyes received the Purple Heart for wounds received in Iraq. Currently, about 30,000 non-citizens serve in the U.S. military.

transportation facilities. However, powerful southern members of Congress blocked most attempts at reform.

The 1954 Supreme Court decision in *Brown v. Board of Education of Topeka, Kansas,* helped spark the modern civil rights movement. The Court unanimously ruled that maintaining racially segregated schools for black students and white students was unconstitutional because such schools could not offer equal educational opportunities. Federal court judges later ordered many school districts to redraw boundary lines and bus children to schools outside their own neighborhoods, if necessary, to achieve racial integration in each district school. Other civil rights reforms soon followed.

Bolstering the Right to Vote. The Civil Rights Act of 1957 made it illegal to prevent people from voting in federal elections. However, the act had many loopholes and proved ineffective in securing the universal right to vote. The Twenty-fourth Amendment, passed in 1964, barred the use of a poll tax (a tax that was often used to prevent low-income African Americans from voting) or any other tax in federal elections. That amendment was later extended to state and local elections. The Voting Rights Act of 1965 banned literacy tests, poll taxes, and intimidation of voters in any state.

Protection from Discrimination. The Civil Rights Act of 1964 prohibited discrimination in public accommodations, such as restaurants and hotels, and in programs receiving federal aid. This landmark legislation also prohibited job discrimination by employers and unions and strengthened enforcement of voting and desegregation laws.

Women's Rights. In the mid-1800s, Elizabeth Cady Stanton and Susan B. Anthony organized the suffrage movement to secure women's right to vote. Suffragists tried to include women in the Fifteenth Amendment, ratified in 1870, which guaranteed the right to vote to all men, regardless of race.

However, that idea was blocked by members of Congress who feared that a provision giving women the right to vote would keep the entire amendment from passing. Despite this setback, the suffrage movement continued. Fifty years later, on August 18, 1920, the Nineteenth Amendment was ratified, extending to women the right to vote in all state and national elections.

Laws Against Gender Discrimination. As the civil rights movement gained momentum in the 1960s, women, too, sought legal protections from discrimination. In 1963, Congress adopted the Equal Pay Act, which guaranteed equal pay for men and women who perform equal work. A 1972 law, known as Title 9, barred gender-based discrimination in all education programs receiving federal support. In 1978, Congress amended the Civil Rights Act to prohibit job discrimination against pregnant women.

Equal Rights Amendment. In 1971, Congress passed a proposed amendment to the Constitution that supporters thought would permanently guarantee equal rights for women. The Equal Rights Amendment (ERA) stated: "Equality of rights under the law shall not be denied or abridged by the United States or by any state on account of sex." However, the hotly debated amendment was never added to the Constitution, falling three states short of the thirty-eight necessary for ratification.

Affirmative Action. Some Americans believe that the government should take a more active role in extending opportunities to certain groups of people to compensate for past discrimination by the government. In the early 1960s, President John Kennedy issued a series of executive orders requiring federal contractors to "take affirmative action" to ensure that their hiring practices did not discriminate because of race, color, or national origin. Presidents Lyndon Johnson and Richard Nixon expanded these programs to include gender and to apply to certain organizations accepting government funds. The policies seek to increase employment and higher educational opportunities for minorities and women and require government institutions to actively recruit qualified minority candidates.

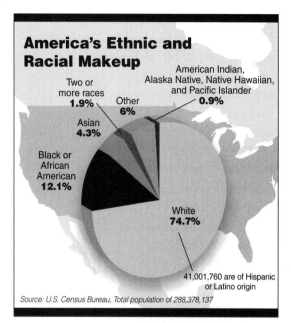

America's Ethnic and Racial Makeup

Two or more races
1.9%

Other
6%

American Indian, Alaska Native, Native Hawaiian, and Pacific Islander
0.9%

Asian
4.3%

Black or African American
12.1%

White
74.7%

41,001,760 are of Hispanic or Latino origin

Source: U.S. Census Bureau, Total population of 288,378,137

Race and ethnicity continue to be dominant issues in the United States, especially with increased immigration and changing demographics. Although non-Hispanic white people are 66 percent—the majority—of the U.S. population, the U.S. Census Bureau predicts that by 2050, they will be less than 50 percent of the total population. Non-Hispanic white people are already in the minority in California, Texas, New Mexico, and Hawaii. Hispanic people are now the largest single ethnic minority group in the United States.

Since then, many colleges and universities have implemented their own affirmative action programs to give opportunities to women and to candidates from minority backgrounds. However, a series of Supreme Court decisions in the 1980s and 1990s defined and limited the scope of affirmative action initiatives in higher education.

Challenges Remain

Issues of Race.

Although some minority groups, such as Asian Americans, have generally prospered in recent decades, some members of other groups still face challenges. In the aftermath of Hurricane Katrina in 2005, many Americans were stunned and surprised by images of severe poverty among black people in the U.S. Gulf Coast region, particularly New Orleans. However, for years, African Americans have suffered high rates of poverty (currently almost 26 percent), along with Native Americans/Alaska Natives (more than 25 percent) and Hispanics (more than 22 percent). Studies consistently show that people from these groups still have less access to good quality health care and fewer educational opportunities, face discrimination in housing, and experience disproportionate rates of incarceration. Civil rights activists argue that these statistics demonstrate that discrimination still occurs and must be addressed.

Voting Rights. Despite the many laws meant to ensure that all men and women can exercise the right to vote, minorities in some areas still report obstacles to enfranchisement. In 2006, the Supreme Court ruled in *League of Latin American Citizens, et al. v. Perry* that the redistricting plan passed by the Texas Legislature in 2003 was constitutional, but that part of it violated the Voting Rights Act. To remedy the situation, the Court ordered a federal panel to adjust the lines of five districts, and to hold new primary elections in November.

Gender and Pay Inequity. U.S. Census Bureau statistics indicate that, on average, women make about seventy-seven cents for every dollar men earn. Typically, professions made up of a majority of women tend to pay much less than professions with a majority of men. Even when women work the same jobs as men, they sometimes receive less pay. Some political leaders have proposed "comparable worth" bills that would equalize wages between jobs requiring similar skills. So far, such proposals have proven too complex to gain widespread support. A 2007 study again showed that women earn significantly less on the whole than do men, even when they perform the same work.

Ready to Start Up?

In 2006, the U.S. Census Bureau revealed statistics showing that growth for minority- and women-owned businesses is far outpacing the national average. Between 1997 and 2002, the bureau reported, the total number of businesses owned by black people grew by 45 percent—four times the national average—for a total of 1.2 million businesses. The number of Hispanic-owned firms grew by 31 percent for a total of 1.6 million; Asian-owned firms grew by 24 percent to total more than 1 million; and women–owned firms grew by 20 percent for a total of 6.5 million. Experts say these firms are among the fastest-growing segments of the economy. Reasons for the increases include laid-off or retired women and minorities beginning their own businesses and recent college graduates choosing to go into business for themselves at an early age.

Sexual Orientation. In recent decades, homosexual men and women have become more open about their sexual orientation and, in turn, have sought legal protection from discrimination. Although federal law does not extend civil rights protections on the basis of sexual orientation, some cities, counties, and states have passed laws that ban discrimination against gay men and lesbians. In 2003, the Supreme Court ruled that gay couples had a constitutional right to privacy with regard to their sexual behavior. The landmark decision in *Lawrence v. Texas* declared that states could not prosecute consenting adults for sexual activities in the privacy of their own homes.

Military Service. Since President Bill Clinton signed the "don't ask, don't tell, don't pursue, don't harass" policy into law in 1993, nearly 11,000 troops have been discharged from the armed forces based on this policy, which says that troops may serve only if they are quiet about their sexual orientation. Defense Department statistics show that discharges under the law accounted for less than one percent of all discharges in 2005. But gay rights supporters argue that the policy discriminates against homosexuals and threatens national security now that the nation is at war and needs skilled service members. They point out that in 2005, nearly 7 percent of the 726 troops dismissed because of sexual orientation were in the medical profession. In March 2007, Rep. Marty Meehan (D-Mass.) introduced the Military Readiness Enhancement Act to repeal the 1993 law.

Marriage Benefits. Many homosexual couples want to receive the same legal benefits conferred by government that married couples receive. Such benefits include favored immigration status, hospital visitation rights, rights of survivorship, the right to adopt a partner's child, and extension of health and dental insurance coverage. Some local governments and private employers give benefits to same-sex domestic partners, though the federal government does not.

CURRENT ISSUES

Same-Sex Marriage. Some homosexual couples argue that they should be able to marry legally, just as heterosexual couples can. However, many Americans disagree.

In February 2007, New Jersey became the third state to issue licenses allowing same-sex couples to enter into civil unions. Here, the mayor of Lambertville performs a civil union ceremony for a lesbian couple the week the new law took effect.

AP photo/Mel Evans

The federal Defense of Marriage Act (1996) allows states to deny legal recognition to same-sex marriages performed in other states and defines marriage under federal law as legal only when between one man and one woman. As it stands now, state governments can decide whether or not to legalize marriage between same-sex partners. Debate has been especially heated since 2004, when court rulings in Massachusetts made that state the only state to permit gay marriage. Local leaders in several U.S. cities and counties further raised the issue's profile by marrying same-sex couples in defiance of their states' laws, and a backlash ensued. Twenty-seven states now have constitutional bans against same-sex marriage. The debate rages on—even in Massachusetts. In January 2007, state lawmakers tentatively passed a constitutional amendment that, if approved by voters in 2008, would ban gay marriages and replace them with civil unions. The amendment requires a second approval from lawmakers before going to the voters.

While a majority of states do not recognize same-sex marriage, a growing number are granting some civil rights and benefits to same-sex partnerships. Before 2003, only Vermont allowed gay couples to legally form a civil union, but as of April 2007, seven states and the District of Columbia granted some civil rights and benefits to same-sex partnerships. And starting in January 2008, Oregon and New Hampshire will also grant legal recognition to partnerships or unions of same-sex couples.

In 2004 and 2006, fearing that state courts, like the one in Massachusetts, could overturn state laws prohibiting same-sex marriage, President George W. Bush and some members of Congress pushed for a "Marriage Protection Amendment" to the U.S. Constitution to ban same-sex marriage across the nation. The efforts failed to acquire the two-thirds majority in Congress needed to pass. Experts say the new Democratic Congress is unlikely to take up the issue again soon, but debate about same-sex marriage will remain contentious.

Supporters of a constitutional amendment argue that traditional marriage is a sacred institution that will collapse unless it is constitutionally protected. Amendment advocates fear that allowing same-sex marriage will inevitably lead to other harmful changes in marriage, such as allowing multiple spouses. They point out that throughout human history, marriage has been defined as between one man and one woman. Furthermore, they say, a heterosexual marriage is vital to raising and educating children. Many supporters of an amendment consider homosexuality to be a morally wrong and unnatural behavior that does not qualify for civil rights protections.

More than 6,500 same-sex couples have been married in Massachusetts alone, opponents are quick to point out, with no adverse effects to society. Amending the Constitution to define marriage would mark an embarrassing first in U.S. history—the first time the nation's founding document had been changed to discriminate against a certain group. Supporters of allowing gay people to marry argue that it is good for family values because it solidifies the family life of children living with same-sex couples. In addition, they point out that gay couples contribute to society just as heterosexual couples do—by paying taxes, supporting public education, and contributing to the economy—and should thus receive the same government benefits. Ultimately, say opponents of a federal amendment outlawing same-sex marriage, decisions about marriage can and should be left to the states.

Affirmative Action. To diversify their student bodies and assist minority students, some colleges and universities use affirmative action policies—such as awarding applicants extra

points in the admission process. But over the years, Supreme
Court decisions have limited such policies in various ways.
In *Board of Regents of the University of California v. Bakke
(1978),* the Supreme Court struck down racial quotas in college admissions, while also stating that race could be used as
one of many factors in deciding who gets accepted. In two
cases that involved the University of Michigan in 2003, the
Court held that taking race into account does not violate the
Fourteenth Amendment—which ensures all citizens equal
treatment under state law—but noted that schools must judge
the individual merits of each candidate rather than rely on formulas that award "points" to certain applicants. Some people
question whether race-based affirmative action is still needed
for admissions.

Supporters of continuing affirmative action argue that students from minority backgrounds still have lower test scores
than non-minorities because of socioeconomic factors resulting from past discrimination. Thus, admissions policies that
take race into account are still important tools for reversing
the damage of the past, proponents say. Furthermore, they
argue that campus diversity serves the entire student body by
building students' skills in working with and learning from
people of different backgrounds. Finally, supporters argue that
the policy encourages colleges and universities to consider all
predictors of a student's success—not just test scores and
grades.

Others argue that affirmative action has run its course and
now unfairly rewards or penalizes prospective students based

on their race, ethnicity, or gender. Such opponents maintain that the best way to end discrimination is to be completely colorblind or to address the economic issues behind low-achieving student groups. Furthermore, they contend that affirmative action does more harm than good by implying that minority students cannot compete on their own merits. These critics agree that the playing field must be level, but insist that the best way to equalize opportunity is to ensure that all students obtain a first-rate K–12 education.

Race and the Public Schools. After the Civil War, the Constitution was amended to abolish slavery and to guarantee newly freed slaves "equal protection under the law." For the next century, however, the daily life of African Americans in the United States was still characterized by discrimination, poverty, and violence. Racist practices were codified into laws that required separate facilities and services (such as public transportation) for each race. In *Plessy v. Ferguson* (1896) the Supreme Court upheld these laws, finding that "separate but equal" accommodations were constitutional.

One area of life in which the "separate but equal" doctrine had dire consequences was in public education. African-American children were often confined to under-funded, over-crowded school buildings and were forced to learn with outdated textbooks and poorly trained teachers. In 1954, the laws requiring separate public schools for black and white children were finally overturned by the Supreme Court in *Brown v. Board of Education of Topeka, Kansas.* Reversing *Plessy,* the Court unanimously held that "separate educational facilities are inherently unequal." In a holding the following year, the Court ordered the public schools to integrate "with all deliberate speed." However, many southern states strongly resisted this effort. Violence prompted the federal courts to directly impose and oversee the integration plans of many school districts over the next few decades.

Although most of these court-imposed plans have ended, many school districts across the country have since implemented their own plans in an effort to achieve racially balanced and diverse student bodies. Because these plans use

race as a factor in deciding which school a child will attend, some critics believe they violate the Fourteenth Amendment's guarantee of equal protection. In 2007, the Supreme Court considered the constitutionality of plans used in school systems in Louisville, Kentucky, and Seattle, Washington. Under these plans, efforts to achieve a specific mix of white and black students sometimes prevented children from attending their first-choice schools.

Proponents of new racial integration plans in public schools say that they are consistent with the spirit of the Court's decision in *Brown* because they seek to provide children with a racially integrated educational experience that will prepare them for life in the adult world. Unlike the race-based policies of the past, they say, these plans represent a good faith effort to create a positive educational experience for children of all races and do not cause undue harm to children of one race since the quality of the schools is relatively equal. Supporters also believe the plans are necessary because many residential neighborhoods from which schools draw their students are still not fully integrated. Since these plans are implemented by the local school boards, and the Supreme Court has long recognized local power over public schools, advocates believe that the Court should allow these plans to stand.

Critics of racial balancing plans in public schools say that any attempt to classify individuals by the color of their skin amounts to unequal treatment, which is inherently unconstitutional under the Fourteenth Amendment. The goal of *Brown* was to move toward a color-blind society, not one in which important decisions—like where a child can go to school—are based on race. A law that classifies people based on their race can be constitutional only if the state can prove that its purpose is important, or "compelling," enough to outweigh the fundamental right of equal treatment under the law. Detractors argue that the goal of achieving racial diversity in the public schools is not a sufficiently compelling interest because its benefits are not proven: just because a student body is racially mixed does not mean that black and white children are more likely to be friends or to understand one another. Therefore, the pursuit of racial balance does not justify assigning a child to a school simply because he or she is black or white. Ultimately, say opponents, if the Court allows governments to make race-based decisions, even with good intentions, the doors will be opened to more harmful race-based policies in the future.

OUTLOOK

Despite the progress achieved in extending civil rights to Americans, some citizens believe that more should be done. Others, however, argue that attempts to treat one group fairly must not come at the expense of other groups, the nation's values, or America's security. As the makeup of the United States continues to change, lawmakers, the courts, and citizens alike will continue to assess what changes to current policies, if any, are needed.

THE DEBATE: MINORITIES AND WOMEN

The U.S. Constitution should be amended to ban same-sex marriage.

PRO: Historically, marriage has been defined as between one man and one woman. Traditional marriage promotes strong families and is a cornerstone of society; homosexual activity is immoral. To protect marriage from being changed forever by activist courts, it must be written into the Constitution. States would still have the power to allow civil unions.

CON: A constitutional amendment banning same-sex marriage would only serve to write discrimination into the nation's most important legal document. Same-sex couples and their children should have the same legal benefits and protections as other families. The state legislatures and courts should uphold equality for gay citizens; doing so supports true family values.

Race-based affirmative action is still needed for college and university admissions.

PRO: Minority students still face major disadvantages in education brought on by past discrimination. Race-based admissions allow for the consideration of factors other than test scores and grades. Furthermore, campus diversity is a worthy goal that better prepares all students for the demands of multicultural workplaces and the global economy.

CON: Minority preferences in college admissions result in reverse discrimination and do more harm than good. Low-achieving students deserve additional resources before they graduate from high school so that they won't fall behind later on. To level the playing field and ensure diversity in higher education, more effort should be devoted to K-12 education.

Racial balancing plans in public schools are constitutional.

PRO: The Supreme Court's ruling in *Brown v. Board of Education* was designed to ensure that public schools were racially integrated. Attempts by local governments to achieve racial balance in their public schools are constitutional because they benefit children of all races. Without these plans, many schools would not be integrated and children would be deprived of the diverse educational experience necessary to prepare them for participation in civic life.

CON: Public school racial balancing plans are unconstitutional because they require important decisions to be based solely on whether a child is black or white. The Supreme Court envisioned a color-blind society, not one where governments would continue to make race-based decisions. The goal of achieving diversity does not outweigh the right to equal protection under the law. Such plans will open the door to more harmful race-based policies.

SCIENCE AND TECHNOLOGY

The worlds of science and technology seem to change every week. Just as the public begins to adapt to the latest communication or wireless service, or begins to understand the impact of a new medical breakthrough, news emerges of an even more astounding device or procedure that promises to further "revolutionize" the way the world's people live.

The pace has continued to accelerate since the beginning of the new millennium. Satellite technology and communications such as cell phones are erasing borders between nations; the ability to clone living organisms—once the domain of science fiction novels—is now a reality; much of the world's food supply is now manufactured rather than grown; and many people's lives, both personal and professional, are integrally tied to their personal computers.

As new technologies race forward, citizens and lawmakers alike are trying to stay alert and address the many legal, economic, and ethical ramifications of technological change. Many researchers and corporations hope to elude proposed regulations that might hinder new creativity and profit, while some citizens and organizations worry that "new" does not necessarily mean better or safer. While most people agree that innovations in science and technology have made their daily lives easier, some are quick to point out that many of these same innovations can also threaten the health of the environment, disrupt economies, challenge long-held belief systems, and destroy human life. Encouraging continued scientific innovation while protecting the world from the possible dangers of new technologies is one of the greatest challenges facing the United States and other nations.

KEY QUESTIONS

- Should the federal government fund embryonic stem cell research?

- Should the federal government act to preserve "net neutrality"?

- Should nanotechnology research be regulated?

BACKGROUND

Making the Modern World: 1900-2000

The twentieth century has been called the "fastest moving century." In 1900, people transported themselves by foot or horse and buggy. By the late 1960s, men were walking on the moon. In 1900, life expectancy around the world was about 30 years; by 2000 it was approaching 65. For most of the century, people relied on the postal service to send messages, waiting days, even weeks, for delivery. By 2000, people were exchanging millions of instant electronic messages with their families, friends, and business associates around the globe.

While science has succeeded in improving life in extraordinary ways, it has also created the technology to destroy it on a vast scale. In 1900, there were no military aircraft or missiles. A mere forty-five years later, a single atomic bomb dropped from an airplane leveled an entire city.

Faster and Faster. In the early part of the twentieth century, transportation became faster and more convenient. Fifteen years after the Wright brothers successfully tested their powered biplane in Kitty Hawk, North Carolina, in 1903, airplanes were being used to carry bombs during World War I. Soon, nonstop commercial flights were carrying passengers around the world. Although the automobile was actually invented at the end of the nineteenth century, the advent of the mass-produced Ford Model T and other "motor buggies" between 1908 and 1914 increased the number of cars in America by about 500 percent, to nearly 2.5 million. By the 1970s, more than 100 million Americans owned a car. Today, there are more than 200 million vehicles on the road.

For many, the most exciting breakthrough of the twentieth century—space exploration—came at the height of the Cold War. The rivalry between the United States and the Soviet Union was largely carried out in laboratories by scientists and engineers, as each side maneuvered for scientific and technological superiority. The 1957 launch of the Soviet satellite *Sputnik* into orbit marked the beginning of the space age and

In 1969, the United States became the first nation to successfully land a man on the moon.

the space race. Only twelve years later, the United States became the first country to send a man to the moon.

Longer, Healthier Lives. The ability to treat and cure diseases increased dramatically throughout the twentieth century, helping to extend the average person's life expectancy by over thirty years. With the introduction of antibiotics and immunizations, previously fatal diseases such as polio, cholera, and smallpox were neutralized by the 1950s. Surgical procedures such as heart and kidney transplants were introduced in the 1960s and became commonplace over the next decade. In the 1990s, the use of fiber optic instruments called endoscopes enabled surgeons to perform intricate, less-invasive surgical procedures.

Mass Technology for Mass Destruction. In the twentieth century, waging war became, in many ways, a contest of technological mastery. World War I (1914-1918) was the first major war to use radio communication and electrical power. New weapons, such as armored tanks, dirigibles (airships), poison gas, airplanes, submarines, and machine guns increased casualties and brought the war to civilian populations.

In 1945, the world witnessed an even more devastating fusion of science and war, when the United States dropped atomic bombs on the Japanese cities of Hiroshima and Nagasaki. Despite bringing about the end of World War II, these bombs destroyed both cities, killing as many as 300,000 people. By 1970, the United States and the Soviet Union had accumulated more than 70,000 nuclear warheads. For the first time, people lived with the knowledge that their leaders could, with a single order, destroy the world. Today, the existence of nuclear bombs and other technologically sophisticated weapons, such as biological and chemical agents, continues to threaten all nations.

The Information Age. Innovations in communication accelerated after World War II. The development and marketing of numerous technological breakthroughs—from television to mobile phones, and transistor radios to the Internet—changed the methods and speed of communication and information dissemination around the world.

See It Now. Television became a major agent of social change in the twentieth century. Derisively called the "idiot box" by social critics, television also exposed audiences to other peoples and places, and brought historic events including wars and space travel into millions of homes. Just three households had a TV in the late 1920s when television broadcasting made its debut. By 2000, roughly 1 billion TV sets existed throughout the world.

A PC in Every Home. In the 1950s and 1960s, computers were large, bulky mechanisms used primarily by governments and large corporations. The invention of the microprocessor in

As science dominated the twentieth century, weapons with enormous destructive powers were created. Here, U.S. soldiers watch the cloud from a Nevada nuclear test blast in 1953.

AP Photo/files

Boris Roessler/epa/Corbis

1971 enabled engineers to shrink both the size and cost of computers, making them affordable and practical for everyday business and household use. Over the next two decades, computer technology rocketed ahead on every front. By the mid-1990s, the personal computer (PC) had become a standard item in most homes and offices across America.

The PC's paramount importance in people's lives was solidified with the popularization of the Internet, once just a data network used by the U.S. Department of Defense. The Internet quickly became the principal instrument of sharing and transporting information around the world. Today, more than 200 million Americans have access to the Internet, revolutionizing commerce, entertainment, news, and politics.

Life in the '00s

Though the twentieth century brought incredible changes and advancement, many experts believe the pace of innovation has actually sped up over the past ten years. Inventions such as the airplane, automobile, and television arrived under what is generally considered a manageable rate of change. But the innovations that have characterized life in the twenty-first century—smaller computer chips, genetic engineering, nanotechnology—are constantly advancing, presenting a daunting challenge. As producers and consumers rapidly devour the "latest and greatest" tools and toys, it has become more difficult for the public and lawmakers to continually evaluate the overall impact of these new technologies, for better or worse, on society.

Biotechnology: Genetic Manipulation. One of the most powerful mergers of computers and science has been in the field of biotechnology, specifically genetics. Biotechnology is the modification or manipulation of organisms to transfer genetic material from one kind of organism into another for perceived benefits. These transfers can be used to create genetically modified (GM) crops and plants, treat disease, and even replicate, or clone, human beings. While marveling at the advances of genetic research, many people are frightened at its seemingly boundless possibilities and wonder if a "Pandora's Box" has been opened.

"Frankenfoods." A genetically modified food is one that contains ingredients from plants or animals that have had their genes altered to produce a desired trait. For example, crops such as corn, rice, and soybeans are routinely injected with genetic materials to make them more resistant to insects or drought. This practice is hardly new; farmers in the United States have been raising GM food crops since the mid-1990s. Nor is it rare. Nearly all foods available in supermarkets today have had their genes altered in some way.

Genetically modified foods are commonplace throughout the United States. It is estimated that nearly 70 percent of the foods purchased in grocery stores contain genetically modified ingredients.

Kozak/zefa/Corbis

Many health care professionals believe that genetically modified foods have higher nutritional value and will help reduce malnutrition in developing countries. But many consumer groups and environmental activists warn that the GM food "experiment" could produce unforeseen health effects and unwanted environmental consequences.

Mapping the Genome. The biggest controversy surrounding genetics is the prospect of manipulating the human genome through the creation of a complete genetic "map" of the human body. In 2000, a group of scientists announced they had "cracked the code" of the human genome, identifying about 30,000 individual genes that guide human development. Scientists and ethicists have been grappling with what to do with this information. Potential applications include manipulating these genes for disease therapy, stem cell development to prevent or cure certain diseases and disabilities, and even cloning.

The Internet: Shrinking the World. In January 2007, more than 1 billion people around the world were using the Internet—surfing the Web on optical fibers, cable television lines, radio waves, and telephone lines. And people are now able to access the Internet and transmit data via electronic devices other than computers, such as cellular telephones.

No industry has gone untouched by the power of the Internet. Business models have been erased and redrawn to adapt to this technology. With an increasing number of people using the Internet to read newspapers and magazines online, media observers believe traditional print publications may one day become extinct.

The public has also been forced to contend with the Internet's "darker side,"—including electronic viruses, spam mail, unwelcome offensive material, and a new arena for criminal activity. Personal Web sites, online communities, and the surge in blogging have prompted a remarkable burst of human creativity, but they have also provided hate groups, pornographers, and terrorists with low-cost ways of spreading their messages to anyone with a personal computer. Addressing the many complex legal and constitutional issues such new realities present has been a challenge to all branches and levels of government.

Innovation and Regulation. Throughout the twentieth century, breakthroughs in warfare, communications, and medicine compelled the government to impose regulations to curb potential hazards produced by these innovations. But the accelerated pace of technological change over the past decade has made it more difficult for lawmakers, scientists, and ethicists to assess the impact of new innovations and reach consensus on regulation. The government, for example, wants to ensure that the public will be protected from medicine that has not been properly tested or that a new technology won't promote environmental degradation. The scientific and business communities, on the other hand, generally believe government regulations curb the incentive to innovate and slow the delivery of exciting and potentially life-saving materials and services to citizens. Finding balance between the two interests can be exceedingly difficult.

Voting In the Electronic Age

After a controversy over voting irregularities in Florida marred the 2000 presidential election, many states turned to new electronic voting systems, which use optical scanners and touch-screens. A 2006 report by the Brennan Center of Justice, however, warned that these systems were not immune to corruption and fraud, posing a "real danger" to the legitimacy of local, state, and national elections. In February 2007, Florida governor Charlie Crist announced plans to spend $32 million to ensure that electronic voting machines throughout the state leave a paper trail of votes. Even with this improvement, experts say "e-voting" machines would still have to be audited on a regular basis to reduce irregularities.

CURRENT ISSUES

Stem Cell Division. The fight over whether to use stem cells for medical research is one of the most highly charged moral, ethical, and legal debates of recent years. Stem cells differ from other kinds of cells in the body. Stem cells can replicate indefinitely and produce specialized human structures. Harvesting these cells may give doctors the ability to create any body tissue, potentially revolutionizing the treatment of many diseases, including spinal cord injuries, multiple sclerosis, diabetes, Parkinson's disease, cancer, Alzheimer's disease, and heart disease.

Stem cells can be derived from several sources. Many scientists believe that those derived from early-stage human embryos and aborted fetuses are more effective than those derived from adults. Despite the potential, many people oppose destroying human embryos for any purpose. Although there is significant support in Congress for federal funding of embryonic stem cell research, President George W. Bush used his presidential veto power to reject bills in 2006 and 2007 that would have loosened restrictions on this type of funding.

Many researchers believe embryonic stem cell research can uncover the greatest potential for the alleviation of human suffering since the advent of antibiotics. They say the research could potentially help more than 10 million Americans who suffer from diseases that eventually may be treated more effectively or even cured with embryonic stem cell therapy. But proponents warn that this potential will be severely undermined if federal funds, the financial engine behind most biomedical research in the United States, are not available. They believe that instead of retreating from the possibilities embryonic stem cell research offers, the government should assist in exploring this science for the betterment of mankind.

Those who agree with the president remind people that stem cell therapy still requires the destruction of a tiny human embryo. They believe that all human life is sacred and that taking one life—even if only in the form of an embryo—to save another is an unacceptable sacrifice. Such critics contend that life is not something to be tampered with in scientific laboratories by scientists "playing God." Critics also point out that stem cell researchers can seek out alternative sources of stem cells. For example, in early 2007, researchers discovered that stem cells derived from amniotic fluid, which surrounds a baby during gestation, may be just as effective as those extracted from embryos.

The End of the Internet as We Know It? In 1995, only 18,000 Web sites populated the World Wide Web. By mid-2004, that number had skyrocketed to 50 million; two years later it hit the 100 million milestone. Even with this meteoric growth, the Internet has always been, essentially, a level playing field where online content is transmitted at equal speeds over the broadband service networks run by cable and telephone companies.

However, Web sites have long ceased to be a collection of text-based pages requiring about the same amount of space to move through cables and lines. Over the past few years, the sophistication of Web content has improved dramatically. Video, audio, and other multimedia applications have become commonplace and demanded by consumers. Cable and phone companies, however, warn that their networks are increasingly becoming overburdened. To prevent the Internet superhighway from becoming "clogged," these companies have proposed the creation of a top tier or "fast lane." Sites, such as Google and Yahoo, which depend on large amounts of bandwidth to deliver content, would have to pay fees to use the faster delivery.

In 2005, broadband providers requested that Congress revise the Telecommunications Bill of 1996 to allow the industry to create this tiered system of service. In response, opponents lobbied the government to pass a Network Neutrality bill to prevent service providers from dividing the Internet into so-called "fast" and "slow lanes." As of mid-2007, neither the House nor Senate had voted on Net Neutrality legislation.

Proponents of so-called "net neutrality" argue that the Internet should treat large and small content providers equally. They believe that if telecom companies are permitted to pro-ceed with a tiered system, they will be granting privileges to content providers with money and power. These critics

contend that if that happens, only content creators who can afford to pay for premium service will be able to get their content or applications to consumers. This threatens to drown out other voices and sources of information, especially those from smaller companies, citizen organizations, and independent bloggers. At worst, say critics, the Internet will end up operating much like cable television does now: users will be dependent on bandwith providers' decisions about what "channels" they can access and how much that access will cost.

Opponents of maintaining net neutrality say they need flexibility and money to substantially upgrade network facilities—cables, lines, and wireless technologies—and to ensure that consumers are able to receive the multimedia content they want and demand. They argue that if they cannot charge fees to companies who are "bandwidth hogs," then they will have to pass on their increased costs to consumers. Broadband providers also caution that technological innovation will grind to a halt if it becomes too expensive for them to make new advances easily available to consumers.

Nanotechnology: No Small Matter. For many years, scientists have been experimenting with the manipulation of atoms and molecules for the purpose of producing the smallest-scale objects—a science called nanotechnology. A nanometer (derived from the Greek word *nano*, meaning "dwarf") is measured as one-billionth of a meter. (For perspective, the diameter of one human hair is about 100,000 nanometers thick.)

All manufactured products are made from atoms, and their physical properties are determined by the arrangement of those atoms. Nanotechnology enables researchers to rearrange atoms to maximize the properties of products to make them smaller, stronger, and more precise than current technologies permit. Nanotechnology is still in its infancy, and scientists are just beginning to understand how it can be used to improve products and processes in fields ranging from semiconductors to medicine and energy. According to devotees, the possibilities of nanotechnology are endless. Imagine computer chips the size of a speck of dust, microscopic medical implants, tiny robotic systems for space exploration, or nano-sized particles that bleach toxic waste from contaminated areas.

Nanotechnology has captured the imagination not only of scientists, but also of entrepreneurs and the federal government, who see a new blockbuster industry—with potential revenue projections of up to $1 trillion—and intriguing national security applications. However, nanotechnology is still a mystery to many and a worry to some.

Those wary of nanotechnology say their main concern is not with the products being created, but with the particles themselves. Such critics cite studies that show that nanoparticles have been found to cause health problems and irreversible environmental damage once they have been dispersed into soil and water. In February 2007, the United Nations called for tighter regulation on nanotechnology, arguing that nations have not done sufficient research into its potential risks. Many products with nanotechnology have already hit the market-place, including sports equipment like golf balls and tennis rackets, clothing, and skin care products. As a result, some lawmakers favor establishing new workplace, health, and environmental regulations to help educate and protect consumers until the risks of nanotechnology have been properly assessed.

Those who oppose increased regulation argue that the last thing this burgeoning new science needs is a drawn-out public debate and intensified government scrutiny. They contend that while the industry is still largely in the discovery and development stage, it is unwise to regulate it too much. Many experts argue that any safety concerns can be adequately addressed with current laws—not a new set of regulations. Nanotechnology advocates also point out that the Environmental Protection Agency is currently developing a strategy for a voluntary reporting program for researchers working in nanoscience. (Such programs have served other scientific pursuits well by allowing public oversight and information sharing without the stifling effects of bureaucratic red tape.) Supporters say that creating an atmosphere of fear and distrust in the public before nanotechnology's benefits can be properly conveyed is unfair and could damage untold economic and scientific potential.

OUTLOOK

The explosion of science and technology during the twentieth century has enriched lives and expanded the possibilities for human progress. At the same time, it has led to new conflicts that will continue to challenge human ingenuity and force citizens and policymakers alike to consider how such changes affect Americans' lives and the ways in which they govern themselves.

THE DEBATE: SCIENCE AND TECHNOLOGY

The federal government should fund embryonic stem cell research.

PRO: Most biomedical science in the United States—particularly in the crucial exploratory phase—is funded by federal dollars. No field of research can prosper without this support. Stem cells provide a historic opportunity to advance treatments for a host of afflictions. The cells extracted from embryos are more effective than adult lines; this is where federal research dollars must be directed.

CON: Using embryonic stem cells destroys human life. Stem cell alternatives, including adult stem cells and those found in amniotic fluid, do not cross this important ethical line. Embryonic stem cell therapy opens a door to darker meddling in human life, including cloning. The federal government should not fund this field, and instead leave it to the private sector to pay for this research.

The federal government should act to preserve "net neutrality."

PRO: The Internet has always operated on the principle of neutrality—all available Web site content is transmitted with equal speed over broadband networks. If broadband providers charge fees for access to "faster lanes," the era of democratic distribution and exchange of media and information over the Internet will end. Without the necessary regulation, telecom companies will be able to block or censor content.

CON: "Net neutrality" is just code for unwarranted federal regulation of the Internet. Broadband providers need to update their networks to meet the heavy demand for sophisticated multimedia content. This will cost a lot of money, so it makes sense for some companies to pay for speedy delivery of their data-heavy content. Otherwise, the costs will be shifted onto consumers, and innovation will dry up.

Nanotechnology research should be regulated.

PRO: Nanotechnology poses serious health-related and environmental risks. Consumer products that utilize the science are already being sold before the public has been educated about the technology's pros and cons. Before it's too late, lawmakers should impose a series of oversights, not to stifle research, but to ensure that nanotechnology development proceeds with practical and effective safeguards.

CON: Nanotechnology is still in its infancy, but it has limitless potential to become a beneficial and lucrative industry that will enhance daily life, scientific study, and national security. Imposing regulations now would hamper innovation and allow other countries to capitalize on the latest, ground-breaking developments. Lawmakers should instead encourage industry self-regulation and educate the public about the science.

FOREIGN POLICY ISSUES

INTRODUCTION

At the end of the last century, international relations were in the midst of what many believed was a new era of global cooperation. The Cold War—a competition between the United States and the Soviet Union for military dominance, influence, and power—had ended, and many nations saw progress on issues ranging from international trade to human rights. However, for Americans, this time of relative tranquility was interrupted on September 11, 2001, when al Qaeda terrorists attacked the United States at home and killed nearly 3,000 people.

Overnight, U.S. foreign policy changed. The government's overriding focus became security—specifically, containing the danger posed by a combination of threats: terrorists, the proliferation of weapons of mass destruction, and the influence of nations dominated by hostile regimes. Setting a new course, President George W. Bush declared that the United States would strike preemptively at countries and groups it deemed as threats. Within months, U.S. troops went to war in Afghanistan and soon thereafter, Iraq.

Today, a host of questions confront Americans and their policymakers as they contemplate the role of the United States in global affairs. What are the best ways to disable terrorist networks? How can the United States promote democracy in war-torn countries? Does the United States have a responsibility to intervene in humanitarian crises? Questions like these and others regarding trade, the environment, and foreign aid lie at the heart of foreign policy—government choices and actions that pursue and protect U.S. interests when interacting with other nations.

In the United States, both the executive and legislative branches are responsible for setting foreign policy. The president serves as the nation's chief diplomat and sets the agenda by appointing cabinet members and ambassadors and by negotiating treaties. The president is also the commander in chief of the U.S. armed forces. The Department of State carries out the president's foreign policy by representing the United States in international negotiations. Congress approves presidential nominations for ambassadorships and top State Department positions; it also declares war, ratifies treaties, funds foreign aid and military programs, and passes laws or resolutions to enact specific foreign policies. The White House and Congress sometimes disagree over how to balance two concerns—dealing with the world's problems and attending to issues at home.

U.S. foreign policy leaders use a variety of tools. They rely on diplomacy—meetings between government leaders or their representatives—to form personal working relationships with other nations. American officials also use trade policies and economic and military aid programs to influence other countries. Through international organizations, such as the United Nations and the World Trade Organization, U.S. representatives meet with world leaders to address common concerns. In addition, the United States sometimes uses military force to protect its interests and those of its allies.

Across many continents, U.S. relations with other nations are constantly changing. As new events unfold, officials routinely reassess what actions will serve the immediate as well as the long-term interests of the country. Over the next year, Americans will continue to debate how to conduct the war in Iraq, whether and how to cooperate with other nations to combat global climate change, and how best to help citizens of the world deal with new threats—like terrorism, poverty, and disease—and embrace new opportunities, such as increased global trade, higher rates of education, and life-saving technological advancements. This work will require careful attention and a strong commitment from citizens and lawmakers alike.

DEFENSE

In the decade between the end of the Cold War and the terrorist attacks in 2001, the U.S. military downsized and reduced its massive nuclear stockpile. U.S. armed forces were still active overseas, helping to restore and keep peace in troubled lands such as Haiti and Kosovo.

Without a large, overarching threat, however, U.S. leaders were slow to formulate a new military strategy for the post-Cold War era.

The terrorist attacks on September 11, 2001—the first foreign attacks on American soil since the bombing of Pearl Harbor in 1941—presented the nation with a new and urgent threat to its national security. Once again, defense policy moved to the top of the federal government's agenda. Over the past six years, the Bush administration has carried out a more aggressive foreign policy and dramatically increased the size of the defense budget. The United States attacked Afghanistan in October 2001 to overthrow the Taliban government that harbored the terrorists responsible for the September 11 attacks. Congress and the administration also took steps to increase domestic safety, creating the Department of Homeland Security.

President George W. Bush also outlined a new priority for the nation's defense: the United States would strike preemptively, and without international backing if necessary, to confront possible threats from terrorists or hostile states. This controversial policy led to the invasion of Iraq in 2003 and the overthrow of dictator Saddam Hussein, who had been suspected of stockpiling weapons of mass destruction (WMD). But by 2007, dissatisfaction with the Iraq war was rampant, causing confrontation between the president and Congress, straining U.S. armed forces, and prompting difficult questions about the sustainability of current national defense strategies. Although U.S. leaders remain committed to combating terrorism, many believe the government should consider different courses of action.

KEY QUESTIONS

- Should the president seek authorization from Congress before ordering military action?

- Should the U.S. National Guard patrol the U.S.-Mexico border?

- Do U.S. enemy detention and interrogation policies violate international law?

BACKGROUND

U.S. Defense Policy

The U.S. Military at a Glance. Approximately 1.4 million men and women currently serve on active duty in the U.S. Air Force, Army, Navy, Marine Corps, and Coast Guard. Another 1.2 million serve in the National Guard and Reserve forces. These troops, with their weapons and equipment, support the nation's military goals and protect and defend its vital national interests, including the sovereignty and territorial integrity of the United States and the lives and well-being of its citizens. In fiscal year 2008, the United States will spend more than $600 billion to maintain its defense and pay for operations in Iraq and Afghanistan.

After World War II, American forces were trained to defend against one principal enemy, the Soviet Union, which competed with the United States for military dominance, influence, and power. This costly and sometimes frightening competition, called the Cold War, shaped worldwide defense strategies and international relations for more than forty years.

The defense policies of the Cold War—deterring nuclear attack, protecting allies, and containing communism—required a large military budget. After the breakup of the Soviet Union in 1991, Congress reduced spending on defense. In the years following the terrorist attacks in September 2001, however, defense spending has increased dramatically.

Nuclear Weapons. During the Cold War, the United States and the Soviet Union produced tens of thousands of nuclear bombs to deter one another from attack. Each country still has between 5,000 and 7,500 nuclear devices today and both have agreed to reduce

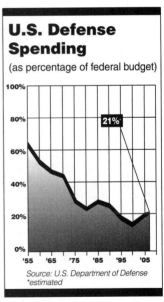

U.S. Defense Spending

(as percentage of federal budget)

Source: U.S. Department of Defense
*estimated

After the September 11 terrorist attacks in 2001, defense spending began to rise. President Bush proposed $481 billion for defense in fiscal year 2008. Adding to that total will be the supplemental funds—as much as $140 billion passed by Congress for operations in Iraq and Afghanistan.

their arsenals to between 1,700 and 2,200 active warheads by 2012.

National Missile Defense. In 2004, Bush administration officials implemented the first phase of a National Missile Defense. When completed, the system will consist of a complex global network of satellites, radar stations, and land- and sea-based communications centers that is intended to detect, intercept, and destroy launched missiles before they reach American soil.

Defending and Supporting Allies. After World War II, the United States helped create and lead the North Atlantic Treaty Organization (NATO), a military alliance meant to defend Western Europe against communist aggression. Today, NATO's twenty-six members include Canada, most western

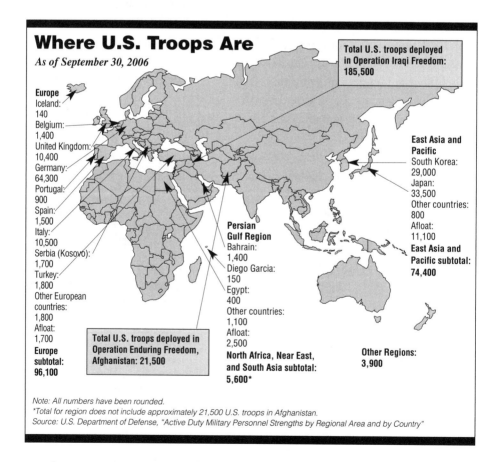

Where U.S. Troops Are
As of September 30, 2006

Total U.S. troops deployed in Operation Iraqi Freedom: 185,500

Europe
Iceland: 140
Belgium: 1,400
United Kingdom: 10,400
Germany: 64,300
Portugal: 900
Spain: 1,500
Italy: 10,500
Serbia (Kosovo): 1,700
Turkey: 1,800
Other European countries: 1,800
Afloat: 1,700
Europe subtotal: 96,100

Total U.S. troops deployed in Operation Enduring Freedom, Afghanistan: 21,500

Persian Gulf Region
Bahrain: 1,400
Diego Garcia: 150
Egypt: 400
Other countries: 1,100
Afloat: 2,500
North Africa, Near East, and South Asia subtotal: 5,600*

East Asia and Pacific
South Korea: 29,000
Japan: 33,500
Other countries: 800
Afloat: 11,100
East Asia and Pacific subtotal: 74,400

Other Regions: 3,900

Note: All numbers have been rounded.
*Total for region does not include approximately 21,500 U.S. troops in Afghanistan.
Source: U.S. Department of Defense, "Active Duty Military Personnel Strengths by Regional Area and by Country"

European countries, Greece, and Turkey, as well as several new members from eastern Europe. All members are legally required to help defend one another's current borders. The United States is also committed by treaty to defend other allies around the world, including Japan, South Korea, and some Latin American countries.

Use of Force. During the Cold War, the United States wanted to "contain" communist influence and expansion. Consequently, U.S. leaders often used military force to support pro-American governments fighting communist-backed invasions or insurrections. For example, in 1954, when communist guerrillas and the army of North Vietnam threatened South Vietnam, the United States began a nineteen-year military involvement with high human, political, and monetary costs. Efforts to contain communism also led to U.S. military interventions in Korea (1950), Guatemala (1954), Lebanon (1958), Cuba (1961), the Dominican Republic (1965), and Grenada (1983).

Persian Gulf War. After Iraq invaded Kuwait in August 1990, U.S. and allied troops organized a successful counter-assault that forced Iraq to retreat. As a condition of Iraq's surrender, the government of dictator Saddam Hussein agreed to a UN resolution to disarm. Later events revealed that Hussein did not abide by this agreement.

Kosovo. From March 1998 to March 1999, a war for autonomy was fought between the Kosovo Liberation Army and Serbian troops in the Serbian province of Kosovo. When NATO-brokered peace efforts broke down in March 1999, the United States—as part of a large NATO military force—began air attacks on strategic Serbian targets. After two months of bombing, Serbian president Slobodan Milosevic accepted NATO's conditions and terminated the conflict.

Afghanistan. In October 2001, the United States attacked Afghanistan's Taliban government for its refusal to turn over the al Qaeda terrorists responsible for the September 11 terrorist attacks. The U.S. military, with help from Afghan opposition forces, overthrew the government, captured or killed al Qaeda members, and disrupted numerous terrorist bases in that country. Major combat operations were declared over in May 2003.

Because the Taliban continues to pose a significant threat in Afghanistan, U.S. troop levels there remain high. An increase in early 2007 brought the total to 27,000—the highest number of troops in Afghanistan since the October 2001 invasion.

Iraq. After U.S. officials judged Iraq to be in violation of United Nations (UN) resolutions to give up its chemical, biological, and other weapons, the United States, Great Britain, and a coalition of allies attacked Iraq in March 2003, overthrowing the government of dictator Saddam Hussein. However, violence from rebels, extremists, and rival ethnic, religious, and political groups continue to keep parts of the country in chaos.

By the end of 2006, progress in Iraq appeared at a standstill and U.S. troops were under continual attack from insurgents. Growing anxiety over the direction of the war led to the resignation of Secretary of Defense Donald Rumsfeld (replaced by Robert Gates) and strong public demands for a new strategy. Many lawmakers proposed a timetable for a withdrawal of U.S. troops from Iraq, an action the White House argued was the equivalent of surrender. Instead, in early 2007, President Bush ordered the deployment of an additional 30,000 troops (bringing the total number of U.S. forces in Iraq to around 145,000) to curtail violence between warring Iraqi factions and improve security in Baghdad. While many applauded this new show of military strength, others feared that the increase in troops would do little to bring stability to the war-torn country.

U.S. Military Stretched Thin. The ongoing commitment in Iraq has significantly strained overall U.S. troop strength, and recruitment efforts in recent years have not reached their goals. The much-anticipated Iraq Study Group Report, released in 2006, warned that the nation's armed forces were at a breaking point, due in large part to repeated deployments in Iraq. It is estimated that less than one-third of U.S. Army units are "currently at high readiness levels."

Many experts believe that the U.S. military has not been so overburdened since the end of the Vietnam War in the mid-1970s. Until the Iraq war is concluded, however, lawmakers

In 2007, approximately 30,000 U.S. troops were stationed in Afghanistan. This marine is guarding his camp near Kandahar, Afghanistan.

Earnie Grafton/epa/Corbis

doubt the government will be able to successfully rebuild the nation's forces.

Defending Against Terrorism

For years, experts warned that terrorism could be one of the largest security threats to the United States in the twenty-first century. Although there is no universally accepted definition of terrorism, the Code of Federal Regulations defines it as "the unlawful use of force or violence against persons or property to intimidate or coerce a government, the civilian population, or any segment thereof, in furtherance of political or social objectives."

Osama bin Laden and the al Qaeda terrorist network that he helped to found are believed responsible not only for the September 11, 2001, terrorist attacks, but also for the 1998 bombings of American embassies in Kenya and Tanzania and for the attack on the U.S. Navy destroyer *Cole* docked in Yemen in 2000. Intelligence experts believe that al Qaeda and other terrorist groups have been seeking biological, chemical, or even nuclear weapons.

Preemption. The United States and its allies went to war with Iraq in 2003 to prevent the regime of Saddam Hussein from using weapons of mass destruction or giving them to terrorists. Although the United States had launched preemptive strikes in the past, (in Grenada in 1983, for example), the war in Iraq represented a broad and explicit expansion of the idea that a nation could make war in self-defense even when no attack had been launched or no clear threat had been made against it. However, after the overthrow of Saddam Hussein in 2003, it was revealed that U.S. intelligence information about the severity of the weapons threat was inaccurate. Since then, the policy of preemption has provoked debates at home and abroad.

Those who support preemptive strikes argue that terrorists and hostile nations do not play by any rules and will strike without warning. They say the only way for the United States to defend itself is to strike first and forcefully against terrorists and the nations that support them. Opponents caution that the doctrine of preemption departs from America's historical efforts to use international diplomacy. They fear that this unilateralist stance has only created resentment of American power and might encourage other nations to adopt the doctrine to suit their own purposes.

Gathering Intelligence. An important element in making defense policy is the information, or intelligence, gathered by several U.S. intelligence organizations. But intelligence efforts failed to head off the September 11 terrorist attacks in 2001, and predictions that Iraq had an arsenal of lethal weapons of mass destruction were proven incorrect. In light of these failures, lawmakers called for comprehensive reform of U.S. intelligence-gathering capabilities.

In 2005, Congress passed, and President Bush signed, legislation creating the position of Director of National Intelligence (DNI). The DNI—currently Mike McConnell—is charged with overseeing and coordinating the nation's intelligence-gathering efforts.

Protecting the Homeland. Before the September 2001 attacks, responsibility for domestic security was divided among many different government agencies. In 2003, Congress and President Bush created a new cabinet department, the

Department of Homeland Security. The new department merged twenty-two federal agencies and now coordinates immigration, border control, customs, transportation security, emergency response, and the Coast Guard, among other functions.

CURRENT ISSUES

War Powers: Congress vs. the President. After the Vietnam War, there was widespread concern among lawmakers that presidents Lyndon Johnson and Richard Nixon had seized too much authority—to the detriment of the conduct of the war and the U.S. Constitution. In 1973, Congress tried to fix this problem by passing the War Powers Act, which was intended to curb presidential unilateralism and ensure that lawmakers would have a significant voice in the gravest decision the federal government can make—sending troops into combat. In the case of Iraq, Congress, by a vote of 77 to 23 in the Senate and 296 to 133 in the House, passed a resolution giving the president authority to attack Iraq if Saddam Hussein failed to comply with UN resolutions.

However, since the 9/11 attacks and the passage of the Iraq resolution, many have argued that the Bush administration has made too many important decisions pertaining to national security without consulting or informing Congress. These include not only continuing the war in Iraq, but also allowing the secret detainment and possible torture of prisoners. The White House has repeatedly argued that Congress may not place limits on the president, including the amount of military force to be used in response to a threat, or the method, timing, and nature of the response. "These decisions, under our Constitution," said one U.S. Justice Department official, "are for the president alone to make."

Many experts agree that the administration has taken extraordinary measures to increase executive powers and that such measures may indeed exceed constitutional boundaries. Supporters argue, however, that the president is exercising executive power to keep the nation aggressive in the war on terror and to ensure success in bringing democracy to Iraq. They maintain that with more threats to national security emerging, including Iran's campaign to acquire nuclear weapons, Congress must allow the commander in chief to act

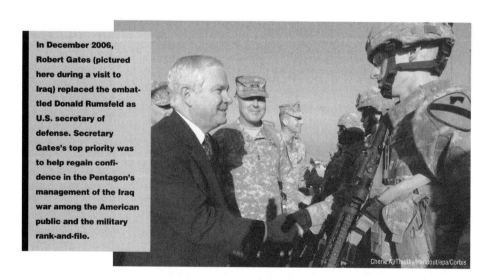

In December 2006, Robert Gates (pictured here during a visit to Iraq) replaced the embattled Donald Rumsfeld as U.S. secretary of defense. Secretary Gates's top priority was to help regain confidence in the Pentagon's management of the Iraq war among the American public and the military rank-and-file.

Cherie A. Thurlby/Handout/epa/Corbis

decisively to prevent possible attacks. Many experts caution that if the legislative body tries to act as a "co-partner," the resulting micromanagement of U.S. defense strategy will greatly jeopardize national security.

Critics of the administration's post-9/11 military actions argue that to regain public trust of U.S. policies in Iraq and the war on terror, the executive and legislative branches must work together. Many members of Congress have questioned the Pentagon's handling of the war in Iraq and contend that one of Congress's roles is to maintain oversight of administration policies and to give advice when members believe it is necessary. They also point out that it is Congress that appropriates taxpayers' money to pay for security measures and reconstruction in Iraq, and that with that constitutional responsibility comes the expectation that the president will consult with Congress and keep its members informed.

"Militarizing" the U.S.-Mexico Border? The 2,000-mile long border between the United States and Mexico is the most frequently crossed international border in the world. In 2006, almost 250 million people crossed legally into the United States from Mexico. Over the past decade, unparalleled trade and exchange between the two nations has accelerated the legal flow of goods and people to historical highs.

The U.S.-Mexico border also has the highest rate of illegal crossings in the world. According to the Department of Homeland Security, there were 2.5 million more illegal immigrants living in the United States in January 2006 than there were in January 2000, with about 850,000 entering the country every year, mostly through Mexico.

Illegal immigration through Mexico has always been controversial, and is especially so in those parts of the nation closest to the border, which have the highest number of immigrants. Now, immigrants are moving into communities across the United States, often bringing with them new ways and cultures and raising questions about the effects of illegal immigration on the U.S. economy and on taxpayers. Many Americans are demanding that the government do something to stem the tide of illegal immigration. In recent years, the debate over U.S.-Mexico policy has expanded to include the national security implications—including terrorism—of a porous 2,000-mile border between the two countries.

In May 2006, President Bush responded to national concerns by deploying 6,000 U.S. National Guard troops to assist border agents in sealing off the U.S. border across California, Arizona, New Mexico, and Texas. Many applauded this move, believing that the time had come to properly address what they view as a national security threat. Such border patrol proponents argue that all nations have a right—and an obligation to their citizens—to properly secure their borders and tightly control the migration of people between two neighboring countries. These advocates contend that deploying troops is not about "militarizing" the border—it's simply a matter of assisting the border patrol in doing its job by providing intelligence and logistics support and training.

Critics, on the other hand, believe the president's decision was a violation of the Posse Comitatus Act, a law established after the Civil War that prohibits the use of U.S. troops for domestic law enforcement. In addition, they contend that the military is already stretched too thin to patrol a border the United States shares with Mexico, a longtime U.S. ally. Critics don't doubt the seriousness of the illegal immigration problem but they argue that it is an issue that requires economic and social—not military—solutions.

How to Treat Suspected Terrorists. With the exception of the decision to invade Iraq, the controversy over the guidelines and legal limitations governing the detention and interrogation of suspected terrorists has been the most divisive anti-terror policy of the Bush administration. These so-called "enemy combatants" include individuals imprisoned at the U.S. detention facility in Guantanamo Bay, Cuba, as well as those who have been detained both in and outside of the United States in facilities administered by the Department of Defense. In a July 2006 decision, the U.S. Supreme Court ruled that these suspects should be protected under the Geneva Conventions, the 1949 international law that prohibits "cruel treatment and torture," and that they cannot be tried by secret military tribunals.

The U.S. government's guidelines on the detention and treatment of "enemy combatants" have provoked controversy worldwide. Here, military police on the Guantanamo Bay Naval Base in Cuba bring a detainee to an interrogation room.

Limited by this ruling, the White House then called on Congress to pass a law that provided the president with the flexibility to order the detention and trial of suspects.

In October 2006, Congress responded by passing one of the most controversial bills of recent years, the Military Commissions Act, which President Bush signed into law. The law establishes procedures governing the use of military commissions to try "unlawful enemy combatants" accused of engaging in hostilities against the United States. Specifically, the law strips the right of detainees to challenge their detention (known as habeas corpus), authorizes the president to order their detention indefinitely, and in some cases provides U.S. officials with immunity from prosecution for using interrogation methods that might be categorized as torture.

Critics have denounced the administration's detainee policies as inhumane, unconstitutional, and reckless. In addition to encoding the brutal treatment of prisoners, critics also argue that these tactics—secret detention, torture, and denial of habeas corpus—clearly violate international law. The United States cannot hold itself up as a "nation of laws" to the rest of the world when it sponsors such egregious violations of human rights, say critics, nor can it expect that other nations will uphold the human rights of captured Americans. Opponents of the administration's policies also contend that there is no evidence that many of the interrogation tactics in question will yield any accurate or useful intelligence on potential terrorist activity.

Supporters of the current U.S. policy respond that constraining efforts to curtail urgent, modern threats by applying dated international law, such as the Geneva Conventions, will not serve the national security interests of the United States or any other nation. They argue that such laws governing treatment were designed for traditional wars and conflicts. The war on terror, however, mandates that new rules and procedures become part of U.S. law. Because terrorists are not typical "enemy combatants"—usually allied with, or agents of, a specific foreign government—they should not be covered by the protective framework of international law.

OUTLOOK

Although U.S. military campaigns in Afghanistan and Iraq succeeded in overthrowing hostile governments, many obstacles remain to restoring stability and keeping the peace in those countries. Meanwhile, terrorists have threatened new attacks on the United States and around the world. To meet these challenges, the government has increased the defense budget and implemented controversial measures that, while designed to improve national security, have also tested strategic, legal, and moral boundaries. Although these policies are now under close scrutiny from lawmakers, experts disagree about whether the nation will actually choose a different course to defend its national security.

THE DEBATE: DEFENSE

The president should seek authorization from Congress before ordering military action.

PRO: According to the Constitution, Congress has the power to declare war. Too often, presidents have ignored or curtailed Congress's influence in the serious decision to send troops into harm's way. Without such consultation or approval, the executive branch is sidestepping the Constitution and federal law and failing to create consensus and unity around military action.

CON: We live in a dangerous time in which seeking congressional approval to protect the nation may cause serious harm. The president and his military advisors are best-equipped to respond to imminent threats and must be trusted to carry out appropriate action to protect the American people. The legislative branch cannot be permitted to micromanage U.S. military policy.

The U.S. National Guard should patrol the U.S.-Mexico border.

PRO: Every nation should properly guard its borders. The United States, through weak enforcement, has been allowing millions of undocumented aliens to illegally migrate across the U.S.-Mexico border over the past few decades. The National Guard and the resources of the Department of Defense can help border agents seal off entry points and curb illegal immigration, thus lessening the serious economic strain it puts on the United States.

CON: U.S. military resources are already stretched thin enough without wasting valuable equipment and personnel along the border shared with a longtime ally. Illegal immigration is a problem that requires non-military solutions because it is not a national security matter; it is an economic and social issue. The Pentagon violates the Posse Comitatus Act when it "militarizes" the U.S. border and uses troops for domestic law enforcement.

U.S. enemy detention and interrogation policies violate international law.

PRO: The inhumane treatment of terror suspects not only violates U.S. constitutional principles, but will lead to multiple violations of international law, namely the Geneva Conventions. By ignoring international law, the United States is surrendering its standing as a moral force in the world and possibly exposing its own troops to similar treatment by U.S. enemies overseas.

CON: The United States cannot be tied down by outdated international law. The Geneva Conventions were not created to protect enemy combatants who target civilians, so terrorist suspects are not protected by its provisions. The war on terror is a new type of conflict, one that requires different rules and procedures for detaining dangerous terrorists and gathering information on potential attacks.

DEMOCRACY AND FOREIGN AID

Tools of U.S. foreign policy include spreading democracy and aiding foreign nations and peoples. By democracy, U.S. officials generally mean American-style democracy—free and fair elections, democratic institutions (like courts of justice, representative government, a free press, and free markets), and individual rights (such as liberty and the freedoms of speech, religion, and assembly). Many policymakers and citizens believe that democracies are more peaceful and friendly to the United States. After the 2001 terrorist attacks, many experts observed that oppressive conditions around the world were giving rise to Islamic extremists and terrorism. To counter that, President George W. Bush has made spreading democracy, often through the use of foreign aid, a cornerstone of U.S. foreign policy.

Attempts to install democracy in Iraq, however, have proven costly and controversial. And elsewhere in the Middle East, recent democratic elections brought radical Islamic groups to power in the Palestinian Territories and Lebanon. These events have prompted Americans to debate whether democracy promotion serves America's national interest.

Controversy exists over foreign aid as well. Giving foreign aid is both a generous and a self-serving act. The United States offers financial and military aid to help nations and peoples in trouble but also to bolster allies and to build better relationships with other countries. Some nations, and some U.S. citizens, criticize the United States for stinginess and for not intervening aggressively enough in humanitarian crises. Others believe the U.S. government does not give wisely. Determining what is in the Unites States' interests—and whether democracy promotion and foreign aid serve those interests—is challenging for policymakers.

KEY QUESTIONS

- Should the United States promote democracy in the Middle East?

- Should the United States reduce its consumption of foreign oil to promote democracy?

- Should nations be required to meet certain criteria to qualify for U.S. foreign aid?

BACKGROUND

Democracy Around the World

Democracy Blooms. The United States is the world's oldest continuous democracy. After the signing of the U.S. Declaration of Independence in 1776, the ideals of representative government—government by the people—began to take root elsewhere, especially in western Europe. From the mid-nineteenth century through the twentieth century, the idea of self-determination received a boost as European nations like Great Britain, France, and Spain relinquished their colonies in Africa, Asia, and Latin America and allowed them to govern themselves. Then, in 1991, when the Soviet Union collapsed, many former Soviet republics and eastern European countries held democratic elections and began converting to market economies. The collapse of the Soviet Union had a ripple effect beyond Europe. Today, most Latin American countries have democratically elected governments. But despite this trend in Europe and the Americas, many governments in Africa, Asia, and especially the Middle East do not hold free elections or honor individual rights.

The United States and the Spread of Democracy. American leaders have long believed that the global spread of democratic government serves the U.S. national interest. Policymakers contend that when government officials are held accountable through fair elections, they tend to act in the best interests of their people—honoring civil liberties and respecting the borders of neighboring countries. Analysts also think that when new democracies adopt free-market reforms, increased international trade benefits the U.S. economy. Throughout its history, the United States has given other nations aid or pursued military strategies abroad to encourage the establishment of stable democracies.

Rebuilding Europe. In the aftermath of World War II, U.S. officials devised the Marshall Plan, a multibillion-dollar aid program to help rebuild the democracies of Western Europe and bolster them against the communist influence of the Soviet Union. In addition, the United States worked to establish democracy in postwar Japan.

The Cold War. From the end of World War II through the collapse of the Soviet Union in 1991, American policymakers focused on containing authoritarian communist regimes and supporting democracy among many U.S. allies. To stop the spread of communism, the United States became involved in the Vietnam and Korean Wars, and also supported anti-communist rebels in nations like Nicaragua and Afghanistan.

Nationbuilding. In the 1990s, the United States became involved in nationbuilding missions in Bosnia, Haiti, and Somalia. The term "nationbuilding" has come to describe the process of using the military to bring civil order and improved government to countries struggling to emerge from war or other unrest. Some policymakers and citizens argued that such missions were costly and unnecessary.

Democracy and Nationbuilding Efforts After 9/11.

Since the 2001 terrorist attacks, the threat of terrorism has replaced communism as the United States' top security concern. Many analysts think that terrorism grows out of political and economic oppression. So, in the war on terror, President Bush has made ending tyranny a major U.S. foreign policy and security goal. To encourage democratic growth, the administration has pursued closer diplomatic ties, military alliances, trade, and military intervention and delivered foreign aid in a number of different countries, most prominently in southwestern Asia and Iraq.

Afghanistan. In October 2001, the United States launched a military campaign against Afghanistan's Taliban government, which was suspected of harboring the al Qaeda terrorists behind the September 11 attacks. After a month of bombing by U.S. warplanes, the Northern Alliance, an anti-Taliban rebel force operating in Afghanistan, defeated Taliban forces on the ground. Since then, with the help of American and, more recently, NATO forces, a democratic government has begun to take shape. In 2004, elected Afghan delegates approved a new constitution, and Hamid Karzai was elected president. However, the country remains unstable because of tribal tensions, attacks from resurgent Taliban fighters, and the opium drug trade.

Not Enough Water

The average American uses 40 gallons of water a day for drinking, washing, cleaning, and cooking. Now, imagine having less than 1.5 gallons of water a day. The 2006 United Nations Development Report noted that more than 1.2 billion people around the globe lack safe drinking water, and 2.6 billion do not have access to adequate sanitation. The result: Dirty water and unsanitary conditions kill 1.8 million children every year, spread diseases, and cause conflicts. UN officials note that progress is being made in providing safe drinking water to more people, but they fear that rapid population growth in water-stressed regions like sub-Saharan Africa and the Middle East could overwhelm those advances.

Iraq. In March 2003, after diplomats failed to verify Iraq's compliance with United Nations (UN) resolutions concerning Iraq's weapons development program, U.S. and British military forces invaded Iraq to expel dictator Saddam Hussein. After the regime toppled, a U.S.-led coalition began to advance a transition to democracy. Despite continuing rebel attacks and sectarian religious strife, Iraqis voted in two major parliamentary elections and swore in a new government in May 2006. More than 140,000 U.S. troops there are trying to establish security, train the police force, and rebuild infrastructure. Despite some progress, Iraq remains mired in sectarian violence that threatens the long-term viability of the new government. By 2007, a majority of Americans were unhappy with the U.S. war effort. Some Americans expressed hope that President Bush's "surge" strategy would work, but critics, including Democratic leaders in Congress, disagreed and pressed the president to set a date for troop withdrawal.

Foreign Aid

Every year, the United States gives assistance in the form of money, goods, services, and technical expertise to more than

100 countries. Although the United States is the world's largest donor in terms of dollars, the amount as a percentage of U.S. gross domestic product is less than 1 percent—a fact that draws criticism from other nations.

Types of Aid. Most aid is either given as a grant—with no expectation of repayment—or as a loan. Most American aid is bilateral (two-sided) and goes directly from the United States to another country. Aside from the huge Iraqi aid program, Israel, Egypt, Afghanistan, Colombia, Jordan, Pakistan, Liberia, Peru, Ethiopia, and Bolivia received the largest amounts of U.S. foreign aid in recent years. The U.S. government also gives multilateral (many-sided) aid to international organizations, such as the United Nations and the World Bank, which then distribute it to countries around the world.

U.S. goals in providing foreign assistance include promoting development, strengthening allies and fragile states, providing humanitarian assistance, supporting U.S. strategic interests, and addressing global health problems such as AIDS. There are several types of foreign aid.

Development Assistance. Development assistance helps needy countries make long-term, sustainable improvements in their economies and living standards. Aid monies support initiatives like building the roads, hospitals, power plants, and other infrastructure that countries need to grow. Today, many development programs also help nations transition to democratic governments and establish market economies. For example, in 2006, Jordan received a grant to help it further democratic reforms.

Humanitarian Assistance. Humanitarian assistance generally offers immediate short-term relief. When countries endure famine, civil war, or other disasters, the U.S. government sends aid to feed the hungry, treat the sick, and shelter the homeless. Recently, the United States allocated nearly $1 billion in humanitarian aid to help victims of the 2004 South Asia tsunami.

Military Aid. When the United States wants to strengthen the armed forces of friendly governments, it provides military assistance. Such programs enable allies to buy U.S.-made

The December 2004 tsunami disaster caused more than 200,000 deaths and widespread destruction across South Asia. Here, U.S. service personnel distribute food to Indonesian survivors.

AP Photo/Bullit Marquez

weapons, airplanes, and vehicles and to train soldiers for their national defense. Since September 11, 2001, many security assistance programs have focused on providing training, equipment, and technology to help other nations fight terrorism. For instance, in 2004, the United States ran a joint counterterrorism training program in the Philippines aimed at helping that country defeat an internal terrorist group with ties to al Qaeda.

AIDS Relief. In fiscal year 2005, President Bush launched the President's Emergency Plan for AIDS Relief (PEPFAR). The program targets resources to nations (mostly in Africa) with the most severe AIDS epidemics. PEPFAR funding supports prevention, care, and management efforts in an attempt to alleviate suffering and prevent the spread of the disease.

Crisis in Darfur. In early 2003, tensions over land use and water supplies provoked an uprising in the Darfur region of Sudan. The central Sudanese government responded by bombing villages. Many world leaders believe Sudan's government also supports the Janjaweed, an Arab tribal militia that has continued to carry out brutal rapes and murders despite several cease-fires. Reports estimate that hundreds of thousands of men, women, and children have died due to the violence and famine engulfing the region—a situation many have deemed a genocide. The United States and other nations provide military aid to the African Union peacekeepers on the ground, but most agree that the force is too small to quell the violence. Meanwhile, the UN has been unable to pass a resolution that the Sudanese government will honor. Frustrated with these circumstances, U.S. leaders are considering other measures to aid the people of Darfur.

CURRENT ISSUES

Democracy and the Middle East. The Iraq war and the ongoing effort to support democracy in Afghanistan represent two major efforts in President Bush's initiative to spread democracy. At first, these nations presented the world with stunning sights: millions of men and women in Afghanistan and Iraq lined up to vote in free and fair elections for the first time. However, the newly elected leaders have thus far struggled to assert their authority over their peoples, deliver basic services, and stabilize the countries against insurgents (the resurgent Taliban forces in Afghanistan and the Sunni and Shiite militias and terrorists in Iraq). The operations have had enormous human and financial costs—since the U.S. invasion of Iraq, more than 3,000 Americans and tens of thousands of Iraqis have died in the war. The United States has spent more than $500 billion on the wars in Afghanistan and Iraq.

Elsewhere in the Middle East, democratic elections again did not lead where the White House hoped they would. In Lebanon and in the Palestinian Territories, citizens participated

U.S. and UN leaders are struggling to respond effectively to help end the humanitarian and military crisis in the Darfur region of Sudan. The United States provides assistance to the African Union peacekeepers (pictured here helping an injured woman).

in free elections with the encouragement of the United States. However, to the disappointment of American officials, members of the terrorist group Hezbollah (which is backed by the governments in Iran and Syria) gained a significant number of seats in the Lebanese government. In the Palestinian Territories, where the United States offered financial development assistance in support of democracy, members from the terrorist group Hamas gained a parliamentary majority. Because Hamas calls for the destruction of Israel, the United States and the European Union are withholding financial assistance to the Palestinian Authority. All of these developments have prompted many Americans to debate the practicality of promoting democracy in the Middle East.

Two Lebanese women cry as they carry a poster of an assassinated anti-Syrian politician in Lebanon. Despite democratic reforms, Lebanon has faced repeated political crises because its government and people are split between supporters of the Syrian-backed terrorist group Hezbollah and supporters of the pro-American, anti-Syrian prime minister Fouad Siniora.

Supporters point out that installing democracy will take generations, and they urge Americans to stay the course despite the setbacks. Everyone deserves freedom from tyranny, say democracy proponents. They insist that the millions of citizens who lined up to vote show that people in the Middle East want democracy and will work for it. Proponents acknowledge that some elections did not turn out in America's favor, but argue that carrying out the duties of elected office and being accountable to voters to retain their power will force extremists like Hamas to moderate their views. As democracy takes root, citizens in other Middle Eastern nations will demand elections and human rights, too. Proponents contend that U.S. democratization efforts will eventually reduce terrorism and bring greater stability to the world—thus benefiting Americans.

Critics of the current policy say the Middle East is not ready for democracy. According to such observers, democratization efforts have increased sectarian violence and given known

IRAQ WAR VICTORY GARDEN

terrorists public platforms to advance their causes. Furthermore, argue detractors, the instability in Iraq threatens to
engulf the entire region and could empower anti-American
states like Iran and Syria. Critics contend that democracy cannot be successfully imposed on nations with polarized populations, weak civil societies, and no history of democratic
institutions or rule of law, and point to Iraq as a tragic example.
According to these opponents of U.S. democratization efforts
in the Middle East, U.S. national interests are better served by
having stable and friendly governments in the region, like
Egypt and Saudi Arabia, even if they are not fully democratic.

Democracy and Energy Security. The United States
imports nearly 60 percent of its oil and consumes roughly 25
percent of the world's supply. The dollars used to buy oil, in
conjunction with rising oil prices, have enriched the governments of oil-producing nations, many of which are autocratic
and unfriendly. Some commentators and analysts contend that
America's addiction to oil and to heavy imports of foreign
supplies directly undermines the Bush administration's goal of
spreading democracy. However, energy security—maintaining
reliable and affordable access to energy resources—is critical
to America's economic health and status as a global super-

power. Thus, policymakers find themselves weighing how to pursue both global democracy and energy security, and trying to determine whether reducing consumption of foreign oil would encourage the growth of democracy.

Proponents of reducing oil consumption cite studies that suggest that as oil wealth increases, democracy decreases. For examples, they point to Russia's recent curbing of its free press and of private business ownership, and Sudan's refusal to end the genocide in Darfur. These advocates insist that American "petrodollars" subsidize autocratic regimes that neglect human rights and oppose U.S. goals. Reducing consumption of oil, they claim, will drastically reduce oil nations' wealth and lessen their ability to control their citizens through subsidies from oil profits or oppress them militarily. As a result, such governments will have to become more accountable to their people and more cooperative on international issues. These proponents say that an America that is less reliant on foreign oil will better promote international democracy to the benefit of Americans and people worldwide.

Others argue that there is no guarantee that reducing American consumption of foreign oil and thus reducing other nations' oil wealth will automatically lead to greater democracy. Even if democracy were a sure thing, they argue, maintaining energy security—the lifeline of American prosperity and power—must always be the United States' first priority. Furthermore, opponents emphasize that given U.S. energy needs, dramatically reducing dependence on foreign oil is simply an unattainable goal for the near future. They say that becoming "energy independent" could even be counterproductive in that rapidly falling oil profits could lead to a worldwide recession. Instead, such critics favor pursuing gradual democratic reforms in foreign countries in conjunction with building strong partnerships with a variety of oil-producing nations.

Aid for Good Behavior. In 2004, President Bush launched the Millennium Challenge Account (MCA), a program that changed the way the United States gives foreign assistance. This fund grants money to developing countries that embrace certain social, political, and economic reforms. To qualify, countries have to agree to meet specific criteria, including democratic governance. But not everyone believes that U.S. foreign aid should be linked with recipients' performance, and some people disagree with the Bush administration's criteria.

Critics of the new distribution plan assert that some nations in great need will not—or cannot—meet the governance criteria and thus will not receive critical help. Others say that such a plan drains money from programs which encourage democratic reforms. Few Middle Eastern countries, for example, qualify for Millennium Challenge money because of their high income levels, corruption, or lack of civil liberties; yet in many of those countries, people desperately need U.S. aid dollars and support. Some opponents charge that the plan is a new form of colonialism; it claims to give aid recipients power, but it is the United States that makes the rules and evaluates the outcomes.

Proponents praise the MCA because it ensures that aid dollars get results by tying them to measurable development progress. Furthermore, they argue that the program provides incentives for countries to make positive reforms in order to qualify for aid. Supporters contend that because MCA funds are tied to measurable progress, the aid program will also attract private investment to recipient nations—as much as two dollars of capital for every aid dollar, thus tripling the effect of the U.S. government's efforts. In such a climate, new businesses will bring even more prosperity to developing countries.

OUTLOOK

Promoting democracy and giving foreign aid will continue to be key tools in U.S. efforts to advance U.S. national interests and create a healthier, safer world. In the coming years however, developments in Iraq, Afghanistan, and other struggling democracies could influence how the United States promotes democracy in the long run. Policymakers and citizens will also continue to assess whether current initiatives achieve the desired results. When and how should democracy be promoted? How much and what kind of aid achieves the best results for both the recipients and the United States?

THE DEBATE: DEMOCRACY AND FOREIGN AID

The United States should promote democracy in the Middle East.

PRO: People in the Middle East want and deserve freedom. Installing democracy in a region so plagued with autocratic regimes will take decades of hard work, but it is worth the effort. The spread of democracy and freedom in the Middle East will eventually reduce terrorism, make the world more stable, and keep Americans safe.

CON: The United States should not impose American-style government on nations without the culture to support it. Democracy in Iraq and the Palestinian Territories has unleashed greater violence and bred terrorism. Fostering stable and friendly governments—even if they are not democratic—better serves the U.S. national interest.

The United States should reduce its consumption of foreign oil to promote democracy.

PRO: Studies suggest an inverse relationship between oil wealth and democracy. As long as America continues to spend billions on foreign oil, the nation will be undermining its goals for spreading democracy and building allies. Reducing the oil wealth of autocratic nations will force them to open up, cooperate, and become more accountable.

CON: There's no guarantee that reducing oil will lead to greater democracy. Besides, achieving energy independence is an impractical goal. Reduced oil consumption could trigger a worldwide recession. The United States must protect its energy and economic security first, and advocate for democracy second.

Nations should be required to meet certain criteria to qualify for U.S. foreign aid.

PRO: The Millennium Challenge Account makes donors and recipients partners in lifting nations out of poverty. As recipients improve their political and social systems, they know they will receive more foreign aid as well as increased private investment. Unfunded countries also have incentive to improve their ratings and apply for grants.

CON: The Millennium Challenge Account will not necessarily help the humanitarian needs of many people because they live in countries that will not quality for assistance. And some countries that need support for fledgling democratization efforts will not meet the criteria for funding, either. This program should not become the new model for international aid.

GLOBAL ENVIRONMENT

Today, most Americans say that they generally support environment-friendly goals. Such support has been building since the 1960s. At that time, the American people started to become more aware that pollution was causing health problems, killing fish and wildlife, and making the air unhealthy. Congress responded by passing laws to clean up polluted lakes and rivers, protect plant and animal species, and improve air quality. Since then, acid-rain causing emissions dropped, lakes and rivers became cleaner, and ozone-depleting compounds were banned.

However, despite some progress, many people remain concerned that the United States—and indeed the world—lags in efforts to ward off serious environmental problems. Of particular global concern is Earth's warming. Six of the warmest years in the last century have occurred since 1998, and more scientists and leaders are blaming worldwide human activities—particularly land clearing, farming, and the burning of fossil fuels to create energy—for the shift.

Some people at home and abroad criticize the United States, the world's largest energy consumer and biggest polluter, for not acting faster and more aggressively to address global warming and other environmental issues. Other Americans, however, warn that protecting the environment requires careful research and thoughtful technological responses that do not harm the American economy. Facing a myriad of environmental concerns, national and world leaders must often balance environmental efforts with economic growth, the preservation of energy supplies, and national and global security.

KEY QUESTIONS

- Should the United States expand the production of corn-based ethanol?

- Should the federal government impose mandatory caps on greenhouse gas emissions?

- Should the United States expand its use of nuclear energy?

BACKGROUND

Environmental Concerns

Population Pressure. More than 6 billion people—double the number in 1960—currently live on Earth. Population experts predict that the planet will add nearly 3 billion people by 2050. Most of this growth will take place in Africa, Asia, and Latin America—regions that still struggle to feed and house their current populations.

Agriculture and Logging. Although necessary for food production, the agriculture industry also poses environmental problems. Large-scale farming requires clearing land and using fertilizers and pesticides, which can run off and pollute waterways. Livestock release methane, one of the greenhouse gases believed responsible for global warming. Meanwhile, uncontrolled logging and burning, particularly in tropical rain forests, destroys ecosystems. Poorly managed forests have fewer trees to release oxygen and absorb carbon dioxide in the air.

Energy. The world's use of energy—particularly the high consumption of energy in the United States as well as a growing demand for it in China and other developing countries—is at the root of many environmental concerns. Creating and using energy often results in air pollution and toxic waste. According to the Energy Information Administration, the United States meets 85 percent of its energy needs through the burning of fossil fuels like oil and coal. Many developing countries also rely heavily on fossil fuels for energy. The process of extracting these fuels and others like natural gas and uranium (for nuclear power) sometimes causes environmental damage and pollution of nearby lands and waterways. But the bigger concern today is the impact on the atmosphere. Burning coal and oil releases small dirt particles into the air that cause smog. Their burning also releases compounds responsible for acid rainfall. And the process is blamed for emitting significant amounts of gases like carbon dioxide and nitrous oxide that many believe contribute to global warming.

SOURCES OF ENERGY

- *Coal* is a combustible substance mined from the land. Power plants burn coal to create electricity. Coal is a cheap and plentiful fossil fuel used to generate around 50 percent of the energy in the United States. However, coal raises environmental concerns not only for the impact of its mining on land but also because burning it typically emits pollutants that cause acid rain and smog, contribute to the greenhouse effect, and contaminate waterways with mercury.

- *Oil* or *Petroleum* is flammable liquid fossil fuel that is pumped from underground or underwater oil fields. It is burned to heat homes, and when refined into gasoline, it fuels transportation. Emissions from cars and trucks release carbon dioxide—one of the main culprits of global warming. Many people worry that the United States relies too much on oil from the politically unstable Middle East.

- *Natural Gas* is a combustible gas fossil fuel that occurs naturally underground. Compared to coal and oil, it burns cleaner overall but still releases carbon dioxide and methane, two greenhouse gases.

- *Nuclear Power,* a clean-burning form of energy, relies on a nuclear reaction that heats water to produce steam. The steam then drives a turbine that generates electricity. Environmental concerns include the risk of radioactive leaks and the difficulty of disposing of nuclear waste.

- *Wind* has been harnessed all over the world through the use of large windmills that generate electricity. Wind energy is clean but expensive and only as reliable as the wind unless backup generators are used. Furthermore, nearby residents complain that windmills are noisy and unsightly.

- *Water* stored behind hydroelectric dams can be used to generate power quite effectively. However, this source of energy is limited; almost all available water sources are already in use. Furthermore, the building of dams can disrupt surrounding ecosystems and pose problems for migrating fish.

- *Solar Power* works by turning the sun's rays into electricity. Many people believe the technology holds promise, but scientists are still struggling to find cost-effective ways to capture solar energy.

- *Hydrogen,* created when water is split into oxygen and hydrogen, appeals to many people looking for an alternative to burning fossil fuels for energy. When hydrogen is burned by fuel cells, it emits only water vapor and heat. Creating hydrogen fuel, however, requires electricity and is only as clean as the process used to produce that electricity. The technology for using hydrogen is still in the developmental stage.

Climate Change. Over the last century, the level of carbon dioxide in the atmosphere has risen, creating what many call a "greenhouse effect." Sources of excess carbon dioxide include emissions from automobiles, factories, and power plants that are powered by fossil fuels such as coal and oil. Many scientists believe that a layer of carbon dioxide and other greenhouse gases traps the sun's heat, thereby raising the temperature of the atmosphere.

According to scientists, Earth's average surface temperature has increased over the past century by around 1.4 degrees Fahrenheit, with most of the increase occurring over the last thirty years. Furthermore, scientists predict that average global temperatures could increase as much as 2.5 to 10 degrees Fahrenheit by 2100. Some scientists warn that rising average temperatures could melt polar ice caps and flood coastal areas, turn productive farmland into desert, extend

Jutto Klee/Corbis

FX Photo/Corbis

Although not all people agree that human activity is primarily responsible for global warming, scientific evidence does show that human activities like driving cars, flying airplanes, heating and lighting buildings, and farming—all on the rise due to population growth and development—release more and more greenhouse gases into the atmosphere every year.

the reach of tropical diseases, cause mass extinctions of plant and animal species, and alter weather patterns around the world.

In recent years, events suggest that global warming is accelerating. Two major polar ice shelves broke apart, startling scientists with the speed and scope of the melting. Diminishing arctic sea ice has strained polar bear populations, which depend on the ice for hunting. And, tropical plants and pests are thriving at higher altitudes.

Foreign Policy and Terrorism. Maintaining energy security—a steady supply of energy resources—is an important U.S. domestic and foreign policy goal. But some people argue that America's oil dependence not only contributes to environmental problems but also hamstrings its other foreign policy objectives, like promoting democracy and fighting terrorism. Some observers point out that some of the dollars Americans spend on oil go to unfriendly and unstable governments, and that even money spent to purchase oil from allies like Saudi Arabia can end up in terrorists' pockets. Furthermore, some argue that the United States gets involved militarily in the Middle East too often because of the region's oil reserves.

Taking Action at Home

Since the 1960s, the United States government has taken steps to address environmental problems.

Acid Rain. In the northeastern region of North America, as well as in many parts of Europe and Asia, air pollution has led to highly acidic rainfall. Most scientists believe that acid rain results when sulfur dioxide and nitrogen oxide (released by power plants, factories, and automobiles) transform into sulfates and nitrates. In the air, these compounds cause smog and can lead to health problems. When combined with moisture in the air, sulfates and nitrates become acids and fall to Earth as acid rain. Acid rain gradually increases the acidity of soil, streams, and lakes, making them less habitable for plants and animals. It also damages buildings and harms forests.

By 2025, China (now the second-largest polluter behind the United States) may lead the world in the emission of greenhouse gases. One of the culprits is the coal industry. The Chinese city Linfen, a major coal industry site where residents cover their mouths against pollution, was among the top ten most polluted cities in the world in 2006.

Wu Hong/epa/Corbis

To reduce acid rain-causing emissions, the United States implemented a "cap and trade" system whereby companies not meeting pollution reduction expectations can buy credits from other companies that are exceeding them. Over time, the number of available credits shrinks, creating a cap that forces pollution levels to decline. According to the U.S. Environmental Protection Agency, levels of sulfur dioxide emissions have dropped more than 40 percent since 1970, and nitrogen oxide emissions have also fallen.

Clean Air and Water. Congress passed the Clean Air Act (1990) and the Clean Water Act (1977) to establish parameters for reducing pollution and increasing the health of America's air and water. The executive branch also issues directives on environmental policy. For example, recently, among other regulations (including ones affecting forest use, logging, and mining), the Bush administration issued new rules for power plant emissions, including mercury, a neurotoxin that humans consume through contaminated fish. The new mercury rules establish a cap and trade system and give power plants until 2018 to reach targeted reductions.

Fuel Efficiency. In the 1970s, the federal government established minimum fuel efficiency (Corporate Average Fuel

Economy, or CAFE) standards for cars. Today, the minimum standard for cars is unchanged from 1985 at 27.5 miles per gallon (mpg). The minimum for light trucks, a separate standard, was raised to 22.2 mpg in 2007. Pickup trucks, sport utility vehicles, and large vans do not currently have to comply with CAFE standards. Some people suggest that the standards need to be revised.

State, Local, and Business Efforts. Individuals, businesses, and local governments act to protect the environment through recycling programs, community clean-ups, the purchase of fuel-efficient cars and appliances, and the construction of highly efficient "green" buildings.

Around the country, governors and mayors frustrated by the lack of a federal effort on climate change have drafted their own policies to curb emissions. New York, New Jersey, and other northeastern states, for example, are working on a regional pact to limit power plant emissions. California adopted strict limits on carbon dioxide emissions from vehicles, and in 2006, passed a law requiring the state to cap its emissions of greenhouse gases. More than 22 states require utility companies to generate a specific amount of energy from renewable energy sources.

In 2006, California governor Arnold Schwarzenegger and British prime minister Tony Blair joined other business leaders to explore solutions to global climate change. California has also passed a law requiring higher fuel economy standards for cars and statewide caps on greenhouse gas emissions.

Rising Temps Threaten Polar Bears

In December 2006, the Department of the Interior announced that it would consider listing polar bears as threatened under the Endangered Species Act. The reason: Warming temperatures have reduced the amount of summer sea ice in Arctic regions, depriving polar bears of ice platforms from which to hunt seals, their main source of food. Some polar bears have drowned while trying to swim long distances between ice islands. If polar bears are officially listed as threatened, they would be the first U.S. mammals to be so identified because of global warming.

Global Efforts

Beginning in the 1940s, world leaders have met periodically to negotiate international treaties addressing different environmental problems.

Ozone Depletion. Ozone is a thin protective layer of specialized oxygen molecules in Earth's atmosphere. The ozone layer shields the planet from the dangerous ultraviolet rays of the sun. Exposure to ultraviolet radiation has been shown to weaken the human body's immune system, cause skin cancer and eye damage, and destroy crops and microorganisms. In the mid-1980s, researchers began documenting a thinning of the ozone layer over Antarctica that occurs at the end of the South Pole's winter. Scientists attributed the destruction of ozone to manufactured chemicals called chlorofluorocarbons (CFCs). Thus, in 1989, forty-six countries including the United States signed the Montreal Protocol, agreeing to eliminate the use of these chemicals. However, the chemicals can linger in the atmosphere for decades. Even with current efforts showing progress, scientists predict that the ozone layer will not be repaired until 2065.

The Earth Summit. World leaders met in Rio de Janeiro, Brazil, in 1992, for the UN Conference on Environment and Development. At this "Earth Summit," nations signed agreements on three important environmental issues: protecting plant and animal species, stabilizing greenhouse gas emissions, and supporting sustainable development (economic growth achieved in harmony with environmental protection). The summit raised the profile of global environmental concerns and highlighted the need for international cooperation.

The Kyoto Protocol. To try to cement and build on progress from the Earth Summit, in December 1997, more than 160 nations met in Kyoto, Japan, and negotiated the legally binding, internationally enforceable Kyoto Protocol. Ultimately signed by more than 150 countries, it requires signatories to lower emissions of six damaging greenhouse gases, most notably carbon dioxide, by 2012. On average, nations must reduce emission levels by 5 percent. However, the protocol places only voluntary limits on some developing nations, such as China and India, because they lack the resources to meet strict

After major oil companies posted record-breaking profits in 2007, the House of Representatives passed legislation rolling back government tax breaks for the oil industry and increasing fees on offshore drilling. Even if the measure does not become law, observers expect Congress to pursue new energy policies.

Jay Dickman/Corbis

reductions. To help countries reach their goals and foster international energy markets, the Kyoto Protocol includes a trading mechanism. Under this provision, countries that cannot meet their own emission goals can buy the excess reductions of nations that are exceeding their goals.

Australia and the United States are the only industrialized nations not participating in the agreement. While the United States signed the treaty in 1998, neither the Clinton nor the Bush administration submitted the treaty to the Senate for approval. The Bush administration has cited concerns about fairness and economic harm to the United States.

Beyond Kyoto. World leaders have begun discussing a new agreement to go into effect when Kyoto expires in 2012. Many are hopeful that the United States will eventually agree to international caps on emissions.

CURRENT ISSUES

Corn in the Tank. To shift America away from its dependence on foreign oil, in early 2007, President George W. Bush called for replacing 35 billion gallons of gasoline with renewable or alternative fuels by 2017 in order to reduce consumption of oil-based gasoline. One possible fuel showing some promise is ethanol. Ethanol is a clear, alcohol fuel made from plant sugars. In the United States, most ethanol is made from corn. Manufacturers offer two blends. E10 is 10 percent ethanol mixed with 90 percent gasoline and can be used in most new cars. E85 blends 85 percent ethanol and 15 percent gasoline and can only be used in specially designed flex-fuel vehicles. Currently, E85 is not widely available outside the Midwestern United States.

To encourage ethanol production, the federal government grants a tax credit to factories that blend ethanol and gasoline. In 2007, Congress will most likely debate whether to continue offering incentives for ethanol. Many people disagree over whether ethanol is worth the investment.

Advocates for corn-based ethanol contend that ethanol is already increasing America's energy independence by reducing its reliance on foreign oil. They insist that corn-based

SLOWLY, ON THE EMPEROR PENGUINS' LONG MARCH TO THEIR WINTER BREEDING GROUNDS, the MEANING of GLOBAL WARMING BEGAN to DAWN ON THEM...

ethanol is energy-efficient to produce and burn, and that it benefits domestic farm communities, the economy, and consumers. Furthermore, advocates stress that ethanol burns cleanly and reduces the emission of pollutants and greenhouse gases. Supporters of ethanol argue that corn is cheap and plentiful enough to meet needs for fuel, livestock feed, and food. Although many supporters also see promise in "cellulosic" ethanol made from crop wastes like stalks or switchgrass, they contend that the technology to produce such cellulosic ethanol effectively is decades away, while corn-based ethanol can make a difference now.

Others argue that corn-based ethanol offers little hope for solving America's energy and environmental problems. They contend that corn-based ethanol requires more energy to produce than it saves in the gas tank, especially because E85 achieves fewer miles to the gallon than regular gasoline. Opponents add that growing more corn requires the use of more harmful pesticides and fertilizers, and more cleared farmland. Beyond that, they say ethanol production will deplete the food supply and inflate prices for corn and livestock. Furthermore, opponents argue, U.S. cornfields could never produce enough ethanol to make the United States energy independent. The government tax credit for ethanol, 51 cents a gallon in 2006, could be better used to promote truly efficient, clean, and renewable energy sources such as solar and hydrogen power.

Capping Greenhouse Gases. In 2007, the UN Intergovernmental Panel on Climate Change, composed of scientists from more than 100 nations, reported that it was 90 percent certain that human activities were the main causes of global warming over the last fifty years. Although some still refute that finding, the growing international consensus on climate change added momentum to efforts to address greenhouse gas emissions in the United States—which emits more than one-quarter of the world's gases. In response to climate change concerns, the Bush administration has favored research, innovation, and voluntary reductions over government regulation. However, more policymakers and citizens began to discuss whether effective change could happen without nationwide mandatory caps (limits) on greenhouse gas emissions.

Supporters of mandatory caps on greenhouse gas emissions argue that global warming requires urgent action and

Japan—Taking Energy Efficiency to a New Level

Perhaps it's no surprise that the Japanese automakers Toyota and Honda have led the way in developing fuel-conscious hybrid cars. Many observers agree that Japan is the most energy-efficient nation in the world. The Japanese government spurred conservation by raising the cost of gasoline and electricity above global market levels, and then investing those revenues in renewable energies, like solar power and home hydrogen fuel cells. And thanks to government campaigns and a cultural sensitivity to conservation, the Japanese people also focus on saving energy at home and at work by turning down thermostats, choosing energy efficient appliances, and recycling and reusing.

that refusing to cap emissions puts the profits of companies ahead of the health of the environment. Such advocates point out that even some business leaders have begun to call for a national policy, because adhering to different state-by-state requirements is becoming too costly. Supporters also refute the argument that caps would harm the economy by pointing out that nothing could hurt the economy more than ignoring the perils of continued warming—flooding of U.S. coastal cities, the spread of diseases, and drought and famine. Finally, proponents argue that U.S. leadership on this issue will spur developing nations to finally adopt more stringent measures.

Those opposed to mandatory caps on emissions argue that caps are not necessary and could be harmful. They point to increasing emissions reduction efforts at all levels—states, cities, and corporations—and say that each entity is taking the amount of action that it can currently afford. Mandatory caps, opponents argue, will harm the economy by requiring businesses to make costly changes—increases which will, in turn, be passed on to consumers. Such critics maintain that the

The U.S. government plans to store 70,000 metric tons of highly radioactive waste material at Yucca Mountain (below), a federally owned site ninety miles from Las Vegas, Nevada. However, completion of the site remains mired in regulatory problems and legal challenges. Meanwhile, the nation's nuclear waste remains in temporary local storage facilities around the country.

Associated Press/Laura Rauch

best approach is continued research into new technological innovations, such as carbon capturing, which isolates greenhouse gases before they are released into the atmosphere. That approach, cap opponents say, will ensure that the United States is best equipped to lead the way to global environmental health.

A Second Look at Nuclear Energy. For many years, nuclear energy was considered too costly and, especially after the 1986 fire at the Chernobyl plant in Ukraine (then part of the Soviet Union), too dangerous. That accident spread more than fifty tons of radioactive fallout and killed more than 500 people in its immediate aftermath and thousands more in subsequent years.

But in spite of these fears, nuclear energy today provides electricity for homes and businesses around the world, powers ships and submarines, and helps treat diseases. In the United States, nuclear power plants generate about 20 percent of the nation's electricity. Amid soaring demands for electricity, rising energy prices, and concerns about greenhouse gas emissions from burning coal and oil, governments worldwide increasingly are turning to nuclear power. Around the world, 31 countries operate more than 400 nuclear reactors, and 29 reactors were under construction in 2007. In the United States, President Bush announced incentives for the construction of new nuclear power plants. But nuclear power remains controversial.

Supporters of expanding nuclear energy in the United States point out that nuclear power plants emit no pollutants, and therefore offer a clean, renewable, domestically produced alternative to fossil fuels. Nuclear power, they say, could help the United States and countries around the world curb greenhouse gas emissions and halt climate change. Proponents stress nuclear energy's good safety record—no one has died of a nonmilitary radiation accident in the United States, and reactors are safer and more secure than ever. They also point to the fact that nuclear power plants are cheap to operate. Furthermore, nuclear power advocates insist that the new generation of nuclear technologies will reduce toxic waste by reusing some parts of spent fuel, thereby alleviating concerns about waste storage.

Those who oppose increasing nuclear energy production argue that nuclear power poses too many risks. Opponents fear a Chernobyl-like accident that could cause death and environmental destruction. Such detractors also worry that more nuclear plants will increase the likelihood that fuel will be diverted and used for weapons. Those concerned about nuclear power argue that although it burns cleanly, it leaves behind dangerous waste—about 2,000 tons each year in the United States alone—that remains radioactive for thousands of years. This waste—and nuclear power plants themselves—are far too attractive as terrorist targets, critics insist. Finally, opponents point out that building nuclear plants is expensive and time-consuming and is not the answer to current energy needs.

OUTLOOK

In 2007, both the Democratic majority in Congress and many Americans supported increasing efforts to protect the environment—to have cleaner water and air, maintain natural ecosystems, and preserve Earth's atmosphere. But citizens and policymakers face tough questions. Will Americans support a cap on emissions of greenhouse gases if it means consumers must pay more for goods and services? Will Americans agree to drive smaller and lighter vehicles to reduce oil consumption or pay a gas tax to raise funds for alternative and renewable fuels? Policymakers must consider both economic impact and energy security as they pursue environmental solutions.

THE DEBATE:
GLOBAL ENVIRONMENT

The United States should expand the production of corn-based ethanol.

PRO: Corn-based ethanol benefits domestic consumers, farmers, the economy, and the environment. Because corn is cheap and abundant, ethanol will help the United States decrease its reliance on foreign oil. Ethanol burns cleanly and reduces greenhouse gas emissions, helping the United States clear its air and set a good global example.

CON: Investing in ethanol wastes taxpayers' dollars and supports a product that does not solve America's energy problems. Producing corn-based ethanol uses more energy through pesticides, fertilizers, harvest, and conversion than it is worth. Furthermore, redirecting more of the corn harvest to fuel production will drive up food prices.

The federal government should impose mandatory caps on greenhouse gas emissions.

PRO: Global warming is an urgent problem that requires a mandatory, national emissions limit. Even business leaders would prefer to have one national standard rather than differing state-by-state standards. It is far more economical to confront the problem now than to wait until the nation faces an environmental disaster.

CON: Mandatory caps will harm businesses and send American jobs overseas. This is too high a price to pay, especially without similar sacrifices from other heavy polluters like China. Instead, voluntary measures, technological advancement, and more research will lead to sustainable and economically viable progress.

The United States should expand its use of nuclear energy.

PRO: Clean-burning and highly efficient nuclear energy solves many environmental and energy problems. Nuclear power is cheap and has an excellent safety record. Careful monitoring of plants and processes can greatly reduce the possibility of terrorist attacks. Furthermore, new technologies will reduce the amount of radioactive waste.

CON: Nuclear energy poses too many risks to be a viable solution to global warming or America's oil addiction. Problems include the risks of accidents, the threat of terrorist attack, and concerns over how to safely dispose of increasing amounts of radioactive waste. Ultimately, nuclear power plants are too expensive and too dangerous to run.

INTERNATIONAL TRADE

Trading goods and services with other nations is vital to the U.S. economy. Industries that export American goods to other nations often provide good wages, and growth in these industries brings money into the U.S. economy, creating more jobs for American workers.

Meanwhile, inexpensive foreign imports give American consumers better choices, allowing them to get more for their money. Trade policy influences the prices citizens pay for everything from socks to toys to car stereos.

Trade is also a cornerstone of international relations. Good trading relations among nations often foster greater cooperation on other issues, such as security. Leaders also use trade as a diplomatic tool. For instance, they may give better trade privileges to friendly nations or impose trade sanctions on nations that violate international law. Today, trade and economic integration, united with other cultural, social, and technological forces, have broken down barriers between nations—a phenomenon popularly known as "globalization."

Many critics charge that the economic effects of globalization—propelled by free-trade agreements—have harmed poorer nations, led to the abuse of human rights, and increased environmental degradation. In the United States, free trade has raised concerns among many Americans who believe that the government must be tougher with nations that put U.S. goods and workers at a disadvantage at home and abroad. On the other hand, proponents of free trade argue that it is the best way to strengthen both the U.S. and world economies and to promote American interests and democratic ideals.

Resistance to free-trade agreements has been mounting in the United States and most observers predict that Congress will insist on further protections for American workers in any future trade partnerships. Some worry about the long-term effects of such a shift, but concede that, for better or worse, the American people want to reexamine their country's role in the global economy.

KEY QUESTIONS

- Do free-trade agreements harm the U.S. economy?

- Should the United States take stronger action against unfair trade practices?

- Should the United States eliminate agricultural subsidies?

BACKGROUND

Trading With the World

Why Do Nations Trade? When a nation tries to produce most of the goods and services its people require, its economy grows slowly. Faster economic growth takes place when a country exports its most plentiful or most easily produced goods to other nations and imports goods that other nations can produce more easily. Most countries have a comparative advantage, such as natural resources, a temperate climate, skilled labor, or technical superiority, which enables them to make certain products at a lower cost than other countries. Comparative advantage allows each country to profit by trading the goods and services it produces most efficiently for those that other countries are better able to produce.

Tools of Trade. Trade agreements among nations generally establish favorable rules of trade and typically reduce trade barriers. Free trade, or trade without restrictions, however, has been rare in the world marketplace throughout history. Most countries use various tools of trade to protect certain industries or to encourage consumers to buy domestic goods and services. This policy is known as "protectionism."

Tools to protect domestic industries include the following:

- *Tariffs* are taxes on imports that increase the price of foreign-made products.

- *Quotas* limit the amount of specific products that can be imported.

- *Subsidies* are payments and other government supports that give an industry a market advantage.

- *Anti-dumping* rules prohibit other nations from selling goods below the real-market value.

- *Trade embargoes* are bans on trade used to entice other nations to change their behavior.

Top U.S. Trading Partners
in billions of dollars

Canada
China
Mexico
Japan
Germany
United Kingdom
South Korea
France
Taiwan
Malaysia

■ Imports to the U.S.
▨ Exports from the U.S.

0   50   100   150   200   250   300

Source: U.S. Census Bureau, as of November 200?

The United States trades with many nations. Shown here is the total value, in billions, of exports and imports for the United States' top ten trading partners in November 2006.

Coordinating Trade. Following World War II, the United States took the lead in expanding international trade. U.S. policymakers urged the nations of Western Europe to coordinate their trade policies. Furthermore, they encouraged the formation of international bodies and agreements to oversee world economic and trade issues.

The International Monetary Fund. Delegates from forty-four nations met in 1944 at Bretton Woods, New Hampshire, to discuss international trade and monetary issues. They created the International Monetary Fund (IMF) in 1945 to provide short-term loans and help stabilize international exchange rates. Today, 184 countries belong to the IMF.

The World Bank. Also founded at the Bretton Woods Conference, the World Bank makes long-term loans to help poor countries develop economically and reduce poverty.

GATT and the World Trade Organization. In 1947, twenty-three noncommunist nations signed the General Agreement on Tariffs and Trade (GATT), establishing a code of conduct for countries that trade. Under the provisions of GATT, a growing number of nations sought to increase world trade by reducing trade barriers. In 1994, GATT members approved a sweeping new trade accord that eliminated import tariffs on thousands of products, phased out quota systems, and established a new global body—the World Trade Organization (WTO)—to settle trade disputes. The WTO's judicial system for resolving trade disagreements has the authority to impose tariffs or sanctions on member countries. Currently, there are 149 nations in the WTO.

Controversy has swirled around the WTO ever since its inception. Critics believe the WTO's broad mandate favors wealthier nations, and strips power from citizens and individual governments. Others credit the WTO for encouraging countries to settle their trade disputes rather than resort to trade warfare.

With 149 members, each with a veto over any final deal, negotiating new or improved rules of trade is always a struggle. The most recent round of WTO trade talks, known as the Doha Round for the city in Qatar where they began, ended in 2006 without an agreement. Negotiators failed to overcome differences on how to make global trade rules fairer for developing countries.

The Group of Eight (G-8). Since 1975, a group of major industrial democracies has been meeting to discuss economic issues, trade relations, and foreign exchange markets. The G-8 consists of Canada, France, Germany, Italy, Japan, the United Kingdom, the United States, and most recently, Russia.

Trade Blocs. Over the past decade, international trade has been further boosted by free-trade blocs—international groups formed to further reduce tariffs and other barriers to trade among member nations.

The North American Free Trade Agreement. On January 1, 1994, the North American Free Trade Agreement (NAFTA) created the world's largest free-trade area. Under NAFTA, Canada, Mexico, and the United States have gradually eliminated barriers on agricultural products and manufactured goods and removed restrictions on cross-border investments.

The European Union. In 1957, six nations in Western Europe created the European Community (EC). The EC, which later became the European Union (EU), abolished import restrictions among member countries and devised common agreements for marketing their products outside Europe. In January 2002, twelve European nations replaced their individual currencies with a single currency called the euro, and created a unified economy. By 2009, five more countries will adopt the euro. European leaders hope their union, representing one-sixth of the world economy, will

New Age Pirates

According to a 2006 study by the Aberdeen Group, a U.S.-based business and technology research group, over two-thirds of manufacturers in the United States believe that over the past two years, the threat to their intellectual property (IP) has grown as they develop and sell products around the world. More than 70 percent of all fake and counterfeit goods—which can include baby formula, airplane parts, and music CDs—seized by the U.S. Customs Department in 2005 originated in China. Estimated trade losses due to Chinese piracy alone amounted to $1.28 billion for business software, $589 million for entertainment software, $244 million for motion pictures, and $204 million for records and music. Other countries that rank high in the counterfeit trade are Russia, Brazil, and India. The United States is wrestling over how best to deal with nations that allow such piracy, since many of those countries are also strong U.S. trading partners.

promote trade and enable their countries to compete more aggressively in the world market. In 2004, the EU formally added ten new members, thus surpassing NAFTA as the world's largest economic zone. The EU now consists of twenty-seven countries and 470 million people with an economy of more than $13 trillion.

The Dominican Republic-Central America Free Trade Agreement. In 2004, President George W. Bush negotiated a free-trade agreement between the United States, the Dominican Republic, and the Central American countries of Costa Rica, Guatemala, Nicaragua, El Salvador, and Honduras. Similar to NAFTA, the zone will reduce barriers to trade. All countries, except Costa Rica, have ratified the agreement, known as DR-CAFTA.

Globalization Backlash. Free-trade blocs have contributed to what many characterize as the "age of globalization"—the expansion of trade liberalization and free-market capitalism to nearly every nation, and the integration of many of the world's economies. Globalization has been implicitly supported by the policies of the WTO, the IMF, and the World Bank. Over the past decade, a backlash against globalization has been brewing, fueled by the belief that corporate interests are driving trade policies at the expense of less-developed nations, the environment, and human rights.

Anti-globalization sentiment is not restricted to poorer nations. Citizens throughout Europe, Asia, and the United States are concerned about the effect that the new, free-trade driven global economy is having on their standard of living. Consequently, free trade is being scrutinized around the world.

Trade Issues in the United States

Free Trade. Over the past few decades and through presidential administrations from both parties, the U.S. government has advocated for free trade. Officials hope that recent agreements will promote global economic growth and spur other countries to enter into similar trade deals. Over the past decade, the United States has signed regional and bilateral trade agreements that have opened markets in Africa, Asia, Latin America, and the Middle East.

Protectionism. Like other nations, the United States implements some protectionist measures when deemed necessary.

China's 1.3 billion people provide an enormous market for U.S. companies. U.S. retail giant Wal-Mart employs 20,000 people and operates 47 stores throughout China, including this one in Shanghai.

For example, in 2002, President Bush announced an emergency steel tariff to assist the American steel industry. The tariff caused friction with a number of U.S. trading partners until the president rescinded it in 2003. The United States also has a long-standing quota on sugar imports that protects domestic sugar growers. Some experts estimate that this quota causes Americans to pay more than twice the world market rate for sugar.

Some critics warn that increasing protectionist measures could cause other nations to retaliate with their own tariffs, thus provoking trade disputes. These critics point to the subsidies given to American farmers as one of the most egregious examples of U.S. protectionism. But proponents argue that this support is essential because EU agricultural subsidies are much larger.

The Trade Deficit. Since the mid-1970s, the United States has imported more goods than it has exported. The trade deficit total (including goods and services) was $764 billion in 2006, up from $716 billion in 2005. Simply put, the trade imbalance means that the American economy is consuming more than it is producing.

Increased foreign imports mean lower prices on the goods that Americans buy. However, more imports can mean fewer jobs for U.S. workers who produce goods. Decision makers largely disagree about the impact of the trade deficit. Those favoring protectionist measures cite the deficit in their calls for tariffs and quotas that will favor domestic industries and counter what they believe are unfair trade practices of other nations. Free-trade supporters view the trade imbalance as a sign that the overall U.S. economy is strong (i.e., that more goods are being purchased), and they say that America's openness to imports helps maintain U.S. prosperity by curbing inflation.

A Slower Track on Trade. In the November 2006 congressional elections, the Democratic Party won control of both houses of Congress in part by trumpeting a more critical view of the trade agreements negotiated by President Bush and previous administrations. Many analysts believe the addition of

these "trade skeptics" to the U.S. Congress will result in a new dynamic between the legislative branch and the executive branch. Congress is now expected to exert more authority on various trade-related matters, including recent trade deals with Peru and Colombia and the renewal of the president's "fast track" authority to negotiate trade agreements without amendment from Congress.

CURRENT ISSUES

Free Trade and the U.S. Economy. Most economists agree that trade barriers lead to higher prices for domestic products because domestic companies don't have to keep prices low to compete with foreign imports. Many economists also agree that free trade lowers prices, but may cause job losses in domestic industries that produce goods and services that are made more efficiently and cheaply in other countries. U.S. manufacturing industries have experienced the most substantial job losses because of reduced trade barriers. However, job losses are also increasingly occurring in white-collar industries. Businesses in sectors such as software development, finance, medical radiology, and telemarketing have lowered costs by hiring highly educated employees in other countries who are willing to work for less pay—a phenomenon known as "outsourcing." A U.S-based health care facility, for example, can e-mail an X ray to a relatively low-paid radiologist in Australia, who can analyze it and e-mail back a report. And these days, many customer service inquiries from U.S. consumers reach call centers located in India.

Critics of free trade cite outsourcing as just one of globalization's many negative effects on U.S. jobs. In addition, they say that free trade has cost more than 2 million U.S. manufacturing jobs over the past few years. Such detractors point to recent trade treaties that encourage U.S. businesses to move their factories and operations to Mexico, China, and other developing nations. According to critics, this movement displaces U.S. workers, many of whom cannot find comparable new jobs. Furthermore, the unemployment and lower wages that result from free trade harm the U.S. economy because consumers have less money to spend. Instead of sacrificing jobs and wages, free-trade opponents insist that the U.S. government should use trade policy and tax incentives to encourage domestic job creation and an improved quality of life at home.

Proponents of free trade contend that liberalized trade policies boost U.S. exports and increase U.S. business profits,

Intellectual property piracy is rampant in Indonesia, scaring off much-needed U.S. investment there. Here, an Indonesian police officer looks at pirated CDs and DVDs to be destroyed during a ceremony at police headquarters in Jakarta.

Mast Irham/epa/Corbis

thereby creating more domestic jobs than are lost through these policies. Furthermore, advocates contend, the new jobs are often higher-paying, putting more money in consumers' pockets. Free trade, supporters say, allows the United States to benefit from its comparative advantage in goods and services like technology, finance, and entertainment—and gives American consumers access to cheaper manufactured goods from abroad. They admit that people in certain industries do lose jobs because of free trade, but say that the best way to help them is to fund job retraining programs, not install protectionist trade barriers.

Policing Fair Trade. Although the United States and China have developed a mutually beneficial economic relationship, the widening trade deficit with China continues to worry U.S. officials. Some say the deficit would not be as large if China had fair and open markets and adhered more forcibly to global trading regulations. In particular, critics are concerned about China's lax enforcement of intellectual property rights and the lack of openness of its markets to American goods and services. In 2006, President Bush announced that his administration would exert more pressure on Beijing to adhere to international trade rules, yet stopped short of calling for any specific sanctions.

U.S. lawmakers also believe that other trading partners, such as Japan and the European Union, have violated fair trade practices. As scrutiny on U.S. trade agreements intensified in 2007, many lawmakers began calling for tougher enforcement of trade rules—including, but not limited to, recommending more cases for prosecution before the World Trade Organization.

An alliance of Democratic and Republican members of Congress—mostly from states with manufacturing bases hit hard by international competition—have proposed the creation of a special "trade prosecutor," who would have the authority to recommend prosecution of trade violations before the WTO. Such an official would work with, or even replace the U.S. trade representative, as the person charged with seeking redress from trade agreement violations.

The WTO Welcomes Russia

In November 2006, after 12 years of negotiations, Russia and the United States signed a bilateral agreement that allows Russia to join the World Trade Organization (WTO). The U.S. government had been lukewarm on Russian membership due to concerns over Russia's human rights record, its state control over key energy resources, and its resistance to sanctions against Iran in response to Iranian nuclear ambitions. But despite these ongoing concerns, say U.S. officials, the full integration of Russia into the global economy is in the national interests of the United States. Before Russia's membership is complete, the deal must be ratified by both countries.

Supporters of the trade prosecutor believe the United States needs an office devoted exclusively to pursuing violations. These proponents argue that a trade prosecutor will stand up for U.S. manufacturers and lead the fight to make other nations follow the rules. They argue that the U.S. trade representative is saddled with a dual role—promoting new global free-trade agreements while seeking out violations—that amounts to a conflict of interest. A "trade prosecutor," on the other hand, would focus exclusively on enforcing international trade rules for the U.S. government.

Critics of the idea warn that sending a "trade prosecutor" after China and other nations is unlikely to produce significant results and may, in the long run, actually invoke negative consequences for the U.S. economy and national security. While they concede that trade violations should be investigated and addressed, opponents of a trade prosecutor point out that some "guilty" nations are also U.S. allies and should not be treated as enemies. For example, the United States needs to maintain China's support in dealing with North Korea and other foreign policy issues. Alienating trade partners through trade prosecution jeopardizes valuable cooperation.

The Fight Over Farmers. The most contentious issue of the Doha Round of global trade talks was the impasse over domestic agricultural subsidies. The United States, EU countries, and other wealthy nations provide in excess of $200 billion to support farm production in their own countries. These subsidies are distributed primarily to increase domestic farm income and encourage production. Subsidies help domestic farmers but they also drag down the prices of agricultural products—cotton, sugar, rice, and other crops—around the world. Lower prices in the global marketplace hurt farmers in less-developed nations that depend on robust agricultural exports to alleviate poverty. The Bush administration has proposed eliminating subsidies, but only if the European Union follows suit. In 2006, negotiations at the Doha Round failed to produce an agreement on domestic subsidies. In February 2007, Secretary of Agriculture Mike Johanns proposed a new plan to cut traditional farm programs by more than $4 billion over the next ten years.

Many U.S. lawmakers oppose what they see as an effort to trade away American farmers' livelihoods. They argue that farm program payments are helping today's farmers survive and compete globally against the trade barriers and huge subsidies employed by the European Union and Japan. They also contend that agricultural subsidies have ensured that Americans enjoy the safest and most affordable food in the world because so much food eaten in the United States is produced

The World Trade Organization's Doha Round of global trade talks concluded in 2006 without an agreement to reduce agricultural subsidies in wealthy nations. Here, a farmer plows a field in Picardie, France.

AP Photo/J. Scott Applewhite

locally and is thus subject to government regulation. Ultimately, defenders say, if subsides are phased out, the added costs to farmers will be passed on to consumers.

Critics of subsidies argue that American farmers can survive and prosper without subsidies, like their counterparts in Australia and New Zealand have done. Such opponents point out that under the current system, even many wealthy farmers receive huge government payouts. They believe that ending farm subsidies would also aid impoverished parts of the world. The International Monetary Fund estimates that abolishing farm subsidies in developed countries would add as much as $100 billion to global income by allowing poor nations to export more crops and food. More jobs, economic growth, and wealth in developing nations, critics say, will in turn promote political stability and democracy, leading to greater security for all nations.

OUTLOOK

Because the United States is one of the world's largest economies, U.S. trade policy affects people around the globe. With discontent growing over free trade in many parts of the country, experts predict that congressional approval and ratification of trade accords with other countries will slow considerably. Many welcome this change in course; others worry that it may result in protectionist legislation that could grind the global economy to a halt. Thus, U.S. policymakers face complex decisions about balancing the benefits of free trade with the concerns of consumers, workers, and business owners at home and abroad.

THE DEBATE: INTERNATIONAL TRADE

Free-trade agreements harm the U.S. economy.

PRO: Existing free-trade agreements have encouraged U.S. factories and businesses to move operations to less-developed countries, where labor is cheap. As a result, American workers lose their jobs, or must accept lower-paying jobs. Unemployment and lower wages diminish U.S. consumers' buying power, thus weakening the economy.

CON: Free trade opens more markets for U.S. goods and services, creating more jobs in the United States in many industries. Mounting protectionist walls will penalize the entire nation to help a few select industries. Job retraining programs are the best way to help those who lose their jobs due to increased overseas competition.

The United States should take stronger action against unfair trade practices.

PRO: For too long, the United States has been lax in enforcing trade violations to maintain economic relationships. China, in particular, has repeatedly ignored its vow to abide by international IP regulations and enforcement. Consequently, the U.S. software and motion picture industries—the largest sectors of the American economy—have been hit with enormous losses. It is time to empower a U.S. official to pursue and prosecute WTO trade violations.

CON: The United States should not create additional tensions with trade partners by pursuing penalties in international arenas. Taking a more strident stand against lawbreakers will be counterproductive in the long run. Some of these countries are also strategic U.S. allies. Instead, the office of the U.S. trade representative should continue to investigate violations while advocating stronger trade relationships and encouraging voluntary trade law compliance.

The United States should eliminate agricultural subsidies.

PRO: American agriculture has been addicted to subsidies for too long and it is time to eliminate this welfare program. Subsidies give an unfair advantage to U.S. and EU farmers and create artificially low prices around the world, harming farmers in less-developed nations. Leveling the playing field will create a more equitable economic system and help to alleviate poverty and foster democracy in struggling countries.

CON: U.S. agricultural subsidies are far smaller than those in the European Union and Japan. These subsidies ensure that American farmers can compete against the trade barriers that dominate the current trading system and also allow American consumers to enjoy the safest and most affordable food in the world. Eliminating these payments will increase domestic farm costs and raise food prices.

WEAPONS PROLIFERATION

The United States detonated the first atomic bomb in 1945. Since then, many nations have sought to acquire nuclear and other highly destructive weapons for the power they represent. Today, nuclear weapons used in heavily populated areas could quickly kill a million people; enough chemical and biological weapons may exist to kill everyone on Earth. Such weapons of mass destruction (WMD), and the know-how to make them, are falling into more and more hands around the world, despite efforts by world leaders to contain their spread.

Of particular concern to U.S. officials is the possibility that terrorists and hostile nations could be seeking, or may be in possession of nuclear, chemical, or biological weapons.

Protecting the United States from weapons of mass destruction has become a major pillar of U.S. foreign policy, especially since the September 2001 terrorist attacks. In 2003, President George W. Bush launched a war against Iraq because the White House believed that country held a large arsenal of WMD. But despite intensive search efforts, such weapons were never found. While the danger posed by Iraq may have been miscalculated, the proliferation of WMDs—particularly nuclear weapons—is one of the gravest threats to global stability. North Korea and Iran's pursuit of nuclear weapons dominated the headlines in 2006 and continues to present a major foreign policy challenge to the United States and the world. While many lawmakers, including the Bush administration, continue to favor a more confrontational policy, others believe the United States should rely more on negotiations and diplomatic pressure to bring these nations into compliance.

KEY QUESTIONS

- Should the United States ratify the Comprehensive Test Ban Treaty?

- Should the United States loosen restrictions on the transfer of nuclear technology?

- Should the United States develop a "new generation" of nuclear weapons?

BACKGROUND

The Arms Race

In August 1945, the United States dropped atomic bombs on the Japanese cities of Hiroshima and Nagasaki. The attacks quickly brought about Japan's surrender and the end of World War II. The stunning show of force, however, raised the threshold for weapons capability. The subsequent Cold War between the United States and the Soviet Union led to an arms race in which each side amassed stockpiles of nuclear weapons as well as conventional, chemical, and biological weapons. (Conventional weapons include explosives, artillery, and small arms, among others.) Some of these weapons were given or sold to allies and proxy governments supported by either the United States or the Soviet Union, thus advancing the spread of dangerous weaponry around the world.

Regulating Nuclear Weapons. Soon after World War II, the United States proposed to the United Nations that an international agency control all nuclear technology and materials. However, world leaders could not reach an agreement, and other nations began pursuing the development of their own nuclear bombs. The Soviet Union exploded its first atomic device in 1949. Great Britain followed suit in 1952, as did France and China in the early 1960s.

During the Cold War, the United States and the Soviet Union stockpiled nuclear weapons—up to 8,000 warheads each. The bitter rivals believed that the only way to avoid a nuclear war was to deter one another by making the consequences of launching a first strike devastating for both nations. This policy was called "Mutual Assured Destruction," or MAD.

UN Nuclear Nonproliferation Treaty. The 1968 UN Nuclear Nonproliferation Treaty (NPT)

A mushroom cloud rises over the Japanese port of Nagasaki on August 9, 1945—the result of an atomic bomb dropped by the United States in an effort to end World War II. Five days later, Japan surrendered.

granted all nonnuclear signatories access to nuclear technology held by participating nuclear powers. In turn, the nonnuclear countries promised that they would not use the technology to make weapons, but only for peaceful purposes, such as uranium enrichment for fuel. Nuclear powers agreed to reduce their arsenals and not help nonnuclear countries build atomic bombs. In 2007, 189 nations were members of the treaty. Cuba, India, Israel, and Pakistan have not signed; all but Cuba are now known to have nuclear weapons. In 2003, North Korea withdrew from the treaty after intelligence data showed that it was pursuing nuclear weapons.

Nuclear Test Ban Treaties. From the 1940s through the early 1960s, the "nuclear club"—the United States, the Soviet Union, Great Britain, China, and France—conducted explosive tests to evaluate and strengthen the power of their bombs. Concerned about environmental damage the tests might cause, leaders from these countries signed the Limited Test Ban Treaty in 1963. The treaty made it illegal to test nuclear weapons in the atmosphere, outer space, and underwater. Underground tests, however, were still permitted.

In 1996, more than fifty members of the United Nations signed the Comprehensive Test Ban Treaty, agreeing to stop all forms of nuclear explosions except for certain maintenance tests. The U.S. Senate has never ratified that treaty. Some U.S. leaders fear that signing the treaty would limit the nation's ability to test and refine its nuclear arsenal.

Arms Reductions. Beginning in 1991, at the end of the Cold War, the United States and Russia signed a series of Strategic Arms Reduction Treaties, under which each country consented to gradually reduce the size of its nuclear arsenal. Currently, the two nations plan to reduce their active strategic warheads to between 1,700 and 2,200 each by 2012.

Loose Nukes. The breakup of the Soviet Union in 1991 left a large number of nuclear warheads and materials scattered across four former Soviet republics—Russia, Ukraine, Belarus, and Kazakhstan. U.S. officials feared that the economically struggling countries might not be able to prevent hostile nations or terrorists from bidding on or stealing these materials. Thus, in 1992, Congress funded a series of

Police officers storm a pretend warehouse during an emergency practice drill at a June 2007 anti-nuclear terrorism conference in Miami. Around the world, law enforcement officials are trying to prepare for the possibility of nuclear terrorism.

AP Photo/J. Pat Carter

measures, known as the Cooperative Threat Reduction Program, aimed at helping Russia and other former Soviet republics destroy nuclear equipment and secure nuclear facilities.

The Nuclear Club's Growing Membership. In October 2006, North Korea, an isolated, communist dictatorship, conducted an underground nuclear test. Although North Korea's ambitions have been known for more than a decade, the test was nonetheless jarring to the international community, who hoped to persuade the communist state to abandon its program in exchange for economic aid. North Korea is the ninth nation known, or generally believed, to possess nuclear weapons. Previously, the "nuclear club" contained seven acknowledged members: the United States, Russia, China, Britain, France, India, and Pakistan, plus an eighth unacknowledged member, Israel.

Another country widely suspected of harboring nuclear weapons ambitions is Iran. Iran has signed the UN Nuclear Nonproliferation Treaty and recently stated its efforts to develop its nuclear energy industry. However, Iran is believed to be operating a parallel clandestine nuclear weapons program in violation of the NPT. Iran's leadership denies those charges. Although there is no consensus among proliferation experts about when Iran might actually acquire nuclear capability, many U.S. lawmakers believe the threat posed by a nuclear Iran is too great to ignore. Accordingly, the Bush administration

Alexander Litvinenko, a former Russian spy living in London, was killed by a lethal radioactive poison, polonium 210, in a bizarre 2006 incident that captured the world's attention. Traces of the poison were detected in numerous locations where Litvinenko had been before he fell ill and died, and British authorities warned that thousands of other people may have been exposed. The killing, still under investigation, brought renewed concerns over the potential use of radioactive elements as weapons of mass destruction.

is determined to roll back that country's nuclear ambitions. While some encourage the president to pursue a more constructive dialogue with the Iranian government, led by President Mahmoud Ahmadinejad, others believe only a military strike against Iran's suspected nuclear facilities will ensure compliance.

Biological and Chemical Weapons.

Biological and chemical weapons include anthrax, smallpox, and bubonic plague, as well as toxins like ricin and botulinum, and nerve gases such as sarin. Both the United States and the Soviet Union produced large quantities of germ weapons during the Cold War. The U.S. Central Intelligence Agency suspects that other countries—including Iran, Syria, and North Korea—possess similar materials. Intelligence reports indicate that al Qaeda has been actively pursuing such weapons as well.

Biological and Chemical Weapons Conventions. The United States and the Soviet Union signed the Biological Weapons Convention in 1972. Signatories agreed not to develop, acquire, or stockpile germs for offensive purposes. Similarly, the Chemical Weapons Convention (CWC) of 1993 bans the use, production, and stockpiling of chemical weapons such as nerve gas.

Conventional Weapons.

Conventional weapons include warplanes, artillery, tanks, small arms, and ammunition. Armies around the world still largely depend on such weaponry as their main line of defense and many nations' economies depend on selling such weapons. Although most arms-exporting countries agree that the spread of weapons in unstable regions of the world is a threat to peace, the profits gained by selling conventional weapons are too great for many arms-selling countries to give up. The United States is the largest exporter of weapons worldwide. U.S. arms sales in 2005 totaled $75 billion, more than the rest of the world combined.

Defending Against the Threat of WMD

Missile Defense. In 2002, President Bush launched an aggressive effort to deploy a preliminary national missile defense (NMD) program. Such a system would provide a type of shield—in the form of radar and ground-based missile interceptors—that would guard the United States against a ballistic missile attack. Over the past few years, deployments at select Air Force bases have been tested with mixed results, ensuring that debate over the costs and benefits of the program will continue.

Missile Defense in Eastern Europe. In late 2006, the United States announced plans to locate early warning missile radar in the Czech Republic and missile interceptors in Poland, bringing about angry protests from neighboring Russia. U.S. foreign policymakers contend that the anti-missile equipment is meant to defend against potential missile launches by rogue nations, specifically Iran. They say that Russia has a stake in protecting its own soil and should not see the implementation as an assault on Russian interests. In response, the Russians

The Iranian government asserts that its nuclear program is intended only to generate power, but some Western governments, including the United States, do not believe such claims. Here, work continues on the nuclear reactor at the Bushehr nuclear plant in southern Iran.

accused the United States of acting unilaterally in the world and threatened action against the former Soviet states if they complied with the plan. Efforts were underway in early 2007 to diffuse the tensions between the two countries through diplomacy.

Preemption. After the 9/11 terrorist attacks, President Bush declared that the United States would strike preemptively at any nation or group deemed likely to threaten the United States with weapons of mass destruction. He immediately demanded that Iraq—thought to have a large stockpile of WMDs—disarm or face disarmament by outside forces. When Iraq failed to comply with the demand, the United States launched a military attack in March 2003 that ousted Iraqi president Saddam Hussein. Despite intensive searches, however, the United States and its allies were unable to locate any WMD in Iraq.

Like many policymakers in the Bush administration, some experts believe that the nonproliferation strategy—using international treaties to induce pledges from nations not to pursue WMD—outlived its usefulness some time ago, pointing to the defiance of North Korea and Iran as evidence. Some argue that a preemptive strike on Iran's nuclear sites will be more effective than a policy of engagement and dialogue. Others contend that such action, in the absence of a direct threat from Iran, will further destabilize the region and enflame anti-American sentiment.

CURRENT ISSUES

Reviving the Comprehensive Test Ban Treaty. North Korea's nuclear tests and Iran's alleged pursuit of nuclear weapons capability have provided fuel for critics who believe the Bush administration's policies have failed to curb weapons proliferation. Some experts believe the United States needs to change its strategy and begin to engage these nations more directly while also working to strengthen international agreements instead of ignoring them. Critics argue that the U.S. Senate should reconsider the Comprehensive Test Ban Treaty

U.S. Weapons at War

According to the Congressional Research Service, in 2006 arms sales to developing countries—many already engaged in armed conflict—grew to the highest level in eight years. The United States supplied $6.2 billion worth of weapons to developing countries, surpassed only by Russia and France. Experts say the figures underscore how the arms trade to the developing world has become a major staple of the global weapons industry, even though the supply often fuels conflicts harmful to U.S. interests. Experts attribute this rise in part to the wars in Iraq and Afghanistan. Some believe that these high-profile conflicts have served as "commercials," allowing foreign militaries in developing nations to see some of the most advanced weapons systems in action.

(CTBT), which it refused to ratify in 1999. (U.S. ratification is one of the requirements to bring the treaty into force.) In general, the Bush administration is skeptical of the value of arms-control treaties as a means of enhancing U.S. national security and has said that it will not seek Senate reconsideration of the treaty.

Some experts, however, believe that Democratic control of the Senate may give the treaty a better chance for ratification. Proponents of U.S. participation in the treaty argue that the United States must start to refrain from its own nuclear testing before demanding that other nations do so. They also assert that a ban on all tests would make it more difficult for existing nuclear states to develop more advanced weapons than they already have, because such testing would carry with it a high risk of detection by the international community. Finally, they say that U.S. implementation of the treaty would also curb the severe environmental and health damage caused by nuclear test explosions.

Opponents of the Comprehensive Test Ban Treaty, including both the Bush and Clinton administrations, have argued that it is a flawed treaty, counterproductive to U.S. national security interests. Critics believe that the CTBT would be no more successful at curbing nuclear proliferation than the

India is one of three nuclear powers—along with Pakistan and Israel—which has declined to sign the UN Nuclear Nonproliferation Treaty. Here, Indian women celebrate India's nuclear policy at a nuclear testing site.

Kapoor Baldev/Sygma/Corbis

UN Nuclear Nonproliferation Treaty has been. They reason that nations such as North Korea and Iran haven't been deterred by such treaties in the past and won't be in the future. Opponents also warn that ratification would carry significant costs to the United States, including the inability to test the safety and security of its own nuclear stockpile, increasingly a lynchpin of the country's national security strategy.

Bending the Rules. The UN Nuclear Nonproliferation Treaty forbids countries from transferring nuclear material, unless the material serves peaceful purposes and is subject to International Atomic Energy Agency (IAEA) safeguards. These export control guidelines were initiated after India—a nation that has refused to sign the NPT—exploded its first nuclear weapon in 1974. The success of India, Pakistan, and others in pursuing nuclear capability, and the emergence of nuclear black markets, has many experts questioning the effectiveness of nuclear export controls.

President Bush views India as a key ally with the potential to counterweigh the growing influence of China in Asia; he therefore wants to engage the populous country, despite its noncompliance with the NPT. In July 2005, the Bush administration announced a new agreement that would allow U.S.

companies to build nuclear power plants in India and supply fuel for nuclear fuel reactors. In return, New Delhi would allow international inspections and safeguards on its civilian nuclear program, while refraining from further weapons testing and arms technology transference to other countries. Supporters of the administration's policy believe that engagement is more constructive to U.S. security goals than isolation and punishment. They also argue that maintaining a flexible position with an increasingly powerful India will foster cooperation between the two countries in efforts to prevent more hostile nations, such as Iran, from acquiring weapons of mass destruction.

Opponents argue that agreements such as the current U.S. policy toward India undermine nuclear export control laws and the rules that have governed U.S. nonproliferation strategy for decades. Many experts believe that this agreement undercuts the basic bargain of the NPT—peaceful nuclear cooperation in exchange for renouncing nuclear weapons. Critics argue that by stepping out of the NPT framework and providing India with nuclear technology while it still maintains nuclear weapons, the United States could prompt other nuclear suppliers, including China, to make similar arrangements with countries hostile to the United States, such as Iran.

Nuclear Weapons: The Next Generation. In December 2006, the U.S. Department of Energy proposed a major new initiative called Complex 2030—a plan to streamline and upgrade the entire U.S. nuclear weapons complex by 2030. Under this plan, the U.S. government would replace the current stockpile of more than 5,500 bombs and warheads with a new series of warheads, to be produced and stored in one main area. Along with recent global developments, this proposal has reenergized the debate in the United States over the strategic value of nuclear weapons in the twenty-first century.

Critics argue that the Bush administration's plans mark a reckless shift in U.S. nuclear policy by undermining global antiproliferation efforts. Opponents of the program doubt that creating a "new generation" of nuclear weapons is necessary and believe it may jeopardize national security by encouraging other countries to do the same. They contend that the United States cannot construct a brand-new nuclear weapons production complex, costing billions of dollars, while at the same time criticizing Iran's stated efforts to develop an enrichment facility for peaceful purposes.

Proponents of Complex 2030 argue that the United States needs different types of nuclear weapons than those stockpiled during the Cold War. The administration contends that new, smaller weapons are more suitable to the types of threats now facing the United States—threats that can be best neutralized by smaller, more precise strike capability. Such modernized warheads, supporters assert, would also be cheaper to produce, easier to maintain, and safer to dismantle.

OUTLOOK

After 9/11, many U.S. leaders reconsidered traditional approaches to deterrence and nonproliferation in favor of a preemptive policy emphasizing confrontation over diplomatic engagement. However, as the "nuclear club" grows and the United States remains mired in war, many experts are calling for a renewal of U.S. commitment to international alliances and treaties to combat weapons proliferation. As the world's dominant power, the United States faces tough policy decisions ahead about how to protect Americans and their interests from attacks at home and abroad.

THE DEBATE: WEAPONS PROLIFERATION

The United States should ratify the Comprehensive Test Ban Treaty.

PRO: The United States must stop its own nuclear testing before insisting that other countries do so. Ratifying the CTBT would demonstrate a commitment to nuclear disarmament. Banning all nuclear tests and increasing international scrutiny of nuclear programs would curb the development of more advanced and destructive weapons, and halt environmental and human health damage.

CON: International treaties, namely the NPT, have failed in the past to curb nuclear nonproliferation and the CTBT will also fall short. Nations such as North Korea and Iran will continue their pursuit of nuclear weapons and the United States, bound to the CTBT, will not be permitted to perform the tests necessary to update its nuclear arsenal and protect against new threats.

The United States should loosen restrictions on the transfer of nuclear technology.

PRO: The laws governing transfers have proven ineffective as more countries move to acquire nuclear weapons capability. With some nations now posing greater threats, the United States cannot afford to punish and isolate strong allies because they have not complied with the NPT. The most practical policy is to remain flexible and foster collaboration on more urgent national security challenges.

CON: Making exceptions to nuclear export control laws will corrode international nonproliferation efforts. Without these internationally agreed-upon and enforceable rules, rogue nations will have few obstacles in their quest for nuclear capability. Maintaining strong relations with countries such as India is important, but should not compromise global nonproliferation efforts.

The United States should develop a "new generation" of nuclear weapons.

PRO: The United States is facing threats that require a new nuclear strategy. The current nuclear stockpile was designed decades ago to deter the Soviet Union. Not only is that threat obsolete, the weapons themselves may no longer be reliable. The United States should begin developing smaller, more surgical nuclear weapons that are better suited for contemporary threats.

CON: The Bush administration's plan to create new nuclear weapons sends the wrong message at a time when the world is trying to curb nuclear proliferation. The U.S. nuclear arsenal existed in the past as a deterrent. Developing new warheads today communicates to the world that the U.S. government now sees nuclear weapons as legitimate weapons of war.

AFRICA

Millions of U.S. citizens trace their ancestry to Africa. Between the 1500s and the 1800s, slave traders captured West African people from present-day Senegal to Angola and forcibly shipped them to the Americas. More recent African immigrants to the United States have fled civil war and famine. Consequently, many Americans have cultural ties to this large, diverse continent.

Sadly, news about sub-Saharan Africa (nations south of the Sahara Desert) usually relays dire events, such as religious violence in Sudan and the ravages of AIDS. Despite significant human suffering, many African countries are rich in natural resources. Nigeria is among the world's largest producers of oil, and gold, diamonds, and iron are mined in much of the continent. In other places around the world, such resources foster prosperity. Why then, are countries in Africa generally undeveloped and their people poor?

Part of the answer lies in Africa's colonial past and in corrupt leadership after independence. When Europeans established colonies, they created states that divided peoples and deepened conflicts. After colonial rule ended, the world encouraged the establishment of representative governments. Yet those hopes have gone largely unfulfilled. Africa's resilient people have endured poverty, famine, and disease, and while the United States has sent assistance, these solutions have so far failed to end the suffering. Today, celebrities like rock star Bono and television host Oprah Winfrey draw attention to the continent's struggles. Should the United States do more to help Africa escape poverty and fight disease? And how can the world encourage democracy and sound governance?

KEY QUESTIONS

- Should the U.S. government provide funding for more AIDS workers in Africa?

- Should the United States impose targeted sanctions against Sudan?

- Should the United States encourage trade with and investment in Africa?

BACKGROUND

Geography Shaped by a Desert

The African continent is divided by the largest desert in the world, the Sahara. For millennia, North Africa, which includes the Sahara Desert and nations such as Egypt and Libya, has been influenced by Mediterranean cultures. Bordering a great trade waterway, the Mediterranean Sea, North Africa has generally been more prosperous than those countries south of the Sahara. Because of the strong influence of the Middle East,

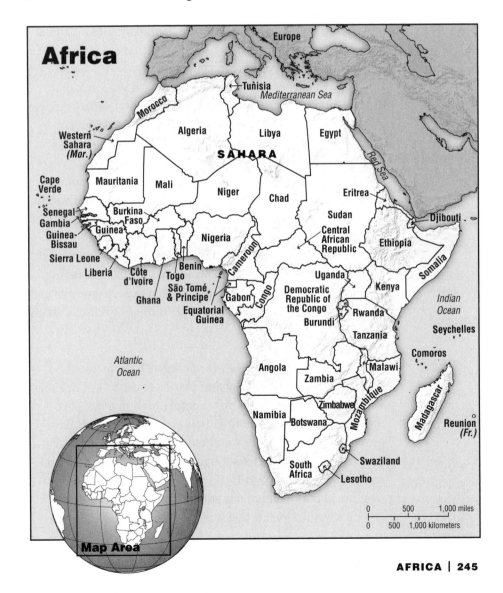

North African countries are predominantly Muslim and their official language is Arabic. Sub-Saharan Africa—the area lying south of the Sahara—has a much greater diversity of climate, geography, culture, religion, language, and history. But sub-Saharan nations share many problems—such as civil war, poverty, and poor health care—and a common aspiration for freedom.

European Colonies in Africa

The Scramble for Africa. In the late 1800s, European countries began the scramble for Africa. African land was partitioned among Belgium, France, Germany, Great Britain, Italy, Portugal, and Spain. By 1920, there remained only three independent countries on the continent.

European leaders colonized Africa for several reasons. Great Britain, for example, wanted control of southern Africa to protect British shipping lanes to India. Most colonizing empires hoped to gain wealth from raw materials. Europeans also believed they were superior, claiming a need to "civilize" natives and spread Christianity. In practice, though, faraway powers exploited local people and resources, without investing in education or other systems that would bring long-term stability.

By the mid-twentieth century, Africa's people demanded their freedom. Europeans had also found that administering distant territories was expensive, and that expected profits had not materialized. Within a short time, dozens of African states gained sovereignty.

The Legacy of Colonialism. Scholars trace many of today's problems in sub-Saharan Africa to aspects of colonial rule. Colonial boundaries, for example, were not designed along religious, tribal, or linguistic groupings. Rather, European countries expressly sought to divide and conquer African peoples. Rival populations found themselves living under the same government, magnifying tensions throughout the continent. In addition, individual groups were often dispersed among several separate countries, causing conflicts along and across borders. When European empires retreated, many of their established boundaries remained. Consequently, ethnic conflict remains a pervasive and devastating legacy.

Experts also blame colonialism for many of today's economic woes. They argue that European powers primarily extracted and exported natural resources—a situation that exploited local people and devastated traditional markets and trade. Export economies left people reliant on foreign sources of manufactured products and cash, rather than producing goods and trading among themselves.

Post-Colonial Leadership and Democracy

When African countries gained independence, the United States encouraged democracy. Elections were held across the region, but the promise of freedom has languished. In many cases, elected officials have resorted to authoritarian or military rule to quell unrest and to extend their power. Corruption and nepotism are rampant. Also, experts note that African leaders have tended to hoard riches and invest them either in military buildups or in banks and property outside of Africa, rather than at home. In so doing, leaders deny their citizens the fruits of their labor.

Today, governments across sub-Saharan Africa span a continuum from functioning democracies to dictatorships. The case studies below show both a democratic success and a failure.

South Africa. Just twenty years ago, South Africa was among the continent's most repressive countries. Today it is heralded as a successful democracy. Until its first inclusive elections in 1994, a white minority led South Africa under a strict segregationist system known as apartheid. Mounting international pressure, economic sanctions, and the threat of civil war prompted the end of apartheid.

South Africa's 1994 elections were the culmination of political and social restructuring that began in 1989. At that time, President F.W. de Klerk introduced democratic reforms and released African National Congress leader and anti-apartheid activist Nelson Mandela from prison. In late 1993,

Democracy in Nigeria

When Nigeria's former colonizer, Great Britain, withdrew in 1960, it left a volatile mix of ethnic groups and a north-south divide between Muslims and Christians. Since then, Africa's most populous nation has endured military coups, ethnic violence, and, despite its oil revenues, persistent poverty. President Olusegun Obasanjo, elected in 1999, was ineligible to seek a third term. The presidential election of April 2007 marked a historic opportunity to transfer power from one democratically elected president to another. The ruling party's candidate Umaru Yar'Adua won a landslide victory, but the process was rife with fraud. Observers noted that the election reflected the widespread political corruption in the troubled nation.

de Klerk and Mandela endorsed a new constitution that extended voting rights to the black majority.

Since then, South Africa has become one of the subcontinent's most effective governments and its richest state. Some analysts attribute this success to the nation's "Truth and Reconciliation" process, whereby human rights violations under apartheid have been publicly acknowledged and forgiven.

Zimbabwe. Formerly the British colony of Southern Rhodesia, Zimbabwe gained independence in 1965 under white minority rule. After a civil war, a new constitution was drafted in 1979 establishing an inclusive government. Robert Mugabe, a key agitator in overthrowing white rule, was elected prime minister in 1980 and president in 1987. He has since retained power by changing the constitution and by crushing dissent and opposition. Observers think he rigged the 2002 election to ensure his continued reign, and he has gained a reputation as one of the continent's most despotic rulers.

Since 2000, Mugabe has led a violent campaign to seize white-owned property in a stated attempt to redistribute land to dispossessed blacks. Land reform has upset the economy, which was largely based on commercial farms, and has led to hyperinflation and chronic food and fuel shortages. In December 2006, Zimbabwe's inflation rate was 1,070 percent, the world's highest. Many residents have fled the country's desperate conditions.

Violence and War

Africa has been marred by civil strife for decades. As of 2006, fourteen sub-Saharan countries were at war or experiencing post-war conflict. Besides civilian and military casualties, there are other costs of war. Extreme violence causes people to flee their homes and results in food shortages and famine. Money spent on war cannot be invested in businesses or human services. When people wage war, they are not earning income for their families or paying taxes to their government. One terrible reality is that children are often recruited as soldiers in Africa.

As a rule, the United States has not intervened in African civil wars unless a humanitarian crisis—such as mass starvation or genocide—has occurred. The examples below describe a humanitarian intervention in the past and a current crisis.

Somalia. When rival clans overthrew Somali dictator Mohammad Said Barre in 1991, the country plunged into civil war. Militias, led by warlords, competed for power and territory. Lawlessness prevailed. In 1992, the United States sent troops into the fray to secure the delivery of food aid to almost a million starving people. A year later, U.S. soldiers attempted to capture warlord Mohamed Aidid, the person blamed for much of the famine. When U.S. troops died in a gun battle, President Bill Clinton withdrew American forces altogether. For more than ten years there was no national government in Somalia.

During the Somali anarchy, radical Islamic groups, including al Qaeda, set up terrorist networks there. In 1998, al Qaeda, led by Osama bin Laden, carried out simultaneous car bombings of U.S. embassies in the African cities of Nairobi, Kenya, and Dar es Salaam, Tanzania.

Finally, in 2004, Somali politicians agreed to create a transitional parliament, which appointed a president, but a working government was slow to form. Warlords and rival clans fueled violence and corruption. Islamic militias then overtook much of the country, including the capital Mogadishu. But in a surprising turn of events in late 2006, Somali government troops, heavily backed by Ethiopian forces, reclaimed the capital and the Islamists fled the city. Days later, U.S. military gunships attacked what they described as an al Qaeda hiding place in the south. With the country still in turmoil, it remains to be seen whether the Western-backed Somali government can pacify and lead the country.

Sudan. Between 1983 and 2004, Africa's longest civil war raged in Sudan, the continent's largest country. Fighting occurred between Arab Islamic fundamentalists of the north and black Africans who practice Christianity and traditional African religions in the south. The Arab-led Islamic government in the capital of Khartoum described the conflict as a holy war. Rebels in the south refused to live according to Muslim law. Also at stake was the country's oil wealth. Facing tough international pressure, the two sides finally reached a peace agreement in late 2004.

Unfortunately, violence and instability have continued in the western Sudanese state of Darfur, near Sudan's border

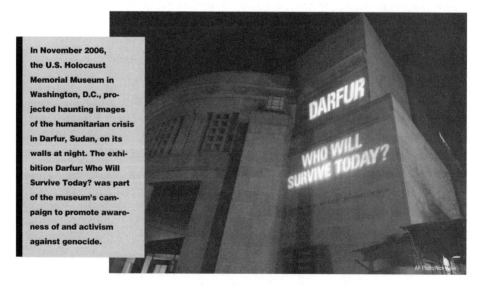

In November 2006, the U.S. Holocaust Memorial Museum in Washington, D.C., projected haunting images of the humanitarian crisis in Darfur, Sudan, on its walls at night. The exhibition Darfur: Who Will Survive Today? was part of the museum's campaign to promote awareness of and activism against genocide.

with Chad. Rebels there continue to battle Sudanese armed forces and the Arab tribal militia, the Janjaweed. Despite the deployment of 7,000 African Union peacekeeping troops, the killing continues, and civilians are the primary targets. Years of bloodshed and disease have claimed hundreds of thousands of lives in Darfur, a situation President George W. Bush has called "genocide."

About 2.5 million people, almost half of Darfur's population, are now homeless. Many of those refugees are encamped in eastern Chad, where they rely on international donations and foreign workers for food and care. As of late 2006, the rebel insurgency in eastern Chad threatened the already tenuous lifeline of humanitarian aid.

Poverty

When people live amid violence and political upheaval, they cannot thrive. Not surprisingly, many people in sub-Saharan Africa live in extreme poverty. According to the World Bank, 300 million people, almost one-half the region's population, live on less than one dollar per day. About 75 percent of residents live on less than two dollars a day. With this level of income, people generally have difficulty meeting basic needs for food, clean water, and shelter.

Food shortages have become a chronic problem. The United Nations (UN) warned in late 2006 that twenty-four countries in the region need food assistance to keep their populations fed. Although situations vary, experts cite common reasons for agricultural failure and malnourishment. During wartime, political instability and violence often cause floods of refugees. Migrating people cannot farm. Also, governmental corruption means that money intended to aid development often does not reach farmers. In some cases, drought causes famine, though some specialists believe famines stem from mismanagement more frequently than from extreme weather.

AIDS

Poverty, war, and poor governance limit people's access to basic services such as education and health care. Because funding for medical professionals, facilities, and supplies is so low, many people in Africa go to Europe or the United States to train to become nurses and doctors. In most cases, they do not return to their homelands to practice. This trend, combined with political instability and other factors, results in a chronic shortage of health care workers in much of Africa. One disease best illustrates the depth of the crisis.

Ever since scientists first identified Acquired Immune Deficiency Syndrome (AIDS) in 1980, the disease—and the virus that causes it, Human Immunodeficiency Virus (HIV)—has spread around the world. People in sub-Saharan Africa have been particularly hard hit by the pandemic.

Although sub-Saharan Africa has just over 10 percent of the world's population, the region is home to about 63 percent of all persons living with HIV—nearly 25 million people. In 2006 alone, an estimated 2.8 million people in sub-Saharan Africa became infected, more than in all other areas of the world combined. That same year, about 2.1 million people in the region died of AIDS, a figure representing 72 percent of global AIDS deaths.

The scale of this tragedy is hard to comprehend. In Swaziland, one of every three adults has contracted HIV. In Zimbabwe, one in five working-age people has AIDS. Consequently, the pandemic has decimated Africa's labor pool of productive young adults. When infected persons become too ill to work, both family incomes and national economies suffer. Children are also increasingly vulnerable. More than 12 million youngsters in the region have been orphaned by AIDS. In Zimbabwe, one in four children is an orphan, the highest percentage in the world.

Because many of the newest and most effective drugs to fight HIV/AIDS are too expensive for African people or governments, leaders from the United Nations, developed countries, and nonprofit organizations have worked to make less expensive, generic drugs available.

CURRENT ISSUES

Providing Funding for AIDS Workers. In fiscal year 2005, President Bush launched an aggressive program to address the

The (RED) campaign enables consumers to support AIDS relief in Africa. In October 2006, Bono, front man for the rock group U2 and creator of (RED), and television host Oprah Winfrey joined together to promote the program, whereby participating retailers donate a portion of their profits to the Global Fund to Fight AIDS, Tuberculosis, and Malaria.

AIDS pandemic. The President's Emergency Plan for AIDS Relief (PEPFAR) allocated $15 billion over a five-year period to make new drug therapies available, to prevent HIV infections, and to care for orphaned children. The program helps victims worldwide, but much of the money assists people in twelve countries in sub-Saharan Africa.

In 2006, President Bush announced that, two years into the program, PEPFAR had helped distribute lifesaving medicines to about 400,000 people in sub-Saharan Africa. At the same time, the United Nations reported that less than one-quarter of the estimated 4.6 million people in that region who need these drugs actually receive them. The percentage of children and babies receiving treatment is even smaller, perhaps as low as 2 or 3 percent in some areas. Analysts point out that while outside nations have helped buy and deliver the drugs, the lack of qualified health care workers inside Africa to provide HIV testing, treatment, and care presents a major obstacle.

In 2006, the World Health Organization's chief on HIV/AIDS said, "The cost of drugs is an issue, but not the only or even the most important issue for children. . . . You need to put the medicines into a system that functions, and the fact that children aren't getting treated is a sign of the frailty of health systems." Advocates say that, in addition to its commitment to PEPFAR, the United States should fund programs to train and retain local pharmacists, nurses, and doctors who can administer AIDS treatment in sub-Saharan Africa. Children lack the power and knowledge to request treatment, so clinics must have personnel to test and identify youths with HIV. Proponents of funding health care workers in the region argue that unless massive investments are made now, population losses will irreparably harm societies and economies throughout Africa.

Opponents of funding AIDS workers in Africa admit that the region's health care systems need to change. However, they do not think that foreign donors can successfully lead that charge. Some note that tampering with Africa's fragile health delivery systems could make matters worse—and possibly hamper the ability to fight other scourges such as malaria and tuberculosis. Detractors also point out that it will take years to train local people in health care professions—and even longer to implement reforms so that professionals will want to remain in Africa. Given these hurdles, critics urge the United States to focus aid dollars on medical supplies, while encouraging Africans to take responsibility for their own personnel and administration networks.

In 2006, rock legend Madonna visited children in Malawi, a country in southeastern Africa, and pledged to set up an orphanage in the AIDS-ravaged country. Her attempt to adopt a Malawian boy met with controversy, as critics claimed that she skirted the proper procedure for the adoption.

AP Photo/Shavawn Rissman

Blood Diamonds

The 2006 film *Blood Diamond,* starring Leonardo DiCaprio and set amid Sierra Leone's civil war in the 1990s, centers on a highly prized "conflict diamond." Conflict diamonds are those that are mined in an area controlled by rebel groups and then sold to fund military action against legitimate governments. A 2000 UN resolution acknowledged that "conflict diamonds are a crucial factor in prolonging the brutal wars of Africa" and underscored that "legitimate diamonds contribute to prosperity and economic development elsewhere on the continent." In Angola, Democratic Republic of the Congo, Liberia, and Sierra Leone, diamond mines have fueled conflict. By contrast, Botswana, a prosperous, stable country, produces a large share of the world's diamonds without violence. Shown here, local prospectors seek diamonds in Sierra Leone in 2000.

Imposing Sanctions on Sudan. Throughout 2006, the Sudanese government refused UN attempts to bolster Darfur's African Union peacekeepers, which had proven insufficient to protect civilians. Sudan's leaders argued that the UN proposal was another form of European colonialism. Skeptics believe that the Sudanese government simply does not want international observers documenting the human rights violations of the Janjaweed, who evidence suggests are backed by the Sudanese government. As violence spreads into neighboring Chad, where many refugees from Darfur are encamped, many worry that a regional war might ensue. Some analysts want to impose strict sanctions against Khartoum to force the acceptance of UN peacekeepers. Some international sanctions are already in place, but proponents want more restrictions, such as enforcing a no-fly zone in Darfur, imposing travel bans and asset freezes for key Sudanese leaders, and targeting Sudan's oil sector. In May 2007, President Bush imposed new sanctions which will prevent specific companies and Sudanese leaders from doing business with the United States.

Supporters of additional sanctions believe that the United States has already given the Sudanese government every opportunity to cooperate, without success. Its unwillingness to allow UN peacekeepers in Darfur proves, at least tacitly, its support for the Janjaweed militias—responsible for the most grave human rights violations in the world today. Advocates of targeted sanctions say that the U.S. government—and other world leaders—must take a hard stance against Sudan to prove their commitment to protecting human rights in Africa.

Opponents of this plan warn that sanctions are complex, imperfect foreign policy tools. By implementing them, U.S. leaders could ultimately enflame the violence they seek to quell. In addition, the Sudanese government does cooperate with the United States in providing intelligence on terrorism—a delicate relationship that sanctions would imperil. Finally, critics of increased sanctions argue that the outside world—whether through sanctions or soldiers—will be unable to subdue the violence in Sudan unless all parties first commit to peace. So far, that has not happened.

Investment in Sub-Saharan Africa. For decades, the U.S. government has tried to encourage development in Africa through grants and loans. Many observers say that aid alone has not succeeded. Some policymakers and the Bush administration advocate opening trade and increasing investment to bring sustainable political and economic development to the region. In 2000, the African Growth and Opportunity Act (AGOA) went into effect. This law offers economic and trade benefits to nations that meet certain requirements—such as promoting market economies, protecting workers' rights, implementing poverty-reduction policies, and enforcing the rule of law. In late 2006, thirty-seven sub-Saharan countries were deemed eligible to export goods to the United States duty-free under this law.

Other nations also want to trade with Africa. In November 2006, thirty-five heads of state from Africa met with Chinese leaders in Beijing to promote trade and investment. Chinese leaders are anxious to secure resources, especially oil, to spur their country's growth. The summit concluded with more than $2 billion in business deals.

Western nations, including the United States, often use the promise of trade deals to encourage reform and better governance in partner countries. In contrast, a key tenet of China's trade deals is that China agrees not to interfere with a trading partner's internal politics. So although China has begun to improve infrastructure such as roads and railroads in Africa, much of the proceeds have enriched corrupt African politicians, not the local people.

Supporters of the AGOA and other business incentives think that the United States must counteract China's influence in the region and ensure that trade helps the African people. When U.S. companies invest there, they aim not only to make money, but also to create jobs and stability. Eligibility requirements, supporters argue, ensure that workers are not exploited and encourage responsible governance. Proponents also contend that increased trade with African countries is good for the American economy, too. The United States needs oil suppliers outside of the Middle East, they say, and Nigeria, Chad, and Sudan can meet that need.

AP Photo/Elizabeth Dalziel

In November 2006, Chinese leaders held a summit with dozens of African heads of state to promote trade and investment. Shown here, President Hu Jintao of China welcomes Olusegun Obasanjo, then-president of Nigeria, to Beijing. China needs vast amounts of natural resources, especially oil, to propel its own development. African leaders like China's policy of not interfering with local politics.

While many policymakers agree that trade and investment in sub-Saharan Africa are good ideas, some are skeptical that such intiatives can replace traditional aid and loans. Critics note that it is still risky to do business in this region. Corruption is rampant. Civil strife and political unrest are all too common. Roads, transportation, and other infrastructure are poor. In addition, diseases have taken a terrible toll on the working-age population. Skeptics say that even when American companies find ways around these obstacles, the most needy people do not necessarily benefit. Such detractors argue that ultimately the African people must take responsibility for their own economic development, creating businesses that draw on local knowledge, skills, and resources to help their societies grow.

OUTLOOK

Africa presents American policymakers with many challenges. Most agree that there is both great potential and a dire need for economic growth. There is also consensus that African leaders must show responsibility for their people through sound governance, improved social services, and anti-corruption programs. But what comes first—economic growth or stable governments? How best can the United States encourage both goals?

THE DEBATE: AFRICA

The U.S. government should provide funding for more AIDS workers in Africa.

PRO: Current programs to send drugs to AIDS victims reach only one-quarter of adults who need them and even fewer children. What Africa needs, in addition to medicines, are well-trained health care professionals to administer HIV/AIDS treatment. If African health care systems are not bolstered with more staff, medicines from abroad will not get distributed, foreign aid dollars will be wasted, and countless more lives will be lost.

CON: Health care systems in Africa must be managed and run by local people who understand the cultures. Training more nurses, doctors, and pharmacists from among local residents and devising a system to retain them will take years, and take money away from supplies. Foreign donors are better off spending money on medicines and leaving health care administration reform to local experts.

The United States should impose targeted sanctions against Sudan.

PRO: As the leader of the free world, the United States has a responsibility to protect innocent civilians from genocide, and it has pursued diplomacy in Sudan—to no avail—long enough. Targeted sanctions against key politicians and the oil sector will prove the United States is committed to the sanctity of human rights and will force Sudan to accept UN peacekeepers in Darfur.

CON: Sanctions, even targeted ones, are unreliable, risky tools. Sanctions against Sudan have been imposed for years, and still its government stands by while militias attack civilians. Warring factions must first come to a meaningful peace accord before peacekeepers—whether they represent the United Nations or the African Union—can protect anyone.

The United States should encourage trade with and investment in Africa.

PRO: Foreign aid has been unsuccessful in bringing economic development to Africa, and free trade is the answer. American programs—unlike Chinese investment policies—seek to positively influence the political and economic systems of participating countries, helping to create jobs and prosperity. Also, the United States needs more sources of oil, such as those in Africa, to decrease its dependence on the Middle East.

CON: Trade will not help the neediest in sub-Saharan Africa. Because of government corruption, business investment is likely to enrich only the powerful few. Corporations will probably act much like empires, exploiting the people and land for their own gain. Africans, with the help of loans and grants from the United States, need to guide their own development to achieve long-term economic success.

ASIA

The largest continent, Asia is home to three-fifths of Earth's population. The region includes the world's most populous nation (China), its largest democracy (India), its most populous Muslim country (Indonesia), its second largest economy (Japan), and four of the five remaining communist nations (China, North Korea, Laos, and Vietnam). For these and other reasons, U.S. policymakers consider relations with these countries important.

After World War II, the United States sent troops into two Asian conflicts—the Korean War and the Vietnam War—to fight the spread of communism. Since then, security concerns have changed, but the American commitment to Asia remains evident. In 2001, U.S. forces stormed Afghanistan to oust the Taliban, a regime that harbored international terrorists, specifically al Qaeda. Policymakers continue to address the threat of terrorism in both Afghanistan and Pakistan. They also have sought to defuse the nuclear standoff with North Korea. In addition, China's growing economy and political influence are changing the region's power structure. American officials debate how to engage that country constructively, particularly regarding trade. Meanwhile, they seek to offset China's arms buildup with regional alliances.

The diverse issues concerning Asia pose many challenges for U.S. foreign policy—problems that require innovative diplomatic, economic, and sometimes military, solutions.

KEY QUESTIONS

- Are negotiations to end North Korea's nuclear program in the U.S. national interest?

- Should the United States restrict Chinese imports?

- Should U.S. lawmakers increase funding for the mission in Afghanistan?

BACKGROUND

Japan

A Changing Japanese Pacifism. After U.S. atomic bombs destroyed two Japanese cities in 1945, Japan surrendered, bringing World War II to an end. The Japanese adopted a new democratic system of government, and its constitution forbade raising an army. In 1951, Japan signed a peace treaty with the United States, ending nearly seven years of American military occupation. Japanese leaders also signed the Mutual Security Treaty, under which the United States pledged to defend Japan in case of attack. In exchange, the United States maintains military bases there, which the Japanese government helps fund. American military personnel in Japan numbered about 40,000 in 2007.

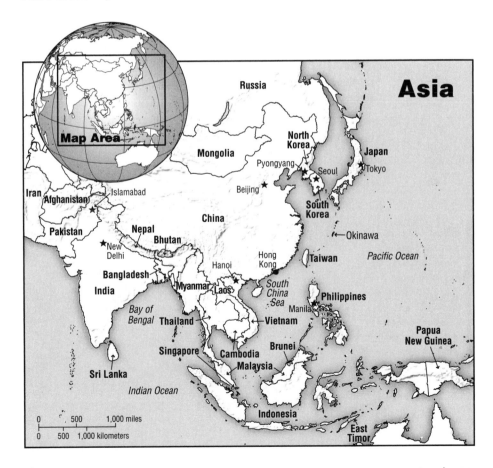

However, Japan's pacifism has evolved over time. During the Cold War, Japanese leaders created "self defense" forces to avert a possible attack by the Soviet Union. A new law in 1992 allowed the Japanese military to conduct peacekeeping and relief operations overseas. Then, in 2001, the Japanese government sent naval vessels to the Indian Ocean to support the U.S. war on terrorism in Afghanistan. This show of military support, welcomed by the Americans, was the first overseas deployment of Japan's armed forces (aside from peacekeeping efforts) since World War II. In 2004, about 1,000 Japanese troops went to Iraq to help with reconstruction. These decisions have gradually shifted the role of the Japanese military—changes that have sparked controversy among the people of Japan.

Many in Japan's leadership support a stronger military. When North Korea resumed its nuclear weapons program in 2003, Japanese leaders considered expanding their defense forces and debated building their own nuclear deterrent. Citing China's military buildup, some officials have proposed altering the Japanese constitution so that the country can develop strong armed forces to deter a possible Chinese attack.

Furthermore, residents on the Japanese island of Okinawa have long protested the presence of American troops there.

In February 2007, residents of Okinawa, Japan, protested the imminent delivery of F-22 jets to a U.S. military base. Okinawans have long resented the noise, crime, and lack of economic development resulting from sprawling U.S. military installations.

According to a deal reached in 2006, Japan is helping to coordinate closure or relocation of several U.S. military bases in Japan, although the total number of U.S. military personnel will remain about the same.

Japan's Economy. After World War II, Japan rapidly industrialized. Thanks in part to its well-educated workers who were able to adopt, and often improve, foreign technology, Japan's productivity rate exceeded even that of the United States. By the 1960s, industries in Japan were making high-quality consumer goods such as clothing, radios, televisions, cameras, and automobiles, and exporting them to the United States and elsewhere. Between the 1960s and the 1980s, Japan's economy grew faster than those of most other countries in the world.

However, during the 1990s, Japan struggled to pull itself out of a recession brought on by inflated land and stock prices. Buoyed partly by growing exports to China, the Japanese economy has grown steadily since 2003. Currently, the Japanese economy ranks second largest in the world, behind the United States. Economic interdependence and shared security concerns about Russia and China make the United States and Japan close allies today.

China

The Rise of Communism. Following World War II, nationalist armies, led by Chiang Kaishek, and communist troops, led by Mao Zedong, fought for control of China. In 1949, the civil war ended with a victory by the communists; Mao renamed the country the People's Republic of China (PRC). Meanwhile, Chiang took his nationalist government to the island of Formosa, now called Taiwan.

U.S.–China Relations. The communist takeover of China in 1949 stunned U.S. leaders, who were dedicated to stopping the spread of communism. At the time, the United States refused to recognize the People's Republic of China. Instead, American officials maintained diplomatic relations with the PRC's rival, the Republic of China on Taiwan. Chinese leaders in the PRC were outspokenly anti-American, and thousands of Chinese soldiers fought against U.S. forces in the Korean War (1950–53).

By the 1970s, China had become a world power, but its relations with the neighboring Soviet Union were deteriorating. In 1972, President Richard Nixon took advantage of strained ties between the two communist giants and made a state visit to China. Nixon's trip led to improved Chinese-American relations, and President Jimmy Carter established full diplomatic ties with China in 1979.

China's Economic Boom. China was isolated from the rest of the world until Mao's death in 1976, when it gradually began to introduce capitalist concepts into its economy. Chinese leaders eventually agreed to share power in the central government and to allow local governments to make more decisions. Furthermore, the government has accelerated efforts to privatize state-owned enterprises and attract multinational companies. China's efforts have paid off. For the last two decades, its gross domestic product (GDP)—the amount of goods and services it produces—has grown by more than 9 percent annually. China's population of more than 1.3 billion forms an immense low-wage workforce that can support economic expansion for many years to come.

Strategic Issues. China has enormous territory, 3.7 million square miles, making it a major strategic concern for its neighbors and the United States. Even though the Chinese government has reduced troops by 200,000 since 2003, its 2.3 million soldiers still constitute the largest standing army in the world. Although American and Chinese officials are wary of each other's military strength, relations between the two countries have generally improved in recent years. China has supported America's war on terrorism and shared intelligence with the U.S. government.

Nevertheless, the two nations still disagree about China's ongoing arms sales to unfriendly nations, including missile transfers to Iran and Pakistan as well as chemical weapons deals with Iran. In addition, for more than a decade, Chinese officials

Insurgency in Southern Thailand

Thailand's 65 million people are mostly Buddhist. However, Muslims form the majority in the country's three southern-most provinces. There, escalating brutality that began in 2004 threatens to become a full-scale sectarian war. Bombings and drive-by shootings occur almost daily. Buddhists and Muslims now live in separate villages, and in some cases Buddhists are fleeing the area entirely. Author Zachary Abuza said, "The social fabric of the south has been irreparably damaged," resulting in a "de facto ethnic cleansing." In this photo, a Thai police officer protects a Buddhist monk in the town of Pattani.

AP Photo/David Longstreath

have been increasing military spending by an average of 15 percent a year. In 2007, it announced an increase of almost 18 percent for a total of just under $45 billion. Concerned about the trend and recent spike, U.S. policymakers wanted to know the intent of China's arms buildup. Chinese officials said the increase was needed for technical modernization.

Human Rights. Another ongoing concern for the United States has been China's treatment of its people. In 1989, the Chinese military brutally crushed demonstrations in Beijing's Tiananmen Square, where more than 100,000 workers and students were appealing for democratic reform. About 800 people died; thousands more were injured. Although China has gradually allowed some personal liberties, it remains largely intolerant of political dissent and squelches religious expression.

As China has pursued rapid industrial development, its society has undergone fundamental shifts. As a result, Chinese leaders have faced increasing protests—both in number and size. Rural peasants often decry environmental pollution, local corruption, and land confiscation. (According to Chinese socialist principles, the state owns all land.) Many who support

Western-style democracy push for greater personal freedoms and protection of private property. Yet the Chinese government faces criticism from socialists as well because free-market economic policies have caused increasing inequality and tension between the rich and poor.

Trade. In 2001, with strong U.S. support, China was admitted to the World Trade Organization (WTO). The United States also established permanent normal trade relations (PNTR) with China, reducing tariffs on Chinese goods and enabling American companies to expand their markets in China. This agreement fostered even greater economic interdependence between the two countries. Americans buy a staggering amount of relatively inexpensive Chinese-made goods. At the same time, U.S. companies continue to invest heavily in businesses in China. Unfortunately, Chinese consumption of U.S. goods has not yet matched trade in the other direction. In 2006, the U.S. trade deficit with China hit a record high— $232.5 billion, or almost one-third of the total U.S. trade deficit. The 2006 trade deficit with China marks the largest with any U.S. trading partner ever.

In short, China's economic growth, geographic size, population, and military strength make it a regional giant and a possible world superpower in coming years.

North and South Korea

War in Korea. Japan controlled Korea from 1894 until 1945. When Japan surrendered to the United States to end World War II, Korea was partitioned into two sections—the North (allied with the Soviet Union) and the South (allied with the United States). In 1948, both superpowers withdrew their forces, but no agreement was reached on reunification.

In June 1950, communist North Korea invaded South Korea. This military action, which was supported by the Soviet Union, was an attempt to unify the two Koreas under communist rule. The United States sent armed forces as part of an allied United Nations "police action" to repel the invasion. The two sides fought to a stalemate and, in July 1953, signed an armistice that suspended combat and established a demilitarized zone between the two Koreas. More than fifty years later, North and South Korea are technically still at war because the armistice did not lead to a permanent peace treaty. For many years, the United States has kept about 37,000 troops on the South Korean side of the demilitarized zone.

North Korea Isolated. North Korea became isolated when its ally, the Soviet Union, abandoned communism and broke apart, and when another important ally, China, established diplomatic relations with South Korea. Through the 1990s, under the hard-line socialist dictatorship of Kim Jong Il, the nation experienced economic collapse and widespread famine. Experts believe that more than 2 million North Koreans died of starvation despite food aid from the United States and international relief agencies. Although not as dire today, hunger continues to be a problem for the impoverished nation. Many officials suspect that North Korea makes matters worse by diverting as much as 30 percent of its gross domestic product to support its military—one of the largest in the world.

South Korea and the Sunshine Policy. Today, South Korea is a modern democracy with a strong economy and good relations with the United States and other world nations. South Korean leaders think that diplomacy, aid, and investment will ultimately bring North Korea's communist system to an end and allow the two nations to reunite peacefully. With this hope, in 2000 it began pursuing a "Sunshine Policy" with regard to North Korea. Some families divided by the war held reunions, but there was little progress in other areas. Soon after President Bush took office in 2001, he withdrew U.S. support for South Korea's rapprochement with the North. In a 2002 address, he named North Korea as part of an "axis of evil."

North Korea's Nuclear Ambitions. One of the most heavily militarized nations in the world, North Korea has long pursued conventional and nonconventional weapons, including biological and chemical agents. In 1994, when North Korea threatened to develop nuclear weapons, the nation struck a deal with the Clinton administration. The United States agreed to help build nuclear power plants in North Korea and supply fuel oil, while North Korea agreed to abide by the UN Nuclear Nonproliferation Treaty (NPT), which it had signed. Signatories to the treaty renounce nuclear weapons and allow international inspections of their nuclear sites.

In January 2003, North Korea withdrew from the NPT and ordered inspectors to leave the country. Leaders from the two Koreas, China, Japan, Russia, and the United States held talks, which finally yielded a breakthrough in September 2005. In a joint statement, North Korea agreed in principle to abandon its nuclear activities in exchange for foreign aid. While an agreement was under lengthy negotiation, the North Korean government test fired missiles in July 2006 and in October detonated a nuclear device near its border with China. These actions spurred renewed commitment to ending the nuclear standoff. Finally, in February 2007, the six nations reached an agreement: North Korea will shut down its main reactor and allow international inspections in exchange for receiving fuel oil, other forms of aid, and relief from financial sanctions.

Central and South Asia

Afghanistan and Al Qaeda. Afghanistan, a mountainous area at the heart of ancient trade routes, has for centuries

Negotiators from (left to right) Japan, South Korea, North Korea, China, the United States, and Russia shake hands after sealing a controversial deal to halt North Korea's nuclear program in exchange for fuel and aid. Talks concluded in Beijing, China, in February 2007.

AP Photo/Michael Reynolds, POOL

Pakistan and the Fight Against Terror

When Great Britain granted the Indian subcontinent independence in 1947, it partitioned the territory into mostly Hindu India and a Muslim homeland, Pakistan. The United States and Pakistan then formed an alliance during the Cold War, when Americans sought to limit communist influence in Asia. In 1954, Pakistan signed a Mutual Defense Agreement with the United States. In exchange, U.S. officials granted Pakistan economic and military assistance.

Since the overthrow of the Taliban, U.S. and Pakistani leaders have renewed their alliance by sharing intelligence and resources in the global fight against terrorism. This cooperation has been crucial, as coalition forces try to rout out al Qaeda terrorists, including Osama bin Laden, who remained at-large as of May 2007, but is widely thought to be hiding along the remote Afghan-Pakistan border. At the same time, Taliban insurgents also sought refuge in the same region and from there have launched attacks on villages in southern Afghanistan.

served as a battleground for competing empires. When the Soviet Union invaded the country in 1979, the United States supported a Muslim rebel group called the Mujahadeen. When the Soviet Union pulled out in 1989, civil war ensued. Finally, in 1996 a hard-line, radical Islamic regime—the Taliban— seized power and provided a haven for terrorists, including Osama bin Laden's al Qaeda network.

Sanctions imposed by the United Nations in 1999 failed to force the Taliban to hand over bin Laden for trial. After the September 11 attacks, the United States and Great Britain launched air strikes on Afghanistan in October 2001. That action paved the way for opponents of the Taliban to seize power in the capital, Kabul, within a month.

Foreign peacekeepers arrived in January 2002, enabling the Afghan people to begin building a democracy. Leaders drafted a new constitution and held presidential elections in 2004, then held parliamentary elections in 2005. Meanwhile, about 19,000 U.S. troops—along with allied forces—continued to fight Taliban insurgents and hunt down al Qaeda members.

As of early 2007, the insurgency had intensified in southern Afghanistan, reflecting the renewed strength of the Taliban and al Qaeda, which had sought refuge along the mountainous border with Pakistan. That fact, combined with rampant corruption and incompetence in the Afghan government, caused concern about the stability of the country.

CURRENT ISSUES

Nuclear Negotiations with North Korea. In February 2007, leaders from the United States, China, South Korea, Russia, and Japan unveiled an ambitious new deal aimed at stopping North Korea's nuclear weapons program. In the first stage, North Korea agreed to shut down and seal production at its main nuclear complex and allow international inspectors back into the country. In exchange, North Korea will receive 50,000 tons of fuel oil and a U.S. pledge to lift financial sanctions. Implementation of the accord will require continuing negotiations and a protracted second phase, wherein North Korea will receive 950,000 tons of fuel oil when it agrees to describe, dismantle, and disable all its nuclear programs and facilities. Also, as part of the deal, the United States intends to remove North Korea from the list of nations that sponsor terrorism and will begin the process to eliminate sanctions under its Trading with the Enemy Act.

Immediately following negotiations, conservatives assailed the plan as a reward for nuclear blackmail. A long-time opponent of bargaining with North Korea, former U.S. ambassador to the United Nations John R. Bolton said simply, "It's a bad deal." He and others argue that U.S. negotiators should have withheld all rewards or incentives until North Korea agreed to fully dismantle its entire nuclear program. (As the current agreement stands, in the short term, the North can hold onto its nuclear arsenal, which could contain enough plutonium to build six nuclear bombs.) Other critics deride the length of time it took to replicate, in their view, the 1994 deal—an agreement which essentially allowed the North to acquire nuclear capability. Many critics say that the new agreement encourages other rogue states such as Iran to move forward with their nuclear ambitions. Finally, some contend that North Korea has repeatedly reneged on its international agreements, and that it will probably do so again.

On the other hand, supporters of the new pact point out that the North Korean nuclear program first had to be frozen before it could be reversed. They note that this multi-phased, multilateral agreement does, in fact, differ from the 1994 plan; it "backloads" the agreement by delaying most of the incentives until after the North has disarmed. Proponents cite the failure and stalemate that resulted from the United States' previous hard-line strategy, and emphasize that North Korea's 2006 nuclear test made a swift agreement absolutely critical. Supporters also assert that because several tough negotiating points have been pushed into the future, North Korea will have plenty of time to prove its commitment to the international community. If it fails again to follow through, North Korea will have lost a tremendous amount of respect—and probably its ally China, which sponsored the last round of talks—leaving itself more isolated and vulnerable than ever.

Trade with China. The record $232.5 billion U.S. trade deficit with China in 2006 is part of a long-term, troubling trend. In 2005, a study on U.S. trade with China found that

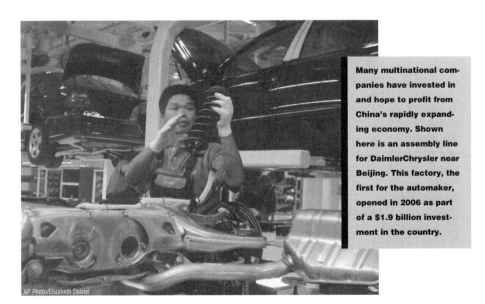

Many multinational companies have invested in and hope to profit from China's rapidly expanding economy. Shown here is an assembly line for DaimlerChrysler near Beijing. This factory, the first for the automaker, opened in 2006 as part of a $1.9 billion investment in the country.

AP Photo/Elizabeth Dalziel

from 1989 to 2003, the U.S. trade deficit with China increased twenty times, while the United States lost an estimated 1.5 million jobs to low-wage workers in that country. Most of these workers are in low-skill, labor-intensive industries like textiles.

Between late 2006 and early 2007, U.S. Treasury secretary Henry Paulson held a series of high-level meetings with counterparts in China to pressure the Chinese to open up their markets to American goods, services, and investment. Because observers have noted little progress, some policymakers are discussing imposing tariffs on Chinese-made goods, particularly paper, steel, furniture, textiles, and plastics—industries that are subsidized by the Chinese government.

Supporters of such tariffs contend that imposing them would make Chinese goods more expensive for U.S. consumers and thus discourage their purchase. Then U.S.-based companies would sell more products and services and employ more American workers to make and deliver them. Meanwhile, industries could focus on retraining Americans for other kinds of jobs. Furthermore, proponents of import restrictions argue that as U.S. companies invest in developing nations such as India and China, the United States becomes far too reliant on shaky economies that might suffer banking crises or other problems stemming from governmental corruption.

Trade is a complicated issue, however, and opponents of new tariffs respond with varied arguments. Some note that since many American companies are invested heavily in China, trade restrictions would hurt them along with Chinese businesses. Other critics point to America's long history of innovation and flexibility, arguing that it is wrong-headed to continue to support dying U.S. industries like cloth manufacturers. As global markets and technology change, they say, millions of jobs will eventually return to the United States. Finally, others assert that maintaining free trade is important because as China's population becomes wealthier, it will become an enormous market for U.S. goods and services.

Increasing Funding for Afghanistan. In early 2007, the top U.S. commander in Afghanistan, Army Lt. Gen. Karl W.

Eikenberry warned that the Taliban's resurgence combined with the weak Afghan government imperiled that country. Said Eikenberry, "The accumulated effect of violent terrorist insurgent attacks, corruption, insufficient social resources, and growing income disparities, all overlaid by a major international presence, are taking their toll on Afghan government legitimacy. A point could be reached at which the government of Afghanistan becomes irrelevant to its people, and the goal of establishing a democratic, moderate, self-sustaining state could be lost forever." Consequently, the Pentagon announced that, at a minimum, it will keep U.S. troop levels near 27,000 into 2008, extending a recent increase in forces. President Bush also asked Congress to provide additional money for two-year operations in Afghanistan.

Many policymakers support President Bush's request and urge the United States to allocate even more resources to counter the serious security threats in Afghanistan. Proponents argue that the mission in that country has been underfunded for at least four years. Speaker of the House Nancy Pelosi (D-Calif.) called Afghanistan "the forgotten war." While the U.S. government was preoccupied with Iraq, Taliban insurgents and al Qaeda chiefs regained strength in their bases along the Afghan-Pakistan border. Meanwhile, persistent poverty and

People in Afghanistan endure daily terrorist attacks, including car bombings, like the one shown here. Much of the violence is carried out by militias and a Taliban-led terrorist network attempting to oust the democratic government.

AP Photo/Rafiq Maqbool

government corruption have driven unemployed youths into militias or the insurgency. Supporters say that only a big surge in spending and U.S. forces can help reconstruct Afghanistan and prevent a militant Islamist government from taking control.

Opponents of a big spending increase for Afghanistan counter that more troops and international aid will probably weaken the Afghan government rather than help it. They say that the Afghan government must reform itself and assume the admittedly difficult task of running and reconstructing the country. While critics agree that a continued U.S. presence is necessary to help fight the insurgency, they think that current American resources can be more efficiently allocated, particularly for training and strengthening the Afghan military, police, and judiciary. Opponents of increasing U.S. funding for Afghanistan cite the enormous financial commitment to Iraq and argue that the United States simply cannot afford to increase funding for Afghanistan as well.

OUTLOOK

The United States faces many obstacles as it continually redefines its relationship with countries in this region of vital economic and strategic interest. Former adversaries such as China have become important trading partners. Yet new concerns arise continually. Afghanistan's government faces an insurgency that could force its collapse, and North Korea poses a nuclear threat, one that U.S. and regional powers will have to work hard to fully defuse. Home to some of the world's largest armies and oldest rivalries, Asia will continue to occupy American policymakers for decades to come.

THE DEBATE: ASIA

Negotiations to end North Korea's nuclear program are in the U.S. national interest.

PRO: The multilateral bargain struck with North Korea in early 2007 uses the pressure of neighboring nations to stop a dangerous nuclear program. The phased implementation of incentives ensures that North Korea will follow through if it wants to receive aid. A nuclear-free Korean peninsula will foster peace in Asia and is therefore in the U.S. interest.

CON: Previous negotiations with Kim Jong Il have failed to resolve the nuclear weapons issue. The current pact, similar to the scuttled 1994 agreement, will fare no better. Offering "rewards" to the pariah nation sends the message that the United States can be manipulated by nuclear blackmail. This precedent encourages other nations, such as Iran, to do likewise.

The United States should restrict Chinese imports.

PRO: In fourteen years, the United States lost 1.5 million jobs while China gained a more than $230 billion trade advantage. Continuation of current free-trade policies will only make matters worse. Imposing tariffs on Chinese goods would put Americans back to work. Besides, the United States should take care not to become too heavily invested in shaky economies like China's.

CON: The United States cannot afford to place limits on Chinese goods because many of them were made with money from U.S. investors and companies. Protectionism cannot replace America's lost jobs. Only international competition will spur U.S. innovation, the engine that secures new jobs for American workers. Continuing free trade ensures a place for U.S. exports—and American profits—in China's enormous market.

U.S. lawmakers should increase funding for the mission in Afghanistan.

PRO: Under siege by a Taliban-led terrorist campaign, Afghanistan has reached a crisis point. Violence, corruption, and poverty now jeopardize the success of the U.S.-backed government. Lawmakers must redouble their commitment to the Afghan people—and to the war on terror—by increasing funding for reconstruction and military operations in the struggling nation.

CON: The federal budget, already straining under Iraq war costs, cannot accommodate big increases in the Afghanistan mission. Current funding could be more effectively spent on critical programs such as training the police. Furthermore, Afghanistan's own government must lead the country's rebuilding in order to earn the respect and trust of the Afghan people.

EUROPE AND RUSSIA

During the Cold War, Europe was divided into two competing camps: Eastern Europe, controlled by the communist Soviet Union, and Western Europe, allied with the United States. For more than forty years, the conflict between East and West dominated U.S. foreign policy.

When the Soviet Union broke apart in the early 1990s, the Cold War ended. Eastern European countries moved toward democratic and free-market economic systems, while Western Europe—free from the Soviet threat—continued with its plan to integrate its economies into a European Union or "United Europe." However, old problems were replaced by new ones. Throughout the 1990s, Europe and Russia struggled with a number of economic and political dilemmas. Ethnic hostilities in the former Yugoslavia prompted NATO—including U.S. forces—to intervene in the conflict in an attempt to bring peace to the region. Ethnic conflict also occurred in the mostly Muslim region of Russia called Chechnya, prompting Russian troops to use force to contain the situation there.

Europe today remains a key political and economic partner of the United States, despite tension in recent years. Relations with Europe suffered their most serious setback in decades when France, Germany, and Russia clashed with the Bush administration over its decision to go to war with Iraq in 2003. This was just one of the rifts that left many observers wondering if the United States and Europe were becoming more like rivals instead of allies. U.S. relations with Russia are even more troublesome. Many differences over key foreign policy issues and Russia's new hard-line rule have strained the relationship and made it unlikely that these one-time enemies can become dependable, trusted allies in the near future.

KEY QUESTIONS

- Should U.S. foreign policy de-emphasize Europe?

- Should the United States pressure Russia to adopt more democratic reforms?

- Should the United States support independence for Kosovo?

BACKGROUND

The Cold War

The Iron Curtain Divides Europe. In February 1945, before World War II had ended, U.S. president Franklin Roosevelt, British prime minister Winston Churchill, and Soviet general secretary Joseph Stalin met at Yalta to discuss the rebuilding of Europe. The three leaders agreed that when the war was over,

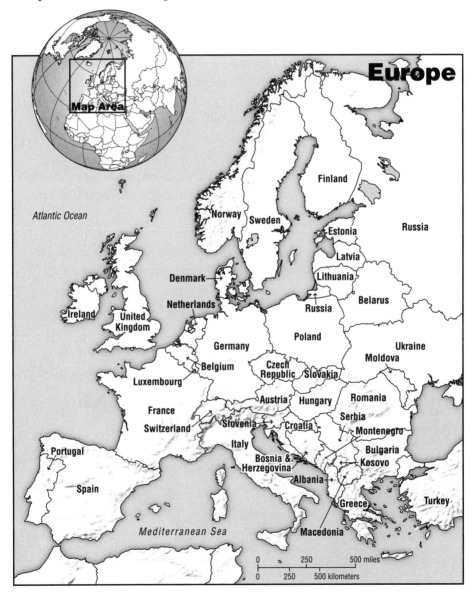

Europe

Map Area

Atlantic Ocean

Finland

Norway
Sweden

Estonia

Russia

Latvia

Denmark

Lithuania

Netherlands

Russia

Belarus

Ireland

United
Kingdom

Poland

Germany

Ukraine

Belgium

Czech
Republic

Slovakia

Moldova

Luxembourg

Austria

Hungary

Romania

France

Serbia

Switzerland

Slovenia

Croatia

Montenegro

Portugal

Italy

Bulgaria

Bosnia &
Herzegovina

Kosovo

Albania

Spain

Greece

Turkey

Mediterranean Sea

Macedonia

0   250   500 miles
0   250   500 kilometers

both Germany and its capital, Berlin, would be divided into occupation zones. France, Great Britain, and the United States would occupy the western zones of Germany and Berlin, while the Soviet Union would occupy the eastern zones. Stalin promised that free elections would be held in all the nations in Europe that his troops had liberated from the Nazis.

However, shortly after the war ended, the Soviets established communist governments in Poland, Romania, Hungary, and Bulgaria. Native communists soon seized power in Yugoslavia and Albania, and Germany was split into two countries. The United States, Great Britain, and France supported West Germany and kept troops in West Berlin, a divided city located 120 miles inside Soviet-controlled East Germany. Thus, a heavily guarded border between East and West that Winston Churchill called the "Iron Curtain" was drawn.

These events marked the beginning of the Cold War— a conflict between the United States and the Soviet Union fought with propaganda, arms buildups, and the use of military and economic aid to win allies.

U.S. Policy of Containment. The United States tried to prevent further expansion of communism by "containing" it

In February 1945, Allied leaders Winston Churchill, Franklin Roosevelt, and Josef Stalin met in Yalta—a Soviet resort town in the Crimea—to set the stage for the post-World War II division of Europe.

National Archives

in areas that were already Soviet-controlled. Containment was carried out on three fronts: (1) economic aid to rebuild Western Europe; (2) military assistance to governments challenged by communists; and (3) creation of the North Atlantic Treaty Organization (NATO) to provide security in Western Europe.

The Marshall Plan and NATO. World War II left much of Europe devastated, its economies ruined, and its people desperate. A foreign aid program called the Marshall Plan (1947-53) provided $13 billion (more than $105 billion in 2006 dollars) in U.S. aid, investment, and trade to rebuild Western Europe. U.S. officials believed that a healthy European economy would prevent a rebirth of fascism or an insurgence of communism and that a strong European military would keep the Soviets from America's doorstep.

NATO, a U.S.-led military alliance, which originally included ten European countries and Canada, was established in 1949 to deter an armed communist attack in Europe. In 1955, the Soviet Union and its Eastern European allies formed a counterpart to NATO called the Warsaw Pact. Both NATO and the Warsaw Pact stationed thousands of troops, tanks, and combat aircraft on European soil and installed nuclear missiles aimed at each other.

Western Europe Comes Together. After World War II, Western European leaders began to think about developing an economic framework that would combine their economic and political strengths. In 1957, they formed the European Economic Community, commonly called the EC. In some ways, EC members operated as though they were one country. Member countries planned their economies to complement one another and, by establishing uniform trade rules and policies, worked together to strengthen European competition in the world market.

From the Berlin Wall to *Détente*. U.S.-Soviet relations were tense over the future of Europe in the 1950s and 1960s. In 1961, the Soviet Union built the Berlin Wall, dividing the German capital and closing off access to West Berlin. This dramatic event solidified the division of Europe into competing camps. Later that decade, leaders in the United States and Western Europe decided it was time to engage the Soviets in constructive negotiations—a policy called *détente.*

Détente (a French word meaning "a relaxation of tensions") reflected the belief that, while the division of Europe was unlikely to change, both the United States and the Soviet Union would benefit from increasing cooperation and reducing conflict. The two superpowers negotiated three important treaties during the period of *détente.*

- **SALT I.** The first Strategic Arms Limitation Talks Treaty, signed in 1972, limited antiballistic missile (ABM) systems designed to intercept and destroy enemy missiles before they reach their targets.

- **Helsinki Accords.** The United States, the Soviet Union, Canada, and thirty-five European countries signed the Helsinki Accords in 1975 to officially recognize the post-World War II borders of Eastern Europe. In return, the Soviet Union promised to increase intellectual freedom and human rights within the Eastern Bloc.

- **SALT II.** The second Strategic Arms Limitation Talks Treaty extended the first SALT agreement, but when the Soviet Union invaded Afghanistan in December 1979, President Jimmy Carter withdrew the treaty. U.S.-Soviet relations again deteriorated.

The Gorbachev Era Begins. When Mikhail Gorbachev became the Soviet leader in 1985, he began a new cooperative phase in U.S.-Soviet relations. Gorbachev established more friendly and flexible relations with the United States, other communist states, and the Soviet people. He also introduced the policies of *glasnost* (openness) and *perestroika* (restructuring). Both policies sought to slowly introduce the Soviet Union to democratic ideals and economic reforms. The results moved the Soviet Union away from its hard-line communist past and closer to a free-market, democratic future.

As political liberalization began to emerge across Eastern Europe, East Germany opened up the Berlin Wall in November 1989. Since citizens were then finally allowed to cross the border, the Berlin Wall was rendered useless. Here, a demonstrator pounds away at the wall during the ensuing celebration.

Reuters/CORBIS

The Soviet Union Unravels

Communism Falls in Eastern Europe. In 1989, communist governments in six Eastern European countries gave up power after thousands of their citizens demonstrated in favor of democracy and free-market economies. Mikhail Gorbachev refrained from sending in troops to keep the communists in power as other past Soviet leaders had done. In Germany, the Berlin Wall—separating East and West Berlin—was torn down before cheering crowds. After East Germany abandoned communism, the economies of the two countries were joined in July 1990 and political union followed in October of that year.

Turmoil in Moscow. Mikhail Gorbachev's popularity at home suffered as the Soviet economy deteriorated. In 1990, independence movements swept through the Soviet Baltic republics of Estonia, Latvia, and Lithuania.

By early 1991, six Soviet republics had declared independence. Meanwhile, the nine remaining republics demanded more autonomy. Eastern Europe was no longer under Soviet control, free-market economics threatened to dismantle communism, and the union was in jeopardy. In August 1991, hard-line communists in the government staged a coup, arrested Gorbachev, and took control of the country. Boris Yeltsin, president of the Russian republic, immediately mobilized opposition in Moscow, which spread throughout the country. After three days, the coup collapsed. Gorbachev returned to power, but his authority and credibility as a leader were gone. More republics announced their independence soon after the failed coup.

The End of the Soviet Union. Although Mikhail Gorbachev was prepared to give the republics more autonomy, he hoped to hold the Soviet Union together. However, on December 21, 1991, Russia's Boris Yeltsin and the leaders of Ukraine and Belarus declared the dissolution of the Soviet Union. Gorbachev announced his resignation on December 25, 1991, and relinquished control of the nuclear arsenal to Yeltsin. Soon thereafter, all of the former Soviet republics became the independent nations they are today.

Russia's Recovery

Because almost none of the basic institutions of a free-market economy—such as private ownership, regulations for business and industry, and banking and loan procedures—were in place when the Soviet Union collapsed in 1991, Russia had to start from scratch. It had to contend with aging factories, the loss of raw materials previously supplied by the now-independent republics, and a workforce unaccustomed to the wage fluctuation and job insecurity associated with capitalism. These problems led to high unemployment, a devalued Russian currency (the ruble), and the inability of businesses to pay their workers.

Growing Pains Under Yeltsin. To encourage worker ownership and entrepreneurship, President Yeltsin instituted an ambitious privatization program to sell state-owned assets to Russian citizens. The results, however, did not live up to expectations.

Yeltsin continued his efforts to move Russia into the global market when he was reelected in 1996. By 1999, however, despite financial help and support from the United States and huge loans from the International Monetary Fund (IMF), Russia's economy had fallen into a state of near collapse. On December 31, 1999, Yeltsin resigned as president, and was replaced by his prime minister, Vladimir Putin. In March 2000, Putin, a former chief of the Soviet intelligence agency (KGB), was officially elected president.

Putin Takes Control. The new Russian leader expressed ideas for advancing democratic standards, such as land ownership, reform of the Russian tax system and judiciary, and the elimination of crime and corruption in government. Many observers believe that President Putin recognizes that a modernized and prosperous Russia depends a great deal upon a constructive—although not deferential—relationship with the United States. He initially won over President George W. Bush with his support for the U.S. military action in Afghanistan in 2001, and the two leaders also pledged to further reduce their countries' nuclear stockpiles.

Russia the Oil Baron

Russia's vigorous oil industry is the engine behind the country's economic growth. Russia is already a major energy supplier in Europe and could become a global energy powerhouse in the future. The European Union's dependency on Russia's oil increases every year. In January 2007, the Russian government cut supplies on the Druzhba pipeline, which runs from central Russia to Germany and accounts for 13 percent of total EU oil consumption. The action was taken to prevent Belarus, through which part of the pipeline runs, from illegally siphoning off oil. By doing so, however, Russia also temporarily cut off supplies for western Europe. The dispute with Belarus was resolved, but the episode reminded European countries of the growing role Russia has in meeting their energy needs and renewed concerns that Russia will use its oil supply as a diplomatic weapon.

A Stable Economy. Many experts give Putin credit for helping push the Russian economy forward. After shrinking throughout Yeltsin's presidency, the Russian economy has grown significantly in recent years—about 6 percent annually since 2000. Although the average Russian's income remains low by European standards, the improved economy has given consumers more choices than ever before. Overall, according to most experts, the Russian economy will continue to grow. Because of this optimism, approval of President Putin's job performance remains very high among Russian citizens.

An Iron Fist. Not all news coming out of Russia has been encouraging for observers. President Putin has rolled back many democratic reforms and instituted harsh measures to control the media. This reversal has alarmed many Western leaders, including President Bush, and caused some officials to rethink U.S. policy toward Russia.

The Russian leader's strong hand has been most visible in the continuing conflict with Chechnya. In 1991, this fiercely independent and mostly Muslim province—located on Russia's mountainous southwest flank—declared its independence and broke from the Russian Federation. Having always maintained that Chechnya—and its strategic location—is too valuable to lose, Russia responded by sending in thousands of troops to bring the province back into line. After five years of brutal fighting between Russian troops and Chechen rebels, Russia pulled out, leaving Chechnya devastated and its independence in question. Despite worldwide denunciation, Russian troops returned in 1999 to try to end the rebellion once and for all. Subsequent terrorist attacks by Chechen militants on Russian civilians have only intensified the conflict. Although Russia has largely succeeded in destroying the leadership of the Chechen separatists, sporadic fighting continues.

The European Union: A United States of Europe?

While Russia and the other former Soviet republics struggled with transitioning to democracy and capitalism during the 1990s, their neighbors to the west were working hard to integrate their economies. In 1985, European Community

(EC) leaders agreed to create a single European market where money, people, and goods could cross borders freely, forming the world's largest and wealthiest free-trade market.

In the early 1990s, the establishment of the European Union (EU) was overshadowed by the discovery that the new-found freedom and autonomy in Eastern Europe had revived conflicts that would bring bloodshed to the continent not seen since World War II.

The Rise of Nationalism. Nationalism—a people's devotion to its religion, culture, or ethnicity—has been the catalyst for many modern world conflicts. In 1991, the country of Yugoslavia fell victim to hatred and chaos generated by nationalism. Yugoslavia, located on the Balkan peninsula and first created after World War I by the merger of six formerly independent republics, became a communist country in 1946. Tensions among Yugoslavia's different ethnic and religious populations date back centuries, but a strong communist central government suppressed potential conflicts for nearly forty-five years.

After communism collapsed, Serbia, the largest and most militarily powerful of the Yugoslav republics, sought to unite the other republics under the banner of "Greater Serbia." In June 1991, another republic, Croatia, declared its independence and seceded from Yugoslavia. Serbian President Slobodan Milosevic then sent troops into Croatia to stop the move, but Croatia won its independence after a bloody conflict. Soon the heavily Muslim republic of Bosnia and Herzegovina, known as Bosnia, followed Croatia's lead and declared its independence. Encouraged by Milosevic, the Serb minority living in Bosnia declared war, with the goal of creating their own Serb-controlled country within the republic.

Genocide in Bosnia. As Bosnian Serbs, Croats, and Muslims fought throughout the early 1990s, the world learned of shocking "ethnic cleansing" going on in Bosnia. Bosnian Serb troops murdered, imprisoned, and uprooted thousands of Muslim and Croat men, women, and children. After almost four years of war that produced 250,000 dead and 3 million refugees, leaders of Bosnia, Croatia, and Serbia signed a peace treaty called the Dayton Accords, which divided Bosnia and Herzegovina into a Muslim-Croat federation and a Serb republic. In December 1995, President Bill Clinton sent 20,000 U.S. troops to be part of a NATO peacekeeping force in Bosnia. In December 2004, NATO handed over peacekeeping duties to the European Union.

In November 2005, ten years after the signing of the Dayton Accords, the leaders of Bosnia's federations vowed to negotiate constitutional reforms that would strengthen state and centralized institutions and help unify the country.

Kosovo. Violence in the Balkans was not limited to Bosnia and Croatia. In the Serbian province of Kosovo, ethnic Albanians—who make up about 90 percent of the population—had for years been pressuring Serbian authorities to grant independence to the province. However, unlike Croatia and Bosnia, Kosovo had never been an independent republic, thus Serbians believed it was rightfully part of Serbia. In March 1998, Serbian authorities, on orders from Milosevic, clamped down on Kosovo as riots and

In 1998 and 1999, Serbia used military force to suppress an independence movement in the province of Kosovo. NATO air strikes eventually forced Serbia to withdraw its forces. Here, Serbian tanks leave the Kosovo capital of Pristina in June 1999.

Anja Niedringhaus/epa/Corbis

violence increased. As fighting escalated, U.S. and European leaders pressured Milosevic to pull his troops back, give Kosovo more autonomy, and allow NATO troops in Kosovo to keep the peace. After the collapse of peace talks in March 1999, NATO air attacks on Serbian military and strategic targets forced Milosevic to agree to NATO's terms. Since hostilities ended, Kosovo and its 2.1 million inhabitants have been under the supervision of the United Nations.

International negotiators have struggled to find a workable solution that will determine, once and for all, Kosovo's "final status." Although Serbia supports granting more autonomy to Kosovo, the government rejects the Albanian Kosovars' demand for independence. This unresolved issue, many fear, could eventually lead to a reemergence of armed conflict and once again destabilize the Balkan region.

The Road to European Unity. In January 1992, after bruising political battles in France and Great Britain over European unification, leaders signed the Maastricht Treaty, which outlined plans for monetary union, the creation of a single currency, and coordination of foreign and defense policies. On November 1, 1993, the European Union (EU) officially went into effect, replacing the European Community. In 2004, its membership grew to include ten eastern European nations, increasing EU membership to twenty-five countries.

The Euro. On January 1, 1999, twelve of the fifteen countries of the European Union began replacing their respective currencies with a single currency, called the euro. The first paper notes and coins went into circulation in January 2002. One notable exception to the adoption of the euro is Great Britain. EU leaders are eager to persuade Europe's second-largest economy, to adopt, and thus add strength to, the euro.

Thus far, the reviews of the euro by participating countries are decidedly mixed. The euro's value against the dollar has climbed steadily since its introduction. Export-dependent countries such as Germany have warned that the value of the currency must be brought down or it will jeopardize the region's economic recovery by making European products too

All European Union member states must ratify the European Constitution before it goes into effect. In May 2005, 55 percent of French voters in a national referendum rejected the constitution. Here, a voter holds the two ballots inside a polling station in Nice, France.

expensive in world markets. Some European leaders, however, do not believe that the euro's high value poses a problem.

The EU Constitution. In June 2004, European leaders agreed on a constitution for the EU, designed to bring together all the assorted treaties and agreements that had been governing the union since 1985. The constitution's main aim is to codify uniform human rights and democratic principles throughout the EU, and to streamline, or centralize, the decision-making process. Members hoped that the constitution would be approved by all twenty-five EU nations—either by referendum or parliament—and take effect by November 2006.

In May and June 2005, however, voters in France and the Netherlands dealt ratification a crippling blow by rejecting the constitution in national referendums. Critics succeeded in persuading the majority in both countries that the constitution would strip away too much sovereignty from individual countries. The failure of the constitution to win popular support in

France and the Netherlands caused other countries to postpone or halt their ratification procedures. By 2007, only sixteen member states had ratified the European Constitution.

CURRENT ISSUES

Rethinking Europe. During the Cold War, the United States developed a strong bond with Western Europe, united against the threat posed by the Soviet Union. Over the years, the U.S. government consistently led efforts to provide necessary security for European allies through NATO and to assist in developing a prosperous economic relationship with the burgeoning European Union. In the 1990s, U.S. leaders also began to encourage and aid Eastern European nations in their transitions from communism to free-market democracy.

However, recent differences with Europe over a series of issues, including the war in Iraq, the Middle East peace process, and global warming, have strained the alliance. While some observers believe low points are inevitable in such a relationship, others argue that these developments are more significant—signaling a permanent breach in the U.S.-European partnership.

Many observers believe Europe should no longer be central to U.S. foreign policy, and that Europe and the United States now need each other less and less. They say that while NATO was critical in the fight against Soviet aggression, it has been sixteen years since the Soviet Union's demise and newer threats to international peace have emerged requiring different alliances. Further, as EU and NATO membership have grown, it has become much more difficult for the United States to reach consensus with Europe on some national security and economic issues. In addition, European governments generally remain wedded to managing international crises through multilateral institutions—a strategy that, some critics argue, is contrary to U.S. national security interests. Many experts believe that the distribution of power in the world is shifting, making it imperative that the United States rely less on the European Union and more on nations, such as India and even China, that are becoming increasingly influential.

Muslims in Europe

In February 2006, a newspaper in Denmark printed a series of cartoons with unflattering depictions of the Islamic prophet Muhammad, triggering a series of violent protests and one of 2006's most controversial international incidents. This explosive episode highlighted the divide between the Muslim and Western world over issues of censorship, free speech, and religious tolerance. For the millions of Muslim men and women who live across Europe, the cartoons were a slap in the face and reignited some claims that European governments have neglected to help Muslim immigrants adjust to life in Europe.

France has the highest Muslim population (10 percent) in Europe, followed by the Netherlands (6 percent). Great Britain also has a growing Muslim population. Most are immigrants from North Africa and South Asia. Many observers say these European governments have a responsibility to help diminish the social and economic isolation of European Muslims. Others argue that the European Muslim community must do more to help fight radical Islamic violence.

Other policymakers argue that although the United States may not always get its way, reaching out and strengthening the transatlantic alliance is the surest path to long-term security success. These experts suggest that with the Soviet threat gone and thus a decreased reliance on the United States for security, European allies now feel freer to voice more robustly their own views—a sign that the transatlantic alliance has evolved into a more mature and open relationship. Instead of diminishing Europe's importance, the United States should adjust to, and embrace, this new dynamic. Many supporters of the alliance also argue that it would be careless to downplay the European Union's importance because the United States will not find another part of the world where political, diplomatic, military, and economic power can be more effectively marshaled in support of U.S. policies.

U.S.-Russian Relations. When Vladimir Putin was elected president of Russia in 2000, many experts hoped that the new leader would help reenergize democratic and economic reform in Russia and foster a constructive relationship with the United States. President Bush believed that he and his Russian counterpart could develop a new strategic framework for U.S.-Russian relations, one that was based on mutual trust and shared economic and security interests.

Putin was elected to a second term in 2004. By then, however, the United States and other countries had become increasingly concerned about changes in the Russian president's leadership style, as evidenced by increased authoritarianism, suppression of the press and political opposition, and the use of iron-fisted tactics to crush the Chechen independence movement. The U.S. government also heavily criticized Russia's decision in 2005 to supply fuel to one of Iran's new nuclear reactors. Nevertheless, in 2006 the United States demonstrated strong support for one of President Putin's top priorities—Russia's accession to the World Trade Organization (WTO). Russia's admittance is not assured; multilateral discussions are still underway.

Despite this support, many believe the United States should begin to treat Russia more like an adversary, rather than the ally U.S. leaders hoped it would become. They say the United States needs to apply greater pressure on Russia to improve its human rights record and restore basic freedoms. Critics say Russia's relationship with Iran in particular is extremely troubling and jeopardizes U.S. anti-proliferation efforts. They argue that because President Bush has touted the spread of democracy around the globe, turning a blind eye to Putin's abuses makes the United States a hypocrite in the eyes of the world.

On the other hand, many foreign policy experts point out that it is necessary for the United States to avoid confrontation with Russia at a time when U.S. influence internationally is on the decline. Despite some anti-democratic policies, they say, Russia has the potential to remain an ally on vital global issues, such as terrorism and trade. Russia's economy has

Though criticized around the world for his government's authoritarian rule, Russian president Vladimir Putin is popular with Russians for facilitating the nation's economic turnaround. Here, president Putin (right) and Russian military officials watch a military parade in Moscow.

Viktor Korotayev/Reuters/Corbis

made remarkable progress under President Putin's supervision. Many experts contend that the U.S. government made the right call in promoting Russia's entry to the WTO, a decision they hope will lead to more cooperation between the two powerful nations.

Independence for Kosovo? Although the Dayton peace process of the mid-1990s largely addressed the wars that tore apart the former Yugoslavia, the situation in Kosovo continues to confound the United States and its European allies. Since the end of the 1999 military campaign that curtailed Serbian aggression, Kosovo has been under the administration of the United Nations, effectively making it made a ward of the international community. Efforts to fully resolve the dispute over the central issue of independence for Kosovo are ongoing. Serbia believes Kosovo should be granted significant autonomy but not the full independence a majority of the country desires. Some expect that the international community—led by the United States, Great Britain, France, Germany, Italy, and Russia—will have to step in and "impose" a settlement. The United States supports independence for Kosovo only if it meets certain benchmarks, namely human rights protections for Kosovo's minority populations. (Ninety percent of Kosovo's citizens are Albanian and they have a contentious relationship with the Serbian minority in the region.)

U.S. proponents of Kosovo independence argue that the residents of the province overwhelmingly favor independence and should be allowed to determine their own status. They say that in addition to honoring the principle of self-determination, granting Kosovo its independence will also help to create long-term regional stability. Some experts argue that continued failure to acknowledge Kosovo's claim will inevitably lead to further conflict—which would almost certainly spread beyond the province's borders. Further, they maintain, the Kosovo government has already begun to build the democratic institutions that will ensure protection of minority rights. Actual independence, advocates say, will create the climate for a prosperous economy by attracting foreign investment and trade, and the desire to maintain this investment will be additional incentive to protect minority rights.

Quite the contrary, say those who oppose U.S. support for Kosovo independence. They argue that true rights for the province's Serb minority have not yet been incorporated into governmental institutions and, despite the insistence of the United States and others, likely never will be. Critics also argue that the Kosovars' campaign for independence is now being viewed as a "model" elsewhere in the world and is providing ammunition for separatist groups to ignite their own violent conflicts as a way to legitimize secession—a dangerous and destabilizing trend for international order. Ethnic conflict should be resolved through mediation and state reform, say opponents, not by dissolving existing states.

OUTLOOK

More than fifty years ago, the United States made a commitment to the economic well-being and security of Western
Europe while containing Soviet communism. However, the
end of the Cold War brought dramatic changes. As the war in
Iraq has demonstrated, the United States is willing to implement its foreign policy objectives with or without its European
partners. Most European nations, in turn, are working to make
their continent a formidable presence that may soon rival the
influence of the United States. In addition, Russia continues to
grow economically and to challenge the role of the United
States around the world. Clearly, U.S. relations with Europe
and Russia will become even more complex over the next
few years.

THE DEBATE: EUROPE AND RUSSIA

U.S. foreign policy should de-emphasize Europe.

PRO: Europe and the United States no longer need each other like they did during the Cold War. The European Union, more powerful and less reliant on U.S. leadership, has interests and priorities not always shared by the United States, including a preference for managing international problems through multilateral institutions. The United States should now consider increasingly powerful nations, such as India and China, for partnerships.

CON: While the United States should build alliances in other parts of the world, it would be a mistake to discount its European relationships. The European Union and the United States differ on some policies, but the two share the same goals overall. No other nation, or group of nations, can provide the United States with such consistent and dependable support. Europe is a formidable global presence that the United States needs to have on its side.

The United States should pressure Russia to adopt more democratic reforms.

PRO: President Putin has stifled democratic reform in Russia with his increasingly authoritarian leadership. Political opposition and a free press are practically nonexistent. President Bush has committed the United States to democracy promotion throughout the world. The United States must now pressure Russia to observe democratic norms, and should consider retracting its support for Russia's WTO membership if reforms are not made.

CON: The United States should be grateful that Putin has succeeded in stabilizing Russia's economy and bringing it back from the edge of collapse. Even though the United States opposes Russia's authoritarian trends, it would be counterproductive to implement punishing policies when global support for the United States is eroding. Russia remains a strategic partner in the war on terrorism and other areas of cooperation too vital to cast aside.

The United States should support independence for Kosovo.

PRO: Kosovo should be granted self-determination. A clear majority of its population favors independence, and democratic institutions have been implemented that signal a commitment to free elections and respect for the rights of minorities. Independence will finally put this conflict to rest. Failure to do so guarantees bloodshed, which may spread beyond Kosovo's borders.

CON: Granting independence to Kosovo will encourage other secessionist movements around the world and provoke greater instability in the Balkan region. Such conflicts must be solved through negotiation and reform, not through the breakup of countries. Given the intensity and violence of past conflict, it is unlikely that minority rights will be protected in an independent Kosovo.

LATIN AMERICA

The United States shares more than a hemisphere with Latin America. Most U.S. communities have residents whose families came from Mexico, Central America, South America, or the Caribbean, and the economies of the United States and Latin America are inextricably linked. As a result, the U.S. government has long recognized the importance of its relationships with the nations in this region.

Throughout the 1980s, Latin America endured economic decline, civil war, communist insurgencies, and brutal military regimes. Hoping to deter communism, U.S. leaders gave economic and military aid to many Central American and Caribbean countries. However, in the 1990s, Latin America transformed dramatically. Dictatorships fell, popular elections were held, and free-market economies emerged.

Recent events have signaled a new period of momentous change. For the first time in decades, there is the possibility of new leadership in Cuba, reviving debate about whether the United States should revise its policies toward this island nation. Meanwhile, some U.S. lawmakers are expressing alarm about the turn toward socialism taking place in some Latin American nations—changes that could jeopardize the future of capitalism in the hemisphere. Some Americans have begun to question whether U.S.-Latin American free-trade agreements are helping or hurting economic development in the region. The resolution of these issues will affect Latin America's future and relations with the United States for years to come.

KEY QUESTIONS

- Should the United States change its policy toward Cuba?

- Should the United States do more to discourage socialism in Latin America?

- Should the United States continue to promote free trade with Latin America?

BACKGROUND

Mexico

Geographically, Mexico is part of North America, but it shares a language and culture with its neighbors to the south. Nevertheless, Mexico and the United States have had close relations for many years. The two countries share a 2,000-mile border, and Mexico is the United States' second largest trading partner (after Canada).

Unlike many countries in Latin America, Mexico has had a relatively stable government. Beginning in 1929, the

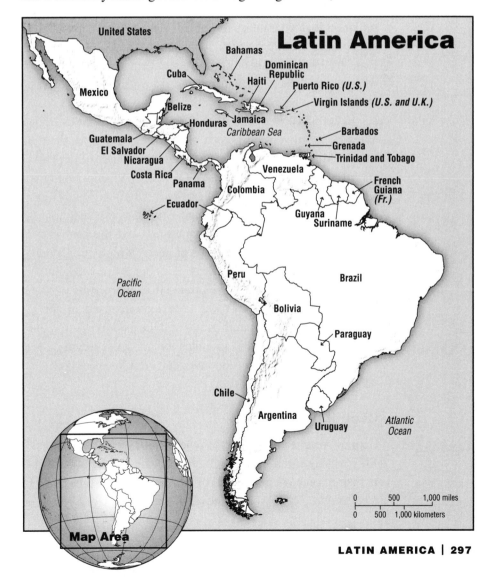

Latin America

United States
Bahamas
Cuba
Haiti
Dominican Republic
Puerto Rico *(U.S.)*
Virgin Islands *(U.S. and U.K.)*
Mexico
Belize
Honduras
Jamaica
Caribbean Sea
Barbados
Guatemala
El Salvador
Nicaragua
Grenada
Trinidad and Tobago
Costa Rica
Panama
Venezuela
Colombia
French Guiana *(Fr.)*
Ecuador
Guyana
Suriname
Pacific Ocean
Peru
Brazil
Bolivia
Paraguay
Chile
Argentina
Uruguay
Atlantic Ocean

0   500   1,000 miles
0   500   1,000 kilometers

Map Area

Institutional Revolution Party (*Partido Revolucionario Institucional* or PRI) held power for nearly seventy years. However, many historians believe that the PRI maintained control through corruption and fraudulent elections.

From 1988 to 1994, President Carlos Salinas de Gortari radically reformed Mexico's economy and helped negotiate the North American Free Trade Agreement (NAFTA). Ernesto Zedillo Ponce de Leon—also a member of the PRI—succeeded Salinas as president in December 1994. During his first month in office, the value of Mexico's currency (the peso) plummeted, causing a severe economic crisis. The International Monetary Fund (IMF) and the United States gave Mexico more than $50 billion in loan guarantees to stabilize the economy, and Zedillo won international praise when his nation was able to repay the loans by 1997. President Zedillo strengthened economic reforms; as a result, the Mexican economy grew significantly in the second half of the 1990s.

In 2000, Mexico held its first presidential primaries, allowing its citizens to directly choose their leader for the first time in Mexican history. Voters elected National Action Party (*Partido Acción Nacional* or PAN) member Vicente Fox Quesada, ending seven decades of one-party domination. In July 2006, Felipe Calderon was elected as the new president of Mexico, but by the slimmest of margins—less than one percent of the vote. Some Mexicans protested the election's outcome, claiming voter fraud. Several recounts followed, but Calderon was eventually inaugurated in January 2007.

As of late, U.S. policy toward Mexico is focused on stopping the flow of illegal immigrants and illegal drugs across the U.S.-Mexican border, and assessing the impact of recent free-trade agreements on the economies and workforces of both nations.

Central America

Central America is a group of seven nations located between Mexico and South America. At times, many of the countries in the region have been ruled by military dictatorships and have endured civil war and poverty. During the Cold War,

Mexicans protest outside the Federal Electoral Tribunal in Mexico City in July 2006, while lawyers inside reviewed claims of fraud in the nation's presidential election. Supporters shown here believed that Andres Obrador of the Party of the Democratic Revolution (PRD) should have been elected, but ultimately National Action Party (PAN) candidate Felipe Calderon was the declared winner.

when the United States and the Soviet Union competed for allies around the world, the United States gave financial or military support to nations such as El Salvador, Guatemala, and Nicaragua to help them fight against communist or leftist guerrillas. Several of these U.S.-backed governments were later accused of committing human rights abuses.

Central American government leaders signed peace treaties with heads of rebel movements in Nicaragua (1982), El Salvador (1992), and Guatemala (1996), ending their civil wars. These leaders promised to implement free-market reforms, to become more democratic, and to reduce their militaries to lessen the chance of future military rule.

For a time, many hoped that Central America would quickly prosper. But in the years since the peace treaties, the region's economies have not improved significantly. Many U.S. policy-makers advocate increased trade to spur growth in the region. In 2004, President George W. Bush signed the Central America Free Trade Agreement (DR-CAFTA) with leaders from a number of Central American countries as well as the Dominican Republic. Congress approved the treaty in 2005.

South America

South America, the fourth largest of the world's seven continents, is made up of twelve nations and one territory (French Guiana) with great geographic, climatic, and cultural diversity. For much of the twentieth century, political elites—primarily military officers—controlled most of the continent's governments. In the 1990s, however, democratic movements brought elections and free-market reforms to South America, a trend that led to expanded diplomatic and trade relations with the United States and the rest of the world.

A Colombian soldier stands guard in the jungles southeast of Bogota, Colombia, in November 2006 in an attempt to keep criminals from using the area to build makeshift drug labs that process coca leaves into cocaine. The United States has assisted in training the Colombian military to combat the production of illegal drugs in that country.

Colombia. The oldest democracy on the continent, Colombia has endured violent political and criminal factions for more than forty years. Drug cartels—powerful groups that produce and sell illegal drugs—control large areas of the country. Despite periodic government crackdowns, drug traffickers continue to wield considerable power and have been responsible for much of Colombia's domestic crime and terrorism. In addition,

AP Photo/ William Fernando Martinez

the nation's armed forces have, for nearly four decades, been fighting rebel groups seeking to overthrow the government. About 90 percent of all cocaine and much of the heroin brought into the United States originates in Colombia.

In 2002, Colombian President Alvaro Uribe assumed office with a hard-line stance on rebels, terrorism, and drug trafficking. Soon thereafter, he reached a peace accord with a large paramilitary group. With disarmament, fighters surrender their weapons in exchange for amnesty and government stipends. Human rights activists criticize Uribe's peace plan as too lenient on criminals who had massacred citizens and gained riches from illegal drugs. From 2000 through 2005, the U.S. government gave Colombia a total of more than $3 billion to stem the flow of illegal drugs into the United States. Uribe was reelected to another four-year term in 2006.

Venezuela. One of the world's top five oil-producing nations, Venezuela is perched on the northern rim of South America. Since the United States is heavily dependent on foreign oil imports, and receives nearly 15 percent of its oil from Venezuela, this nation is considered one of the United States' most important Latin American economic partners.

Despite Venezuela's oil wealth, the majority of the country's population lives in poverty. Voters elected President Hugo Chavez in 1998 in part because he promised to help the poor. In April 2002, opposition leaders mounted a coup d'etat and ousted Chavez for a short period. Although he quickly resumed leadership, Chavez continued to face fierce opposition, including a recall election in 2004, but survived and was reelected easily in 2006. During his tenure, Chavez has attempted to address Venezuela's economic problems by pursuing a number of socialist reforms and has steadily increased government control over businesses and industries. In January 2007, Chavez announced plans to nationalize the country's energy and telecommunications sectors, causing panic in the stock markets and stirring concerns worldwide. Chavez has also publicly criticized the United States and its policies on a number of occasions. During a fiery speech before the United Nations General Assembly in September 2006, Chavez called

President George W. Bush "the devil" and likened the U.S. government to a "world dictatorship."

The Caribbean

The Caribbean Sea holds a group of ethnically and culturally diverse island nations beginning near the southern tip of Florida and stretching to the northern coast of South America. Because of its close proximity, the region has long been of interest to the United States.

Cuba. The large Caribbean island of Cuba, located just ninety miles from Key West, Florida, has the only remaining military government in Latin America and one of the few remaining communist regimes in the world. Cuba's leader, Fidel Castro, came to power in 1959.

By 1960, Castro's belligerent anti-Americanism, human rights violations, and growing ties to the Soviet Union had seriously strained Cuba's relations with the United States. When Castro seized U.S. assets in Cuba, President Dwight Eisenhower retaliated by stopping trade with the island nation. In 1962, during a tense incident called the Cuban Missile Crisis, President John Kennedy put U.S. military forces on alert

This image from a broadcast on Cuban television shows Cuban leader Fidel Castro speaking at an unidentified location on October 28, 2006. The 80-year-old Cuban leader temporarily ceded power to his brother Raul in July 2006 following surgery. As of May 2007, he was reported to be in frail health.

AP Photo/Cubavision via AP Television News

until the Soviets agreed to abandon their plan to place nuclear missiles in Cuba.

When the Soviet Union dissolved in 1991, Cuba lost its historical lifeline of economic and political support. Meanwhile, the longstanding U.S. trade embargo continued. Although the United States has made some exceptions in recent years, allowing limited amounts of food and medicine to be sent to Cuba, the decades-old embargo endures despite the fact that other nations have traded with and traveled freely to Cuba for years. Meanwhile, Cuba's severe economic and social problems have persisted and as long Castro remains in power, it seems Cuba will remain communist. When reports surfaced in late 2006 that Castro's health had deteriorated and he was near death, intense speculation began about the future of Cuba and the fate of the hemisphere's only communist nation.

Haiti. In 1804, Haiti gained independence from France; it was the first Latin American country to break away from its European colonizer. Today, Haiti is the poorest country in the Western Hemisphere.

Throughout most of its history, Haiti was governed by authoritarian regimes. In 1990, Jean-Bertrand Aristide became Haiti's first democratically elected leader. However, Aristide was overthrown by the Haitian military in September 1991, and he returned to power only after the United States and the United Nations (UN) intervened with an economic embargo and the deployment of U.S. and UN soldiers to the island. In February 1996, the presidency was peacefully transferred from Aristide to his prime minister, René Préval.

In January 2000, U.S. troops were withdrawn from Haiti. In December of that year, Aristide was elected president again despite claims of election fraud from his opposition. From 2002 to 2004, renewed accusations of government corruption caused instability. Thousands of Haitians—both opponents and supporters of Aristide—protested in several cities. In response to waves of violence, the United States sent 1,000 marines to Haiti in February 2004; UN peacekeepers took over that June. Meanwhile, Aristide resigned and fled the country. In a turbulent election in 2006, René Préval was elected president. In January 2007, the United Nations announced that to maintain stability in Haiti it would keep its nearly 9,000 military personnel and police officers there until at least 2008.

U.S. Foreign Policy in Latin America

Throughout most of the twentieth century, U.S. leaders tried to implement policies in Latin America that would contain communism and counteract conditions—such as poverty—that encouraged communist rebellions. As democracy and economic reform spread throughout the region in the 1990s, American officials developed policies to strengthen economic relations between the United States and many Latin American countries. Since the terrorist attacks of 2001, U.S. policy has also stressed security issues, particularly combating terrorists and the illegal drug trade.

Origins of Economic Aid. In the 1960s, President Kennedy created the Alliance for Progress, an economic aid program that provided government funds for roads, schools, hospitals, and water projects in Latin America. In 1982, Congress passed the Caribbean Basin Initiative, which gave large amounts of economic aid to countries in the Caribbean and Central America, special duty-free status to products made in the Caribbean, and tax incentives to U.S. businesses that invested in the region.

The Reagan Doctrine. When he took office in 1980, President Ronald Reagan began supplying large amounts of economic and military aid to friendly governments in Central America. He believed that communist rebels—supported by the Soviet Union and Cuba—threatened U.S. security. President Reagan also sent U.S. troops to the small Caribbean island nation of Grenada to quell a communist rebellion there in 1983.

During his second term, President Reagan lobbied Congress to support rebels, called Contras, who were trying to unseat the leftist leadership in Nicaragua. In 1986, Congress approved $100 million in aid for the Contras. Later that year,

Fence Them Out?

In September 2006, lawmakers responded to mounting concerns about the economic impact of illegal immigration by passing a law requiring the construction of a 700-mile fence along the Mexican border to stem the flow of people illegally entering the United States. Calling the actions a publicity stunt, many critics argued that trying to fence in U.S. borders would be both costly and ineffective. Now that Democrats control Congress, they are threatening to withhold funding for this project. Instead, they want to revive other immigration proposals, such as instituting a guest worker program or streamlining the citizenship application process. Serious debate about the issue was underway by June 2007.

the Reagan administration revealed that White House staff member Marine Lt. Col. Oliver North had already secretly sent millions of dollars to the rebels in Nicaragua without congressional approval by diverting profits from clandestine U.S. arms sales to Iran. This controversial policy became known as the Iran/Contra affair.

Promoting Free Trade. In the mid- to late-1990s, many Latin American countries underwent democratic reform and economic growth. Economists attributed much of this revival to the promotion of free trade in the region. The North American Free Trade Agreement (NAFTA) went into effect on January 1, 1994, lowering barriers to trade among Canada, Mexico, and the United States. The historic agreement gradually lowers and eventually eliminates tariffs on U.S. industrial and agricultural exports to Mexico.

Since NAFTA's passage, policymakers have disagreed over its effect on the U.S. economy. After an initial boom in U.S. exports to Mexico, the peso crisis weakened Mexico's buying power and resulted in a large U.S. trade deficit. Although some U.S. corporations moved their operations below the U.S.-Mexico border to take advantage of lower wages, some economists think that the overall effect on the U.S. job market has been minimal.

Since taking office in 2001, President Bush has promoted free trade throughout Latin America. Chile signed a free-trade pact with the United States that took effect in January 2004. President Bush also brought about the Central America Free Trade Agreement (DR-CAFTA) that includes Costa Rica, El Salvador, Guatemala, Honduras, Nicaragua and the Dominican Republic; it was approved by Congress in 2005. Since then, the president has lobbied other countries in the Western Hemisphere to join a NAFTA-like "Free Trade Area of the Americas." However, in 2005, only twenty-nine of thirty-four countries supported free-trade expansion, so an agreement was not reached. Despite this setback, the Bush administration continues to pursue free-trade accords with individual countries and successfully reached agreements with Colombia, Peru, and Panama in 2005 and 2006. As of early 2007, those agreements were awaiting congressional approval.

CURRENT ISSUES

U.S. Relations with Cuba. During the Cold War, U.S. leaders considered Fidel Castro a serious threat to the peace and political stability of the Western Hemisphere. They cited his ties to the Soviet Union and human rights abuses, particularly his treatment of dissidents. Consequently, U.S. officials imposed a trade embargo to choke off Cuba's economy and weaken Castro's regime. Although there have been a few exceptions to the Cuban embargo in recent years—to allow food and medicine in for humanitarian relief for example—a succession of U.S. presidents from both parties have refused to back down on this policy.

In late 2006, when it became known that Castro's health was failing, speculation about the future of communism in Cuba began. Some believed that Fidel's brother Raul, thought to be more supportive of free-market capitalism, might be poised to take control. The mere possibility of new leadership in Cuba prompted some to renew their calls for the Bush administration to end the embargo. Others simply urged that the United States take steps soon to improve its relations with Cuba, laying the groundwork for future trade opportunities and helping to prevent a large number of Cuban immigrants from fleeing their impoverished nation upon the end of the restrictive Castro regime.

Opponents of the embargo say that the forty-year policy has failed and should be abandoned because it has not and will not encourage governmental reform; instead, they say, it has contributed to the poverty and isolation of the Cuban people. They point out that other governments around the world routinely denounce the U.S. embargo, making American resolve appear arrogant. (In 2006, for the fifteenth straight year, the United Nations voted overwhelmingly to demand an end to the embargo.) Human rights activists say that the embargo hurts the people of Cuba, not Fidel Castro, by depriving them of economic opportunity, consumer goods, and technological advancements. Detractors also argue that, ironically, the embargo has actually empowered

From left to right, the presidents of Venezuela (Hugo Chavez), Nicaragua (Daniel Ortega) and Bolivia (Evo Morales) greet supporters in Nicaragua in January 2007. All three leaders have initiated socialist policies in their countries.

AP Photo/Moises Castillo

Castro because it allows him to blame U.S. policy—not his own failed economic programs—for Cuba's poverty. These critics contend that opening trade relations will expand U.S. influence in Cuba, thus promoting the free enterprise and political reform long-sought there.

Those who believe the embargo should continue argue that Cuba is still a dangerous neighbor because it is a known human rights abuser and state sponsor of terrorism. The embargo is working, supporters say, because it bolsters the influence of Castro's critics within Cuba and has crippled Castro's efforts to expand his communist influence elsewhere. Embargo supporters say that without knowing who will succeed Castro, and what economic or governmental system might follow, it would be premature to make changes to this long-standing U.S. foreign policy. Lifting the embargo now would amount to a public defeat for the U.S. government, giving Castro a victory—and legitimacy—that he does not merit.

Socialism Spreading in Latin America. Throughout Latin America over the last thirty years, many nations have made the difficult transition from military dictatorship to representative democracy. While this change has led

The USNS *Comfort*, a floating hospital with 1,000 beds, will sail to Latin America in 2007 with plans to offer treatment and surgeries to thousands of poor people throughout the region. The visit is part of the Bush administration's efforts to show that it is engaged with the region after coming under attack for ignoring Mexico and its southern neighbors in favor of involvement in the Middle East.

to freer and generally less violent societies, in many countries, poverty and economic instability have persisted, creating environments ripe for the spread of socialism. As a result, several Latin American nations—including Brazil, Bolivia, Chile, Argentina, and Venezuela—have elected socialist-leaning leaders in the last ten years. In 2006, voters brought to power even more leaders who support socialist reforms, such as Daniel Ortega in Nicaragua and Rafael Correa in Ecuador. Hugo Chavez was reelected in Venezuela after he promised to continue a "socialist revolution" in his country.

"Socialism" is a political doctrine that supports government or collective ownership of agriculture, business, and industry. A socialist economy contrasts sharply with one based on capitalism, like that of the United States, where individual ownership and market—not government—forces shape the production, sale, and distribution of goods and services. Historically, nations have pursued socialism as a means of addressing poverty, unrest, or great differences in wealth or status in their societies. The United States and other capitalist countries have generally opposed the spread of socialism because they believe it threatens international trade and curtails individual freedoms and democratic rights, all of which run counter to U.S. ideological interests.

Some foreign policy experts believe the United States should do more to prevent the spread of socialism in Latin America, arguing that continuing to promote democracy and capitalism there will ensure that these neighboring nations are home to fair and prosperous societies, conducive to American business. If, as is happening now in Venezuela, a foreign government decides to seize the assets and land of U.S. owned industries, U.S. companies stand to lose millions of dollars. These experts suggest that increasing U.S. foreign aid to leftist-leaning nations will better help to alleviate the poverty and strife that cause citizens to turn to socialism for relief. Moreover, by increasing diplomatic outreach to the leaders of these nations, the United States can convince them that democracy and capitalism are in the best interests of their countries and the world.

A farmer sells pineapples at a market in Managua, Nicaragua, in March 2006. A few weeks after this picture was taken, Nicaragua sent its first shipments of agricultural goods to the United States, officially initiating such exports under the DR-CAFTA agreement.

Other foreign policy experts disagree with this strategy and say that the United States should not attempt to wield influence over Latin America's burgeoning socialist governments. The leaders of these countries were popularly elected by citizens who believed that socialist reforms were the best way to address lasting problems in their homelands. Furthermore, observers argue, if increased government control of state economies helps these nations improve living conditions, then citizens there will be better able to trade with and buy goods from the United States. Some Latin America watchers even suggest that the United States should support socialist reforms in Latin America because such initiatives will prevent the wealth disparities and unrest that have led to political instability there in the past.

Expanding Free Trade. More than ten years after NAFTA's implementation, lawmakers, businesses, and workers in the

United States and Mexico continue to debate whether NAFTA and other free trade agreements are positively affecting the economy. In the United States, labor and manufacturing leaders have stepped up criticism of NAFTA recently, saying it draws jobs and industry away to Mexico where labor and operating costs are cheaper. Meanwhile, Mexico has begun to voice its own concerns that NAFTA is harming its agricultural sector by flooding the Mexican market with U.S. agricultural imports.

Such ambivalence over NAFTA has thwarted recent attempts to expand free trade to all of Latin America. In 2005, President Bush failed to persuade five of the thirty-four countries that the proposed Free Trade of the Americas Agreement (FTAA) would benefit them. Argentina, Brazil, Paraguay, Uruguay, and Venezuela blocked passage of the FTAA mainly because they feared it would disadvantage their farmers. Although President Bush continues to pursue the overall goal of reducing trade barriers in the Americas, the new Congress may not support him. Some of the Democrats who now control Capitol Hill are beginning to lose faith in free trade because they are concerned that it is harming American workers.

Supporters of free trade contend that both U.S. businesses and struggling Latin American economies prosper when they have more opportunities to sell their goods to one another. Although free-trade advocates acknowledge that some U.S. workers might lose jobs to Latin America in the short term, they argue that these drawbacks are outweighed by the long-term benefits of free trade, such as cultivating new consumers of U.S. goods and improving economic stability in neighboring countries. Such supporters view free trade as an important tool in growing and supporting new democracies in Latin America.

Opponents of pursuing more free-trade agreements with Latin American nations represent a number of diverse interests. Labor unions believe that the stark difference between U.S. and Latin American wages encourages agricultural and manufacturing companies to relocate to Latin America, putting U.S. laborers out of work. Environmentalists and human rights activists warn about the lack of pollution control and workplace safety laws in these countries. And some Latin American nations are beginning to oppose free-trade agreements because they fear they lead to an influx of U.S. goods which depress profits for Latin American producers, and an outflow of Latin American workers who leave for better paying jobs in the north.

OUTLOOK

At one time, U.S. foreign policy in Latin America focused on helping fight communism. Today, U.S. policies in the region often promote economic interests. With the possibility of new leadership in Cuba for the first time in many decades, the United States must re-evaluate its economic embargo of the island. And despite recent democratic reforms in the region, some Latin American governments increasingly are turning toward socialism as the solution to persistent poverty. These issues, and ongoing debate about immigration and free trade, will drive U.S. policymaking over the coming year.

THE DEBATE: LATIN AMERICA

The United States should change its policy toward Cuba.

PRO: The U.S. embargo against Cuba is not working, makes the United States seem arrogant, and should be abandoned in anticipation of new leadership in the country. Keeping Cuba isolated only harms the Cuban people and angers much of the world. Expanding trade and travel to Cuba will increase the chance of democratic reforms there, improve the Cuban economy, and provide new customers for U.S. businesses.

CON: Fidel Castro is a dangerous dictator perched only ninety miles from the U.S. coast. The U.S. embargo sends a message that human rights abuses will not be tolerated and prevents Castro from extending his influence beyond Cuba's borders. Without knowing who will succeed Castro, or what type of governmental reforms may follow, it would be premature to abandon the embargo.

The United States should do more to discourage socialism in Latin America.

PRO: The United States should be alarmed by the spread of socialism in Latin America. As more governments increase state control and attempt to nationalize business and industry, international trade and U.S. business interests will suffer. The United States should increase aid and diplomatic outreach to the region to protect democracy and freedom, ideals hurt by socialist governments in the past.

CON: Interfering with the political choices of Latin American nations is a mistake. If citizens of certain Latin American nations believe that socialism is the answer to their economic problems, then they should be free to support those reforms. Increased government control may even improve the nations' economies and abilities to trade. If socialism prevents civil unrest, the United States will benefit.

The United States should continue to promote free trade with Latin America.

PRO: Just as NAFTA has brought economic improvements to Mexico, Canada, and the United States, expanding free trade to other Latin American countries would have similar benefits. U.S. businesses would profit from new markets while Latin America's poor will have access to better jobs and more stable economies. These improvements will strengthen the region's new democracies and guard against unrest.

CON: NAFTA's mixed reviews show that free trade should not be expanded to include all Latin American countries. The loss of U.S. jobs and the damage done to the Mexican agricultural market are only two of the negative impacts of free trade. When manufacturing moves south of the border, the health of the environment and workplace safety suffer. Free trade should not be expanded until these issues are addressed.

THE MIDDLE EAST

The Middle East is a critical area for U.S. foreign policymakers. Several major initiatives converge in this complex region—the war in Iraq, energy security, the Israeli-Palestinian peace effort, and the struggle against terrorism.

The United States became significantly engaged in the Middle East when it struck a security-for-oil agreement with Saudi Arabia in 1945. Since then, the United States has been involved in several conflicts around the Persian Gulf to ensure the safety of oil supplies as well as to protect its allies. Periodically, American leaders have worked to facilitate peace between Israel and the Palestinians.

Focus on the Middle East and on Islamic fundamentalism intensified after the September 11, 2001, attacks. The United States first overthrew Afghanistan's Taliban government, which had harbored the al Qaeda terrorists responsible for planning and financing the attacks. Then U.S. leaders turned their attention to other potential threats. President George W. Bush announced new policies designed to confront and defeat terrorists before they can attack America. He identified Iran and Iraq as particularly threatening nations.

Foremost among national concerns today is the war in Iraq. Launched in 2003 to overthrow Iraqi dictator Saddam Hussein and dismantle his weapons of mass destruction, the war remains highly controversial as efforts to quell civil unrest and establish a stable Iraqi government continue. Citizens and policymakers are deeply divided about whether and how to withdraw from Iraq and the consequences for America's long-term national security interests.

KEY QUESTIONS

- Should the United States withdraw from Iraq?

- Should the United States take a more active role in brokering peace between Israel and the Palestinians?

- Should the United States strike Iran's nuclear facilities?

Because of the region's volatility, we've developed a special electronic chapter to provide updates. You can access it via **closeup.org**

FOR FURTHER READING

The following Web sites provide useful information on topics covered in *Current Issues*. Some sites are impartial sources of statistical or historical information. Others represent a cross section of political thought. Several are news sites with archived coverage of specific issues and regions. These sites are a small sample of what is available online. As always, take care when using online sources to confirm the accuracy and validity of any information you find.

The Federal Government

Bureau of Justice Statistics	www.ojp.usdoj.gov/bjs
Bureau of Labor Statistics	www.bls.gov
Congressional Quarterly	www.cq.com
Federal Statistics	www.fedstats.gov
Library of Congress	www.loc.gov
Social Security Administration	www.ssa.gov
Supreme Court of the United States	www.supremecourtus.gov
U.S. Census Bureau	www.census.gov
U.S. Department of Homeland Security	www.dhs.gov/dhspublic
U.S. House of Representatives	www.house.gov
U.S. Senate	www.senate.gov
White House	www.whitehouse.gov

The Federal Budget

Concord Coalition	www.concordcoalition.org
Office of Management and Budget	www.whitehouse.gov/omb

Constitutional Rights

American Civil Liberties Union	www.aclu.org
American Center for Law and Justice	www.aclj.org

Crime and Security

Coalition to Stop Gun Violence   www.gunfree.org
National Rifle Association   www.nra.org
Office of National Drug Control
    Policy   www.whitehousedrugpolicy.gov

The Economy

AFL-CIO   www.aflcio.org
U.S. Chamber of Commerce   www.uschamber.org

Education

National Education Association   www.nea.org
Alliance for School Choice   www.allianceforschoolchoice.org

Health Care

AARP   www.aarp.org
Centers for Medicare and
    Medicaid Services   www.cms.hhs.gov

Immigration

Center for Immigration Studies   www.cis.org
The Federation for American
    Immigration Reform   www.fairus.org
U.S. Citizenship and
    Immigration Services   www.uscis.gov

Minorities and Women

Center for Equal Opportunity   www.ceousa.org
Southern Poverty Law Center   www.splcenter.org

Jobs and Welfare

The Urban Institute   www.urban.org
Employment Policies Institute   www.epionline.org

Science and Technology

National Academy of Engineering:
   Greatest Engineering Achievements
   of the 20th Century   www.greatachievements.org
National Nanotechnology Initiative   www.nano.gov
National Human Genome
   Research Institute   www.genome.gov

Defense

Center for Defense Information   www.cdi.org
Council for a Livable World   www.clw.org
U.S. Department of Defense   www.defenselink.mil

Democracy and Foreign Aid

Amnesty International   www.amnesty.org
UN High Commission
   for Human Rights   www.unhchr.ch
U.S. Agency for
   International Development   www.usaid.gov

Global Environment

UN Environment Programme   www.unep.org
U.S. Environmental Protection Agency   www.epa.gov

International Trade

Washington International Trade
   Association   www.wita.org
World Trade Organization   www.wto.org
U.S. Trade Representative   www.ustr.gov

Weapons Proliferation

Arms Control Association   www.armscontrol.org
Center for Nonproliferation Studies   www.cns.miis.edu